Adolf Grünbaum

D1171190

Classics in Psychiatry

This is a volume in
the Ayer Company collection

Classics in Psychiatry

Advisory Editor

Eric T. Carlson

Editorial Board

Erwin H. Ackerknecht
Gerald N. Grob
Denis Leigh
George Mora
Jacques M. Quen

See last pages of this volume
for a complete list of titles

MANIC-DEPRESSIVE INSANITY

AND

PARANOIA

BY

EMIL KRAEPELIN

AYER COMPANY, PUBLISHERS, INC.
SALEM, NEW HAMPSHIRE 03079

Reprint Edition, 1987
AYER Company, Publishers, Inc.
382 Main Street
Salem, New Hampshire 03079

Editorial Supervision: EVE NELSON

———◆———

Reprint Edition 1976 by Arno Press Inc.

Reprinted from a copy in
  The University of Virginia Library

CLASSICS IN PSYCHIATRY
ISBN for complete set: 0-405-07410-7
See last pages of this volume for titles.

Manufactured in the United States of America

Publisher's Note: The colored tables have
been reproduced in black and white for this
edition.

———◆———

Library of Congress Cataloging in Publication Data

Kraepelin, Emil, 1856-1926.
   Manic-depressive insanity and paranoia.

   (Classics in psychiatry)
   Translation of selections from Psychiatrie.
   Reprint of the 1921 ed. published by E. & S.
Livingstone, Edinburgh.
   1. Manic-depressive psychoses. 2. Paranoia.
3. Psychiatry--Early works to 1900. I. Title.
II. Series. [DNLM: WM207 K89m 1921a]
RC516.K66213   1975   616.8'95   75-16712
ISBN 0-405-07441-7

MANIC-DEPRESSIVE INSANITY

AND

PARANIOA

MANIC-DEPRESSIVE INSANITY

INSANITY

AND

PARANOIA

BY

Professor EMIL KRAEPELIN of Munich

TRANSLATED BY

R. MARY BARCLAY, M.A., M.B.

From the Eighth German Edition of the "Text-Book of Psychiatry,"
vols. iii. and iv.

EDITED BY

GEORGE M. ROBERTSON, M.D., F.R.C.P. (Edin.)

Professor of Psychiatry in the University of Edinburgh
and Physician to the Royal Asylum, Morningside

EDINBURGH

E. & S. LIVINGSTONE

17 TEVIOT PLACE

1921

EDITOR'S PREFACE

THE conception of Manic-Depressive Insanity as a definite form of mental disorder, various and antithetical though some of the symptoms appear to be in different attacks and even in different phases of the same attack, is one of Professor Kræpelin's most happy generalisations. Naturally, so startling a departure from older classifications was not at first accepted by all, though the way for recognition had been paved by the differentiation and description of Folie Circulaire by French alienists, but further experience and familiarity with the idea led to the almost universal admission of its truth. It is to Professor Kræpelin's credit that he also has developed his own views with increase of knowledge, for he now includes what is often called Involution Melancholia in this group, his failure to do so in his original statement having been regarded by many as a mistake.

Professor Kræpelin's account of Manic-Depressive Insanity, conjoined with that of Dementia Præcox, forms probably his greatest achievement in psychiatry. The last word, however, has not been said on the subject. Many important problems have yet to be solved. Professor Kræpelin, for example, apparently takes the physiological view that the essential feature of Mania is excitement and excitability, and of Depression or Melancholia, inhibition and depression of function. This leads to difficulty when Anxious or Excited Melancholia comes to be dealt with, which is avoided if the psychological view be adopted, that the symptoms in Mania are but morbid developments of the feelings of elation or anger, and in Melancholia of depression and despair, or of fear and anxiety, a species of caricature of these feelings as Maudsley has suggested. Kræpelin's group of mixed states of Mania and Depression, into which he places Anxious Melancholia, would be reserved under the above hypothesis for those cases' comparatively few in number, occurring usually after several attacks, and suffering probably from some degree of disintegration of function, in which the feelings get strangely mixed up, as well as the secondary or associated symptoms. This point is mentioned to give but one illustration of the suggestive and stimulating nature of Kræpelin's work.

The latter part of the book is devoted to an account of Paranoia, which title is employed in the narrowest sense and is restricted in application to those forms, which are very often described as " true " or non-hallucinatory Paranoia. The more numerous allied and hallucinatory forms are mainly grouped by Kræpelin under the title Paraphrenia, though some may be included under Paranoid Dementia Præcox, to which disorder its relationship is undoubtedly very close. Further, it may be added that as true Paranoia has also affinities to some varieties of Mania, all these forms of insanity seem to merge into one another at their so-called boundaries or limits, as do the colours of the spectrum, though the fully developed and typical forms are as distinct from one another and as recognisable as the primary colours.

The medical profession is under a debt of gratitude to Dr Mary Barclay for her faithful rendering into English of these classical studies. She has now completed the translation of Professor Kræpelin's careful descriptions of those forms of mental disorder which are commonly known as The Psychoses, namely, Dementia Præcox, Paraphrenia, Manic-Depressive Insanity, and Paranoia. These disorders form a definite group and provide the most effective illustrations of Professor Kræpelin's accurate methods of analysing and investigating mental disease. His orderly descriptions will be found of great value to the medical officers of our mental hospitals, and to all engaged in the study of clinical psychiatry, particularly to those reading for a Diploma in Psychological Medicine.

GEORGE M. ROBERTSON.

UNIVERSITY OF EDINBURGH,
    December 1920.

TRANSLATOR'S PREFACE

IN translating *Manic-Depressive Insanity and Paranoia*, I have, as in *Dementia Præcox and Paraphrenia*, tried to reproduce the original as literally as possible. Professor Robertson suggested that I should translate these two sections in order to complete the psychoses, and I am grateful to him for the suggestion, as Professor Kraepelin treats his subjects in such a way that, even although one may not always agree with him, one is bound to admit that he shows most exhaustively what can be done in the examination of patients, and in the classification of symptoms singly and in groups. I' hope that the translation may lead to further detailed study of those diseases among English-speaking peoples.

I have again to express my thanks to Dr Walker for kindly reading the proofs.

R. MARY BARCLAY.

LONDON, *November 1920.*

CONTENTS

MANIC-DEPRESSIVE INSANITY

PARANOIA

LIST OF ILLUSTRATIONS

SPECIMENS OF WRITING

Manic-Depressive Insanity

CHAPTER I.

DEFINITION.

MANIC-DEPRESSIVE insanity,[1] as it is to be described in this section, includes on the one hand the whole domain of so-called *periodic and circular insanity*, on the other hand *simple mania*, the greater part of the morbid states termed *melancholia* and also a not inconsiderable number of cases of *amentia*.[2] Lastly, we include here certain slight and slightest colourings of *mood*, some of them periodic, some of them continously morbid, which on the one hand are to be regarded as the rudiment of more severe disorders, on the other hand pass over without sharp boundary into the domain of *personal predisposition*. In the course of the years I have become more and more convinced that all the above-mentioned states only represent manifestations of a *single morbid process*. It is certainly possible that later a series of subordinate forms may be described, or even individual small groups again entirely separated off. But if this happens, then according

---

[1] Kirn, Die periodischen Psychosen, 1878 ; Mendel, Die Manie, eine Monographie, 1881 ; Pick, Circuläres Irresein, Eulenburgs Realenzyklopädie ; Hoche, Über die leichteren Formen des periodischen Irreseins, 1897 ; Hecker, Zeitschr. f. praktische Ärzte, 1898, 1 ; Pilcz, Die periodischen Geistesstörungen, 1901 ; Thalbitzer, Den manio-depressive Psykose, Stemmingssindsygdom, 1902 ; Seiffer, Deutsche Klinik. 1904 ; Deny et Camus, La psychose maniaque-depressive, 1907 ; Antheaume, les psychoses périodique, 1907 ; Binet et Simon, L'Année psychologique, xvi., 164 ; Pierre-Kahn, La cyclothymie, 1909 ; Rémond et Voivenel, Annales médico-psychol., 1910, 2, 353 ; Thomsen, Medizinische Klinik, 1910, 45 und 46 ; Stransky, Das manisch-depressive Irresein, 1911 (Aschaffenburgs Handbuch) ; Homburger, Zeitschr. f. d. ges. Neurol. u. Psych., Refer. II., 9-10 (Literatur).

[2] Confusional or delirious insanity.

to my view those symptoms will most certainly not be authoritative, which hitherto have usually been placed in the foreground.

What has brought me to this position is first the experience that notwithstanding manifold external differences certain *common fundamental features* yet recur in all the morbid states mentioned. Along with changing symptoms, which may appear temporarily or may be completely absent, we meet in all forms of manic-depressive insanity a quite definite, narrow group of disorders, though certainly of very varied character and composition. Without any one of them being absolutely characteristic of the malady, still in association they impress a uniform stamp on all the multiform clinical states. If one is conversant with them, one will in the great majority of cases be able to conclude in regard to any one of them that it belongs to the large group of forms of manic-depressive insanity by the peculiarity of the condition, and thus to gain a series of fixed points for the special clinical and prognostic significance of the case. Even a small part of the course of the disease usually enables us to arrive at this decision, just as in paralysis or dementia præcox the general psychic change often enough makes possible the diagnosis of the fundamental malady in its most different phases.

Of perhaps still greater significance than the classification of states by definite fundamental disorders is the experience that all the morbid forms brought together here as a clinical entity, *not only pass over the one into the other without recognisable boundaries, but that they may even replace each other in one and the same case.* On the one side, as will be later discussed more in detail, it is fundamentally and practically quite impossible to keep apart in any consistent way simple, periodic and circular cases ; everywhere there are gradual transitions. But on the other side we see in the same patient not only mania and melancholia, but also states of the most profound confusion and perplexity, also well developed delusions, and lastly, the slightest fluctuations of mood alternating with each other. Moreover, permanent, one-sided colourings of mood very commonly form the background on which fully developed circumscribed attacks of manic-depressive insanity develop.

A further common bond which embraces all the morbid types brought together here and makes the keeping of them apart practically almost meaningless, is their *uniform prog-*

nosis. There are indeed slight and severe attacks which may be of long or short duration, but they alternate irregularly in the same case. This difference is therefore of no use for the delimitation of different diseases. A grouping according to the frequency of the attacks might much rather be considered, which naturally would be extremely welcome to the physician. It appears, however, that here also we have not to do with fundamental differences, since in spite of certain general rules it has not been possible to separate out definite types from this point of view. On the contrary the universal experience is striking, that the attacks of manic-depressive insanity within the delimitation attempted here never lead to profound dementia, not even when they continue throughout life almost without interruption. Usually all morbid manifestations completely disappear; but where that is exceptionally not the case, only a rather slight, peculiar psychic weakness develops, which is just as common to the types here taken together as it is different from dementias in diseases of other kinds.

As a last support for the view here represented of the unity of manic-depressive insanity the circumstance may be adduced, that the various forms which it comprehends may also apparently mutually replace one another in *heredity*. In members of the same family we frequently enough find side by side pronounced periodic or circular cases, occasionally isolated states of ill temper or confusion, lastly very slight, regular fluctuations of mood or permanent conspicuous colouration of disposition. From whatever point of view accordingly the manic-depressive morbid forms may be regarded, from that of ætiology or of clinical phenomena, the course or the issue—it is evident everywhere that here points of agreement exist, which make it possible to regard our domain as a unity and to delimit it from all the other morbid types hitherto discussed. Further experience must show whether and in what directions in this extensive domain smaller sub-groups can be separated from one another.

In the first place the difference of the states which usually make up the disease, presents itself as the most favourable ground of classification. As a rule the disease runs its course in isolated attacks more or less sharply defined from each other or from health, which are either like or unlike, or even very frequently are perfect antithesis. Accordingly we distinguish first of all *manic states* with the essential morbid symptoms of flight of ideas, exalted mood, and pressure of activity, and *melancholia or depressive states* with sad or anxious moodiness and also sluggishness of thought and action. These two opposed phases of the clinical state have given the disease its name. But besides them we observe also clinical "*mixed forms*," in which the phenomena of mania and melancholia are combined with each other, so that states arise, which indeed are composed of the same morbid symptoms as these, but cannot without coercion be classified either with the one or with the other.

CHAPTER II.

PSYCHIC SYMPTOMS.

BEFORE we proceed, however, to the description of the manifold states which make up the whole clinical course, it will be convenient to obtain a general view of the individual psychic disorders peculiar to manic-depressive insanity.

The **Perception** of external impressions is in *mania* invariably encroached upon, sometimes even very considerably. Only in very slight forms of the malady do we find values which correspond perhaps to the lower values of normal individuals, but which are decidedly below the average.

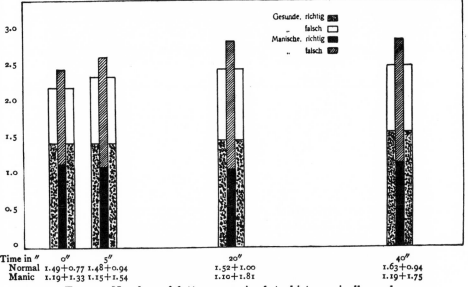

FIG. 1.—Number of letters perceived tachistoscopically and remembered by normal and manic individuals.

Paton, in experiments on sensation in manic patients, obtained strikingly poor results. Wolfskehl, who investigated tachistoscopic perception of series of letters, found that the patients yielded on the average about one quarter fewer correct results than the normal controls. The comparatively large number of mistakes made was noticeable, which, however, was not nearly so large as in dementia præcox, but yet was larger than in normal individuals. This ratio is represented by the first vertical of Fig. 1, in which the correct and the wrong results of normal individuals and of manic patients are compared. The patients apparently perceive carelessly and inaccurately ; but on the other hand isolated experiences lead to the belief that their pressure of speech readily tempts them to make statements when they have really seen nothing. Frequently the severity of the disorder of perception is in remarkable contrast to the insignificance of the clinical manifestations.

Extraordinary **Distractibility of Attention** certainly plays an essential part in defective perception. The patients gradually lose the capacity for the choice and arrangement of impressions ; each striking sense-stimulus obtrudes itself on them with a certain force, so that they usually attend to it at once. Accordingly, if their attention can for the most part be quickly attracted by the exhibition of objects or by the calling out of words, yet it digresses again with uncommon ease to any fresh stimulus. The picture of their surroundings and of events remains, therefore, for them more disconnected and more incomplete than it would be, if it suffered merely from encroachment on the process of perception.

Perception frequently appears to be less severely disordered in *depressive states* ; the tendency to mistaken readings especially is in general absent. Franz and Hamilton found in inhibited patients that the threshold values were raised for touch, pressure, and pain stimuli. Further, in severe cases, according to the often very characteristic utterances of the patients, a slowing and sluggishness of recognition is apparently invariably found, which is caused by defective reaction to external impressions in consciousness. In the process of perception those memory pictures do not appear rapidly or in any number, which make it possible for us to connect at once what is perceived with former experiences, and to place it without difficulty in the familiar circle of ideas. Through this the patients become more or less incapable of working up their experiences mentally or of understanding them. They often declare that in spite of every effort they are not able to understand the meaning of what they read or to follow an explanation. " Like a mist it lies over everything," complained a patient, and another said he was " no longer so capable of noticing anything " as formerly. In the most severe grades of the disorder, in states of stupor, the patients may regard the external world with a complete lack of understanding, even when individual sense perceptions are fairly well appreciated.

The fact must also be taken into consideration that as a rule *facility* of attention is distinctly disordered. The patients are not able to turn their attention easily and quickly to any impressions or ideas. They are not able either to pay attention, or to turn away of themselves from ideas which emerge in their own minds or which are suggested to them from without. This lack of freedom of attention certainly displays innumerable gradations.

Consciousness is in the severe forms of the malady invariably somewhat clouded. At the height of excitement impressions and ideas become dim and indistinct. In consequence accuracy of *orientation* suffers. The patients do not know properly where they are. Everything is enchanted, " not right "; they are in the " freemason house," in the " resurrection house," underground, in purgatory, in heaven, " quite away from the world." They mistake people, think that the nurses are spirits, the physician the devil. A female patient takes the patient in the next bed for the Virgin Mary, a former sweetheart of her husband, for her husband himself. They greet physicians and fellow-patients by the names of relatives or acquaintances. These mistakes are sometimes connected with remote resemblances; in other cases they appear to be more an amusing game in which the patient takes pleasure, partially conscious of the arbitrariness of the designations. That occurs especially at the decline of excitement, when the wrong designations are still adhered to, while from the other conduct and occasional utterances of the patient it is evident that he is quite clear about his place of residence and the people round him. In states of depression also we encounter more or less deep clouding of consciousness up to almost complete oblivion. Here and there a peculiarly dreamy stupor develops, in which the patient experiences the most extraordinary and confused delirious adventures.

Memory is not permanently encroached upon by the disease, but the patients frequently lose for a time the mastery over their range of ideas. Especially in states of depression they are often incapable of recollecting, and are sometimes not able to call to mind the simplest things. They have to consider for a long time before they can work an arithmetical exercise or narrate an experience. They are occasionally unable to name the year of their birth or to give the names of their children. They become entangled in obvious contradictions, which, however, are often corrected after a quite short interval.

Retention in manic patients is, according to Wolfskehl's investigations, disordered in a similar way to perception. This is represented in Fig. 1, in which the values are given for the retention of letters in normal individuals, and in patients, after periods of 5, 20, and 40 seconds. It is seen that the number of correct results in patients is invariably smaller, and on the other hand the number of mistakes considerably greater than in normal individuals, especially after the longer intervals. Erroneous processes are obviously developed which cause falsification of the memory pictures. As investigation of the mistakes shows, divergence to linguistic associations plays a certain part here. The fact is also perhaps not unimportant, that the average values of the manic patients in the shorter periods show much more clearly than those of normal individuals a diminution of correct values (from 1.19 to 1.10), a behaviour which in individual patients is still much more in evidence. Certain experiences give ground for the belief that this is a sign of greater fluctuation of attention.

Distinct **Pseudo - memories** are not infrequently met with in the patients, especially in mania ; they correspond to the results of the experiments. Occasionally they show in a pronounced manner a tendency to delusional fabulation, to descriptions of wonderful experiences out of the past, which the patients more or less seriously believe. Memory of the period of disease itself is usually somewhat indistinct, especially after severe manic excitement or after states of stupor. Experiences from childhood are often constantly and in good faith represented essentially otherwise than they actually occurred, a circumstance which prevents the patients even on recovery from taking up the right attitude towards their own conduct and towards their surroundings.

Isolated **Hallucinations** are observed frequently and in the most different states, although they do not very often appear conspicuously in the foreground. It is generally a case of illusionary occurrences, the appearance of which is favoured by the incompleteness and slightness of perception, but especially by the lively emotions peculiar to the disease. The substance of the illusions therefore is invariably in close connection with the trains of thought and the moods of the patients. Their surroundings appear changed to them ; faces are double, dark ; their own faces look black in the

mirror ; they see a blaze of light, white fumes, " opium-
morphia-chloroform vapour," flickering, the shadow of a
man at the window, a figure in the corner.   People are
changed ; they look like " phantoms " ; their children appear
exchanged ; the physician is " only a sort of image " or the
devil.   The chairs are moving ; the pictures make signs with
their eyes ; a piece of brown paper is changed into the skull
of a princess.

The patient hears a murmuring and a whispering, a roaring, the crackling of hell ; he hears someone coming up the
steps, going to the " larder," " the devil carrying on in the
walls," death gnashing his teeth in the wall, noises " as if a
corpse were being thrown out at the window," an uproar in
the stove as if a man wanted to get into it.   There are noises
in his head ; it sounds like tolling of bells and the murmur
of the ocean, like cries for help, shooting, the death rattle and
groaning, screaming and howling, weeping, entreating and
lamenting, clamouring and cursing.   " In all the noises there
is something," said a patient in very significant tones.
Spirits buzz about each other ; others snarl something which
has some connection with the patient.   Occasionally the
illusions are related to definite impressions.   The birds call
out the name of the patient ; they whistle, " Come, Emily."
The clock says, " You dog, you're still here, you've brought
your father into the madhouse, you're the devil, a swine."
The rhythmic vascular murmur in the ear becomes a reproach, " bad, bad," or " whore, whore," which then is
ascribed to the devil.

Besides these illusions which clearly betray the influence
of emotions, real hallucinations also appear often enongh.
At night disguised figures come into the room.   The patient
sees an open grave, his dead wife, the apostle Paul with good
angels, the Saviour on the cross, the Virgin Mary, Jesus with
roses, the eye of God, the devil.   He sees corpses, skeletons,
" sad spirits," monsters, the heads of his children on the wall,
fiery rings which signify his sins.   In the daytime also
caricatures appear before him, coloured figures, and faces like
the one in Fig. 2, which was drawn by a female patient.
They grin at him out of the book which he wishes to read,
from the bedclothes, from the wall ; they look in at the
window.   Worms swarm in the food, and small heads which
have been cut off.   A patient saw a nail with a noose, which
was a summons to hang himself.

Through wall and window sound warning voices, cries,

the devil's laugh, the weeping of the dead mother, the screaming of children, the song of angels. The content of the hallucinations of hearing is usually unpleasant and alarming. All possible sins are brought before the patient as if he were a criminal ; he is enticed to suicide. " Do something to yourself," " Hang yourself," " If he would only hang himself, otherwise we must keep him for ten years yet," " You dog of a parson, Prussian dog, thief and murderer," are among the things called out, also " masturbator," " poisoner, wild swine," " swine," " you skunk, camel," " frightful creature," " Cinderella, cattle," " base female,"

FIG. 2.—Caricature seen in hallucination.

" O, how she stinks ! " " You must die like a beast," " You must go along," " Do away with him ! " the voices threaten, " You're going to hell," " Get out of this, you've no right here ; God does not die," " Now someone's coming for you," " He's running up there, he'll never get away," " We'll drive her out and make the maid the mistress," " She daren't go away now ; she'll be cut," " We'll put something into him and then he'll sleep and no mistake." Much more rarely pleasant things are announced by the voices. A female patient heard singing which made known to her that she was the Virgin Mary ; another heard that her son had gained millions. A male patient heard " sacred things of God."

Auditory hallucinations frequently appear only in the night-time, or at least much more then. They seem, as a rule, not to possess complete sensory distinctness. They are voices " as in a dream," " from the underworld," " voices in the air, which come from God," more rarely gramophone or telephone voices, wireless telegraphy. Their origin is relatively seldom referred to the external world. The bed speaks ; God speaks ; the dead sister is calling ; the voice of.Jesus is heard ; a white violet says, " It is the will of God " ; the dead father declares, " I am behind you, I am speaking." Much more frequently the hallucinations have their seat in the patient's own body. There is speaking in his stomach, in his left ear ; words are whispered inside him. The devil speaks out of the heart of the patient ; he swears in him ; the patient hears him " inwardly, not with his ears." " An inward voice from the heart says filthy things about God," said a female patient. Another heard " voices coming from within, which lament." " There is talking in my head along with my thoughts," declared a third.

The voices generally stand in the most intimate relation to the remaining content of consciousness. The patients declare that they are questioned ; their thoughts are repeated loud out after two or three minutes. Others carry on conversations with their voices. A female patient said that she heard talking in her body, to which there were answers, " more as if thought " ; another stated that people said what she herself had already said. Now and then commanding voices are heard, for the most part in the sense of self-destruction, as mentioned above.

As the illusions do not usually reach the degree of importunate sensory distinctness which they do in, for example, alcoholic insanity or in dementia præcox, the patients are generally unable to give the words of longer sentences, but only the substance. Nevertheless a female patient wrote that she had heard how her neighbour said, " Her blood is being decomposed, and all nourishment goes to her flesh, and then her face will be swollen like a pig's, and her eyes will quite disappear," whereupon another replied, " But that can't come of itself—she must have been a dreadfully bad girl—and think of the number of young people, who were always in and out of the house," It is, however, very doubtful to me after former experiences whether such utterances, which in this case reproduced the constant self-tormenting of the patient, are really heard word for word.

Compared to illusions of sight and hearing, those of other senses are quite insignificant. There is a strong smell in the house ; the exhalation from the patient's body has a frightful stink ; his food tastes mawkish or putrid, like human flesh or privy manure. The bed is moving ; electric currents pass through it. On the other hand dysæsthesiæ appear in great number and variety, and they sometimes dominate the whole state Extraordinarily frequent are headaches, attacks of migraine, dull oppression, the feeling of a band round the forehead, of a heavy helmet, of a lead plate. In the rest of the body also pains of all sorts are felt. Schröder observed them in 62% of his cases. The tongue is sensitive ; the back aches as if it had gone to pieces, pains shoot from the urethra to the larynx ; there is raging and burning in the body. In one of my patients the disease began with such violent lumbago, that when all other remedies failed, the coccyx was amputated as an attempt to procure alleviation. There are also sensations of crawling, pulling, beating in the head, dragging in the legs, crackling in the bowels, pangs and " shameful feelings " in the abdomen.

As an illustration I quote the following fragment from the description which a female patient gave of herself. She thought that she had brought a serious disease (syphilis) on herself by onanism.

" Six months ago the patient was awakened by two violent blows on the body ; at the same time violent beating in body, heart, backbone, and the back of her head, trembling in hands and feet, in which the veins were greatly swollen. Leaden pallor of her face ; flatulence. After a few weeks the veins went down, and on her hands and especially on the joints, pricks as of a thousand needle-pricks. The skin on her hands became shrivelled and leathery, especially in her bath as if it could be pulled off. When it was pricked or cut, scarcely any blood appeared, sometimes a whitish fluid. Violent burning in her eyelids, lips, tongue and palate, thereafter spots and holes in her skin, as if made with a red-hot point. Small, red spots as in old people. Then a trickling in her whole body as if the vital fluid were curdling, and in her joints like red-hot lead. Whites. Irregular period, which was for long absent, and when it came back, the blood was thinner than formerly as if the blood had no sticky substance in it. At first a great flow of urine, then very slight and a motion only after an enema. Later a strong smell of urine and fæces, and her feet which were mostly cold and shrivelled, as if dead, perspired at times copiously with the same smell. The pulsation of the blood and the great beating decreased, but finally a crackling in her head, as if something were drying up, was specially alarming ; in her ears ticking as of a watch, so that lying on the pillow became a torment. The trembling of her hands and arms increased very much. Great emaciation of the abdomen, a falling in of the thorax. When she lay down, her body hot as lead. Decrease of eyesight. Flesh withered. Her skin peels off in small flakes. Sometimes a slight smell of burning in the skin. Her blood is so hot, as if it were boiling away. For some time patient has increased in body-weight—but apparently everything goes to flesh and nothing to blood, for the veins continue to disappear. At her elbows her flesh is painful, as if it were coming away from the bone. The pulse at her wrist is becoming harder. A feeling at her temples as if a hot hand were laid on them. Increasing indifference. In her skin no activity. When her hands perspire, small secretions like splinters of glass are seen, and so on.''

One sees here that it is largely a case of simple hyperæsthesia, but also of delusional interpretation of harmless sensations. That becomes very clear when the patients say that they feel their food going straight into their blood-vessels, their mucous membranes and glands corroded, their nerves loosened, fat, marrow, and albumen lacking in their blood, the inward working of their bodies, white worms drawing everything out of their bodies and creeping about between their different skins.

This heightened sensibility for the processes in their own bodies is in vivid contrast with the lowering of central excitability in manic states. We observe here a very striking lack of sensibility towards heat and cold, hunger and thirst, pain and injury. The patients expose themselves for hours at a time to the most burning sunshine, take off their clothes in a winter temperature, forget to eat and drink, regardlessly tear off the bandages from their sores, and ill-treat diseased parts of their body or their fractured limbs without giving any sign of discomfort. Nor do fears for health and life, fully justified by the circumstances, appear in them, or they are without hesitation treated as of no consequence.

The **Train of Ideas** of our patients invariably exhibits very important and well marked disorders. In states of excitement they are not able to follow systematically a definite train of thought, but they continually jump from one series of ideas to a wholly different one and then let this one drop again immediately. Any question directed to them is at first perhaps answered quite correctly, but with that are associated a great many side remarks which have only a very loose connection, or soon none at all, with the original subject. In consequence of these continuous interpolations and incidental remarks the patients are quite incapable of narrating any fairly complicated event, unless they are always brought back anew to the subject by constant interruptions and questions. The train of ideas is accordingly no longer dominated, as in normal people, by a general idea, which at the time admits only *one* definite direction of thought-association and inhibits all secondary and chance ideas. Therefore, at every moment the ideas favoured by general

habits of thought gain the upper hand, and not those required by the whole connection.   It thus comes to digression
from one idea to others similar or frequently associated with
it, without regard to the goal of the original train of thought.
The coherence of thinking relaxes more and more ;   there
arises that disorder which we have come to know as *confusion
with flight of ideas*.

The **Flight of Ideas** often becomes very distinctly
noticeable to the patient's own perceptions.   They complain
that they cannot concentrate or gather their thoughts together.   The thoughts come of themselves, obtrude themselves, impose upon the patients.   " I can't grasp all the
thoughts which obtrude themselves," said a patient.   " It
it is so stormy in my head," declared another, " everything
goes pell-mell."   " My thoughts are all tattered," " I am
not master over my thoughts," " One thought chases the
other ;   they just vanish like that,"—these are further utterances, which give us a glimpse into these processes.

In *depressed* patients also flight of ideas occurs not altogether infrequently, though certainly without being very
recognizable in the scanty speech of the taciturn patients ;
sometimes it appears distinctly in copious written utterances.
The patients complain that they " have so many thoughts
in their head," that they cannot pray, cannot work, because
other thoughts, " interpolations," come between, that they
have " no settled thoughts," that they have to think of
everything possible.   Even an immediate change between
flight of ideas and inhibition of thought, which is to be discussed later, appears to occur often.   " My thoughts stand
still," complained a female patient ;   " then they come again
of themselves and run where they will."

As the flight of ideas only represents a partial phenomenon
of the heightened distractibility, we generally observe that
patients with flight of ideas, so far as they are at all accessible
to external impressions, can be caused by these to let their
train of thought take a new turn which is then reflected in
their talk.   An object, on which their eyes fall, anything
written, a chance noise, a word, which sounds in their ears,
is immediately woven into their talk and may call forth a
series of similar ideas which often are only associated by
habits of speech or are related by sound.   The capacity to
observe and to perceive is by no means raised thereby.
Rather do the patients perceive as a rule only very super-
ficially and inaccurately, and they do not take themselves

up specially with what goes on around them. But when they notice anything, their train of thought is immediately influenced by it and generally also their flow of talk ; they express their perception in words and let themselves be aimlessly driven along by the impulse given by it.

Association Experiments have yielded very important conclusions about the train of thought of patients with flight of ideas. These experiments have been carried out principally by Aschaffenburg and Isserlin.[1] The former was able to demonstrate that the association reaction times in manic patients are by no means accelerated, but often even definitely retarded, contrary to the idea which originally was the fundamental signification of the expression " flight of ideas." To this the experience corresponds, that well-marked flight of ideas is observed not altogether infrequently even in quite slow talk. Franz also arrived at the same result. Isserlin has specially investigated the duration of ideas in manic patients. He found that their associations show heightened distractibility in the tendency to "diffusiveness," to spinning out the circle of ideas stimulated and jumping off to others, a phenomenon which in high degree is peculiar to mania. Kilian and Gutmann emphasize further the frequent repetition of the stimulus word. Isserlin was able to ascertain also with help of continuous associations that a change of direction of the train of thought took place in normal individuals about every 5 or 6 seconds, in a female manic patient on the other hand even after 1.6 or 1.7 seconds. The duration of an isolated idea in consciousness could be reckoned on the basis of phonographic records for the patient mentioned at about 1 second, while for two normal people it fluctuated between 1.2 and 1.4 seconds. The essential characteristic of the manic train of thought is therefore above everything the *fleetingness* of isolated ideas ; they do not persist in consciousness but vanish very quickly, when thay have scarcely reached development. " My thoughts are so rapid that I cannot hold them fast at all," said a patient.

Inhibition of Thought appears to form the exact opposite to flight of ideas. It is observed, more or less strongly marked, almost everywhere in depression, further in certain manic-stuperous mixed states and in forms of manic excitement related to these. The patients exhibit an incapacity, often very painfully felt by themselves, to order

[1] Isserlin, Monatsschr. f. Psych. u. Neurol., xxii., 302.

their own ideas aright. As it appears, isolated ideas develop slowly and only in response to very powerful stimuli. In consequence of this an impression does not of itself awaken rapidly and easily a great many associations, among which only a choice has to be made. Association, therefore, occurs mostly according to the content of the ideas, not according to external, linguistic or sound relations. Generally nothing at all occurs to the patients at first, and the train of thought must be laboriously spun out by a special effort of volition. Thus arises a great dulness and retardation of thought, thoughtlessness in answering simple questions, lack of understanding and poverty of ideas. "I cannot think any longer, I cannot imagine anything any more, cannot reflect any more, my head is empty," the patients complain, "my mental capacities are going back, I am as if mentally dead," "I am as in a dream, apathetic, and I don't know anything." Sometimes another complaint is associated with these, that their ideas are colourless and faded, the patients feel themselves incapable of recalling any impression, or occurrence, landscape, painting, or the appearance of their dear ones. They know quite well how the things look, and can even describe them, but the sensuously coloured memory picture is lacking in them.

Such patients produce only a conspicuously meagre number of ideas, even when apparently they are not at all hindered from expressing their thoughts. They are then generally considered very weak-minded, while the further course shows distinctly that here it was only a case of thought having become difficult, not of an annihilation of the store of ideas.

On the other hand the ideas once developed are not ousted by the emergence of fresh series of thoughts, but they fade slowly and often persist with great tenacity, especially when they are firmly rooted in temperament. The consequence then of this is an extraordinary *uniformity* of ideational content. The patients ever again bring forward the same thoughts, do not let themselves be turned aside to other domains, return after every intervening question immediately to the old complaints. "I have to rack my brains for hours about everyday reproaches and things," declared a patient. Now and then the ideas, which ever anew force themselves on the patients against their will, acquire completely the stamp of obsessions. The patients are tormented against their better knowledge by the constant fear that they have killed someone, pushed some one into the water, trodden under foot the host, swallowed a needle, driven a splinter into their foot, soiled the water-closet.

Association Experiment gives a wholly different picture in *depressive* patients from what it does in manic patients. A good idea of this relation is given by the following table taken from the work of Isserlin. It compares two association experiments on a patient, who at the time of the first one on April 25th was in a manic state, at the time of the second on September 8th was suffering from depression :—

	Internal Association. Per cent.	External Association. Per cent.	Digression. Per cent.	Clang Reaction. Per cent.	Repetition of Stimulus Word. Per cent.	Median. Sec.	Middle Zone. Sec.
April 25 .	18	81.5	56	22.3	43	1.0	0.2
Sept 8 .	81	17	—	1.9	—	5	6

The duration of the association time has risen fivefold in depression, and the " middle zone," which cuts out the middle half of the values gained, thus giving a good idea of the scatter of the numbers, also shows a considerable increase ; the association times have not only become longer, but also much more unequal. The relation between internal and external associations has been completely reversed ; whereas in mania the associations according to external relations, especially after linguistic practice, are greatly in excess, they decrease greatly in the depressed patients in favour of associations dependent on content. As a further expression of this displacement the almost complete disappearance of pure clang associations may be taken, which play such a large part in mania. In the same way digression which is so characteristic of the distractibility of manic patients is completely absent in depression, and lastly also the repetition of the stimulus word, which is frequent in manic patients and is probably caused mostly by inattention.

Mental Efficiency is invariably lowered in *mania*, with the possible exception that in the very slightest cases of manic excitement, the volitional excitement which accompanies the disease may under certain circumstances set free powers which otherwise are constrained by all kinds of inhibition. Artistic activity namely may by the untroubled surrender to momentary fancies or moods, and especially poetical activity by the facilitation of linguistic expression, experience a certain furtherance. This favourable effect is usually particularly conspicuous in comparison with the inhibitions of the depressed periods. In all the more pronounced forms of manic excitement, however, the unfavourable influence of heightened distractibility and of unsteadiness of volition is predominant. It is moreover easy to convince oneself that the patients in their desultory trains of thought are by no means rich in ideas but only rich in words ; often enough it comes to very monotonous repetitions. The occasional jokes of such patients are almost always simple plays on words, just as they are called forth by the tendency to clang associations. We find them as we find the tendency to speak in foreign languages, and a series of similar features in acute alcoholism, in which the paralysis of intellectual activity can be demonstrated with complete certainty. In spite of this and in contrast with the results of measurement we frequently meet with the self-deception of heightened mental efficiency. There is just as little evidence for it as there is for the idea of special mental freshness and health which arises from the manic feeling of well-being.

In contrast to that, the feeling of mental inhibition in states of *depression* is often greater than the actual lowering of efficiency, probably because the inhibition of thought can be overcome up to a certain degree by volitional effort, but just by that it becomes especially distinct to consciousness. The patients complain that they feel themselves " as if under a ban," as if fettered, that their thoughts are paralysed, that they now need hours for the simplest mental activity, as for example writing a letter, which formerly they could accomplish in a few minutes.

In order to ascertain more accurately the value of the mental efficiency, I have repeatedly had arithmetical experiments carried out with manic-depressive patients according to the procedure usual in fatigue measurements. Rehm investigated, one after the other, twenty-four normal individuals and thirty-four patients in the most varied states. He found that the work of the patients remained on an average about one-third behind that of the normal individuals. In manic patients the results were in general better than in depressed patients. The patients whose efficiency was most encroached on were those who exhibited clinically distinct inhibitions, and also depressed patients with excitement. The progress owing to daily practice was on the average less than in the normal individuals, once even negative, but a few times it exceeded the highest values of normal individuals. These experiences point to the fact that here probably, sometimes in the course, sometimes in the beginning of the experiment, inhibitions have lowered efficiency to an unusual degree. In the same sense the observation has to be interpreted that the recovery effect of a pause interpolated in the work remained in almost half of the patients behind the lowest values of the normal individuals, and in more than one-third of the cases was even negative, a result that might never occur among normal individuals. Here, even in the pause, inhibitions must have been developed, which in certain circumstances prevailed over the recovery effects.

The experiments carried out by Hutt on eight manic and seventeen depressive patients also gave in general as result a lowering of arithmetical efficiency, which, however, in the former was only very trifling, so far as the difference in education at all allows a comparison to be made with the normal individuals investigated. Improvement due to daily practice remained behind that of normal individuals and in one case was negative. Likewise in several cases negative values were recorded for the recovery effect of the pause ; the unfavourable effect on the output of the interruption due to the pause was throughout greater than in the normal individuals. Lastly, the experience is very noteworthy that in some cases, wholly contrary to the behaviour of normal individuals, an increase of output in continuous work without a pause was connected with the lowering of output after the pause, a circumstance which can only be related to a removal of influences inhibiting work by continuous work, this removal of influences being stronger than the effects of fatigue. It appears, accordingly, what moreover completely corresponds to clinical experience, that in our patients the hindrance to work may be weakened with comparative rapidity by effort and stimulus, while on the other hand after cessation of activity it soon returns and in certain circumstances to a greater extent.

Delusions are in manic - depressive insanity very frequent, especially in states of depression. Their simplest forms are connected with the feeling of mental inefficiency, and exhibit a *hypochondriacal* content. The patient has the idea that he is incurably ill, hopelessly lost. He suffers from cancer, syphilis, softening of the brain, is becoming demented, is having an attack of apoplexy, is ill in his body and soul, a desperate case ; his future will be a slow and tedious death. His body has taken on a quite different form ; his nerves are dried up, his organs withered ; his brain is obstructed with mucus, everything internal is dead, his voice is like tin ; the blood does not circulate in his brain any longer ; his penis does not recover itself again. Occasionally these ideas acquire a very extraordinary content, so that one is reminded of the delusions of paralytics. His brain is only pulp, his head the size of a finger joint ; his lungs and stomach are gone, his genitals are shrivelled ; his palate is withered, his gullet is done for ; in his body everything is sewn up and entangled ; there is a bone in his throat.

Ideas of Sin are almost more frequent. He reflects on his past life, finds that he has not fulfilled his duties, has committed many sins, has been disloyal to his Saviour. He was not grateful enough to his parents, has not taken good care of his children, has treated them badly, has not sent for the doctor immediately when there was illness, has not looked after them well enough. He has not discharged bills punctually, has committed lese-majesty, has neglected religion, has been dishonest about taxes, has masturbated, has committed adultery, has confessed and communicated unworthily ; he has been "frivolous in every relation," "a thoroughgoing rascal." Even these ideas may become more and more remote not only from reality, but also from possibility. The patient has committed perjury, offended a highly placed personage without knowing it, carried on incest, set his house on fire, killed his brothers and sisters. He has poisoned a prince, is a fivefold murderer, is to blame for every misfortune, is a damned soul, the refuse of humanity.

Ideas of Persecution are comewhat rarer ; they are frequently connected with the delusion of sin. The patient sees that he is surrounded by spies, is being followed by detectives, has fallen into the hands of the secret court of justice, of an avenging Nemesis, is going into the convict prison, is to be slaughtered, executed, burned, nailed to the cross ; all his teeth are being drawn out, his eyes dug out ; he is inoculated with syphilis ; he must putrefy, die in a filthy manner. He is despised by his neighbours, mocked, is no longer greeted ; they spit in front of him. There are allusions in the newspapers ; the sermon is aimed at him ; his sins are publicly made known on large placards. Burglars, anarchists, force their way into his house ; people are hidden in the cupboards. The patient notices that there is poison in the coffee, in the water for washing, feels himself hypnotized, magnetized ; people try to lead him astray by putting money in his way ; there is a conspiracy against him. His relatives also become involved. His family must die of

hunger ; his mother is being dismembered, his brother be-
headed ; the husband of a female patient is being arrested.

The domain of religion usually plays a considerable part
here. The patient thinks that he is spied on in the con-
fessional ; he is shut out of the church, is excommunicated,
has lost eternal salvation, must do penance for everyone,
take the sins of the whole world upon himself. Satan has
power over him, is hiding inside him, will command him to
swear, will take him away because he is no longer worth anything. God Almighty does not like him any longer ; his
prayer has no longer power ; hell-fire is already burning
under the bed.

Ideas of Greatness.—While all these delusions usually
go along with profound emotional agitation and are brought
forward and defended by the patient with the greatest conviction, the ideas of greatness, which not infrequently accompany the manic state, often bear more the stamp of half
jocular swaggering and boastful exaggeration, which also in
contrast to the depressive ideas for the most part uniformly
adhered to, change frequently, emerge as creations of the
moment and again disappear. In more sensible patients,
however, delusions may be observed which are psychically
finer spun and which persist more obstinately. To the first
group belong the assertions of the patients that they are
Messiah, the pearl of the world, the Christchild, the bride of
Christ, Queen of Heaven, Emperor of Russia, Almighty God,
that they have ten thousand children. Others allege that
the Czar is their fiancée ; they have been overshadowed by
the Holy Ghost, have annihilated the devil, can cure all
patients by hypnosis. The ideas are less nonsensical, that
they are a great artist or author, a baron, " physician by
birth," honorary doctor of all the sciences, a knight of high
orders, illegitimate son of a prince, that they have a higher
mission, speak seven languages, can hold up two hundredweight. A patient described himself as " a man of action,
immediately after Nietzsche." Large inheritances also usually
play a part. A patient who fancied that he was of aristocratic origin, alleged that his share of the inheritance would
shortly be paid ; another represented himself as the son-in-
law of Rockefeller, and boasted of the dowry of a hundred
million which he had in prospect.

Insight.—A clear understanding of the morbidity of the
state is, as a rule, present only in the slightest states of depression ; nevertheless here also it readily takes on a hypo-

chondriacal colouring with the idea of the hopelessness of the malady. Very commonly it is asserted that the disease is a greater torture than any other, that the patient would far, far rather endure any bodily pain than disorder of the mind. When the delusions are more pronounced, consciousness of the illness is generally lost, even when former and similar attacks are regarded correctly. At most once in a while the patients reply to the representations of the physician, that they would be glad if he were right ; unfortunately everything is only too true of their torments. A female patient begged to be allowed to make her will, as the fear was forced upon her that on the next day she would be completely confused. In manic states the patients mostly reject with emphasis the suggestion of mental disease. "Whoever thinks that I am mad, is himself mad," said a patient. At most they allow that they have been rather excited, " a little bit jolly." Afterwards they occasionally even make fun of the ideas to which they had given utterance ; it was " a little bit of delirium," " of course megalomania." A female patient said on her morbid behaviour being pointed out to her, " Doctor, you too sometimes do nonsensical things."

Mood is mostly exalted in *mania*, and in lively excitement it has the peculiar colouring of unrestrained merriment. The patients are pleased, " over merry " or " quietly happy," visionary, " more than satisfied," " cheerful in this beautiful world " ; they feel well, ready for all possible sport and banter, " penetrated with great merriment," they laugh, sing and jest. They are " enraptured with everything," " the happiest woman " ; happiness has come upon them ; " now the days of roses are coming." The group of patients in manic excitement (Fig. 3) reproduces the expression of this mood in varied colouring from quiet cheerfulness and proud self-consciousness to unrestrained cheerfulness.

Sexual excitability is increased and leads to hasty engagements, marriages by the newspaper, improper love-adventures, conspicuous behaviour, fondness for dress, on the other hand to jealousy and matrimonial discord. Several of my patients displayed in excitement homosexual tendencies. When merriment is associated with poverty of thought, it easily acquires the stamp of foolishness and silliness which then may lead to the assumption of a state of psychic weakness. Further, by the admixture of an unpleasant colouring the disposition of the manic may assume the form of angry irritation. The patients become arrogant and high flown ;

FIG. 3.—Manic Patients.

when they are contradicted, or on other trifling occasions, they fall into measureless fury, which is discharged in outbursts of rank abuse and violence.

But the circumstance is very important for the manic mood, that it is invariably subjected to frequent and abrupt fluctuations. In the midst of unrestrained merriment not only are sudden attacks of rage interpolated, but also uncontrollable weeping and sobbing, which certainly give place again just as quickly to unrestrained cheerfulness. " I don't know whether to laugh or cry," said a female patient. In this alternation of mood, which in a similar manner, although far less pronounced, is frequently found also in states of depression, the close internal relationship of the clinical states, apparently so fundamentally different, is seen.

The fundamental mood in the states of *depression* is most frequently a sombre and gloomy hopelessness. The patient has " whole hundredweights on him," is lacerated with grief, has lost all spirit, feels himself deserted, without any real aim in life. His heart is like stone ; he has no pleasure in anything. As it appears, it is here a case not only of gloomy and sullen humour, but also of a certain inhibition of the emotions which is the antithesis of the free flow of the feelings in mania. It is exactly this decrease of emotional interest, the loss of inner sympathy with the surroundings and with the events of life, which the patients usually feel most bitterly. Within them all is empty and vain ; everything is indifferent to them, is no concern of theirs, seems " so stupid " to them ; music " sounds strange." They have a feeling as if they were wholly out of the world ; they cannot weep any more ; they experience neither hunger nor satisfaction, neither weariness nor refreshment after sleep, no longer any bodily desire ; God has taken away from them all feeling. A female patient complained that she was annoyed, if she saw other people doing anything with interest. " I am like a stock," complained another patient, " and feel neither joy nor sorrow." Indeed it is easy to convince oneself that the patients are surprisingly little affected by bad news. Natural grief usually breaks out first in convalescence. Even when their relatives visit them, they often show no interest, scarcely look up, make no enquiries. On this account they sometimes appear dull and without feeling, although it is not a case of annihilation of emotions, but only of inhibition.

More rarely than the sombre and sad melancholy just described anxiety is the principal feature of mood. Sometimes it is more " inward anxiety and trembling," a painful tension, which can rise to mute and helpless despair ; sometimes it is an uneasy restlessness, which finds an outlet in the most varied gestures, in states of violent excitement, and in regardless attempts at suicide. In other cases again, we meet with a peevish, insufferable, dissatisfied and grumbling mood. The patients are discontented with everything ; they loathe the whole world ; everything torments, annoys, irritates them, fills them with bitterness, the sunshine, people enjoying themselves, music, everything done or left undone in their surroundings. These moods are most frequently found in the periods of transition between states of depression and mania ; they are, therefore, probably most correctly regarded as mixed states of depression and manic excitability.

The torment of the states of depression, which is nearly unbearable, according to the perpetually recurring statements by the patients, engenders almost in all, at least from time to time, weariness of life, only too frequently also a great desire to put an end to life at any price. " There's nothing to be done with me but powder or in water," said a female patient, and another expressed herself thus, " Millstone round my neck, and then to the bottom of the sea." The patients, therefore, often try to starve themselves, to hang themselves, to cut their arteries ; they beg that they may be burned, buried alive, driven out into the woods and there allowed to die. In carrying out injuries on themselves they are often quite indifferent to bodily pain. One of my patients struck his neck so often on the edge of a chisel fixed on the ground that all the soft parts were cut through to the vertebræ.

Out of 700 manic-depressive women, whom I observed in Munich, 14.7% made serious attempts at suicide ; of those, who on admission were over 35 years of age, 16.2%. Among 295 men 20.4% attempts at suicide were reported. The otherwise much greater difference in the tendency to suicide of the two sexes is thus largely obliterated by the disease.

Even in states of depression the mood, as already indicated, is not necessarily always the same, although the fundamental feature here often persists with hopeless obstinacy. Without taking into account the fact, that not at all infrequently for a short time there may be a complete change to the manic state, we are often surprised by a forlorn smile, a sudden gaiety, which appears quite abruptly in the midst of self-accusation and ideas of persecution. " It's a misery," said a patient with a contented look. Occasionally the patients develop a certain grim humour ; they scoff at their own complaints and treat them ironically, calling themselves with a querulous laugh silly cattle. One patient called himself a " magnificent masturbator." Specially characteristic, and in certain circumstances of definite diagnostic significance is the experience that, when the moodiness is not too severe, it is frequently possible to persuade the patients to look pleasant. The suddenness with which the relaxed and troubled features then assume an expression of merriment and high spirits, is extraordinarily startling.

Pressure of Activity.—By far the most striking disorders in manic-depressive insanity are found in the realm of volition and action. In manic states the morbid picture is dominated by pressure of activity ; here we have to do with general volitional excitement. Experiment certainly teaches that the duration of simple and discriminative reactions is invariably lengthened, sometimes even very considerably. Many circumstances, however, point to the fact that the lengthening essentially concerns the connection of actions with external requests, which moreover are often imperfectly understood. On the other hand every chance impulse seems to lead forthwith to action, while the normal individual usually suppresses innumerable volitional impulses immediately as they arise. The disorder might to a certain degree conform to that which we can produce artificially by alcohol ; from this arises the great similarity of many manic patients to light or heavy drinkers. It is true that in drunkenness the encroachment on perception and thought is comparatively much greater than in our patients ; and besides in the former the appearance of paralysis and uncertainty in movement soon makes itself conspicuous.

Manic pressure of activity naturally leads to more or less pronounced restlessness. In the slightest grades it is only a certain restless behaviour, always busy about something, which strikes us, an agitated desire for hurried enterprise. The patients make all sorts of plans, wish to train as singers, to write a comedy ; they send suggestions for reform to the police magistrate or to the railway managers ; a clergyman wrote a letter to the Pope concerning the marriage of priests. They busy themselves with the affairs of other people, but not with their own ; they start senseless businesses, buy houses, clothes, hats, give large orders, make debts ; they wish to set up an observatory, to go to America. One patient made the journey to Corsica and there bought property for 85,000 marks, which involved him in endless law-suits. They make plans of marriage, enter into doubtful acquaintanceships, kiss strange ladies on the streets, frequent public houses, commit all possible acts of debauchery. A young girl went about with men in taverns and paid for their beer. An elderly married man went walking on the street with a negress from a music-hall. While they appear in company as jovial fellows, give large tips, stand treat, they quarrel with their superiors, neglect their duty, give up their situations for trifling causes, leave public-houses without paying. A female patient travelled on the tramcar without a ticket, and then asserted falsely that she had a season ticket.

Acute Mania.—In more severe excitement a state of genuine mania is developed by degrees. Impulses crowd one upon the other and the coherence of activity is gradually lost. The patient is unable to carry out any plan at all involved, because new impulses continually intervene, which turn him aside from his original aim. Thus his pressure of activity may finally resolve itself into a variegated sequence of volitional actions ever new and quickly changing, in which no common aim can be recognised any longer, but they come and go as they are born of the moment. The patient sings, chatters, dances, romps about, does gymnastics, beats time, claps his hands, scolds, threatens, and makes a disturbance, throws everything down on the floor, undresses, decorates himself in a wonderful way, screams and screeches, laughs or cries ungovernably, makes faces, assumes theatrical attitudes, recites with wild passionate gestures. But, however abrupt and disconnected this curious behaviour is, it is still always made up of fractional parts of actions, which stand in some sort of relation to purposeful ideas or to emotions ; it is a case of movements of expression, unrestrained jokes, attacks on people, amusement, courtship, and the like.

Only in very severe excitement may these relations be effaced, sometimes even beyond the possibility of recognition. The patients roll their eyes, turn their heads, roll about on the floor, hop, bellow, turn somersaults, beat rhythmically on the mattress, throw their legs about, beat as on a drum, behave convulsively, gnash their teeth, spit and bite about them. The movements may then in certain circumstances be very monotonous and senseless, and may occasionally give quite the impression of compulsion. A female patient declared to me that she must always carry out peculiar movements with her arms and head and say certain sentences,

" Laissez moi-laissez-moi travailler " ; another stated that she must always beat the wall with her fist ; a third that she had got out of bed " on command".

The pictures reproduced, Figs 4 and 5, afford so far an idea of manic behaviour. The first shows a patient who has plaited her hair for a joke in innumerable small plaits. The second represents a patient who has made a picturesque

FIG. 4.—Manic patient with numerous plaits.

costume for herself from old garments, scarfs, and blankets, and is displaying a number of works of art made of paper on the lid of a cardboard box. I further reproduce some pictures, Fig. 6, from a series taken by Weiler, which show a patient with a lively play of gesture in various impressive attitudes rapidly alternating one with the other.

An Increase of Excitability also is invariably present in our patients as well as excitement. Perhaps this is even to be regarded as the essential fundamental manifestation. The patients are often fairly quiet as long as they are, as far as possible, protected from every external stimulus, but if they are spoken to, or some one comes to see them, or their

FIG. 5.—Decorated manic patient.

fellow patients begin to scream, excitement, rapidly growing worse, appears with uncommon facility. The more they are allowed to talk and to do as they please, the greater does pressure of activity usually become, an experience very important for treatment.

The Feeling of Fatigue is completely absent in the patient in spite of the most intense motor excitement which occasionally persists in the highest degree for weeks, indeed

Fig. 6.—Changing attitudes of a manic patient.

for many months, with slight interruptions. He is not weary and relaxed ; the ill usage of the muscle tissue produces no sensation of discomfort, partly, perhaps, because of the blunting of sensibility previously discussed, but specially perhaps because of the ease with which his activity discharges itself. In him the slightest impulse is sufficient to call forth abundant movement, while for· the attainment of the same result the normal individual would require an incomparably greater expenditure of central energy. On this ·account also every attempt to imitate this state must necessarily in a very short time fail, because· of the impossibility of overcoming the paralyzing feeling of fatigue by a mere effort of will. This circumstance, as also the regardlessness with which the patients use their limbs, has led to the widely-spread, but incorrect, view that they possess very great bodily strength. But on the contrary the working capacity of their muscles is invariably proved in ergographic experiments to be considerably decreased. On the other hand the movements are more quickly carried out than by normal individuals, especially when there is a continuous series of the same movements and the patients fall into rapidly rising excitement.

Towards their surroundings the patients behave in very varying fashion. As a rule they are easily influenced, approachable, often importunate, erotic. At times they become irritated, threatening and violent, but are then for the most part quickly calmed by kindly or humorous persuasion. Many patients are repellent, pert, abrupt, unapproachable ; now and then waxy flexibility and echolalia or echopraxis are observed.

Pressure of Speech, which is often very marked in the patients, is a partial manifestation of the general pressure of activity. The conversion also of verbal ideas into the movements of speech is morbidly facilitated. Isserlin was able to prove that the number of syllables spoken in a minute by a manic patient amounted to 180 to 200, while the normal control produced not more than 122 to 150. As we have already remarked just this circumstance might play a certain part in the peculiar form of the manic flight of ideas. The easily stimulated ideas of the movements of speech gain too great an influence over the flow of the train of thought, while the relations of the contents of the ideas pass more into the background. Thus it comes about that in the higher grades of the flight of ideas, just as happens under the influence of alcohol, forms of speech, which have been learned as such, combinations of words, corresponding sounds and rhymes, usurp more and more the place of the substantive connection of ideas. As is already recognisable from the examples given above, the pure clang-associations, in which every trace of an inner relation of ideas has vanished, assonances and rhymes, even though quite senseless, gain more and more the upper hand.   To what a height the disorder may rise, is shown in Fig. 7, in which, according to Aschaffenburg's investigations, the percentage of clang-associations in five normal individuals and five manic patients is reproduced.   The numbers for the normal individuals fluctuate here between 2 and 4% ; but they may with peculiar personal disposition once in a way even be considerably higher.   On the other hand they never reach the high values of the manic patients which here rise to 32 to 100%.   A female patient wrote on a piece of paper, Nelke—welke—Helge—Hilde—Tilde—Milde—Hand—Wand —Sand.

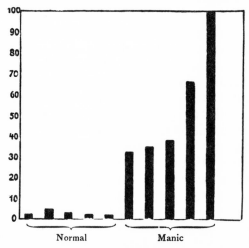

Fig. 7.—Frequency of clang-associations in normal individuals and manic patients.

In the talk of the patient the flight of ideas and the pressure of speech are both at the same time conspicuous. He cannot be silent for long ; he talks and screams in a loud voice, makes a noise, bellows, howls, whistles, is over-hasty in speech, strings together disconnected sentences, words, syllables, mixes up different languages, preaches with solemn intonation and passionate gestures, abruptly falling from high-sounding bombast to humorous homeliness, threats, whining, and obscenity, or suddenly coming to an end in un-restrained laughter.   Occasionally it comes to lisping or affected speech with peculiar flourishes, also, it may be, to talking in self-invented languages which consist partly of senseless syllables, partly of strangely clipped and mutilated words.   Among these are interpolated quotations, silly puns, poetical expressions, vigorous abuse.   Many patients speak like children, in telegram style, in infinitives.

An example of manic conversation is given in the following notes :—

" Notieren Sie genau, es scheint mir alles so grau ; die Uhr (a watch was held in front of the patient) bedeutet den Kreislauf der Zeit; Herr N. hat einen Chronometer bereit.   Mein Magen tut mir weh, immer hipp, hipp, hurrah !   Der Geibel ist der Dichter, der Genius der Zeit gewesen, été, der Sommer muss kommen, die Bäume schlagen aus, und du bist nicht zu Haus. Röslein, so hold am Haag, mich doch niemand holen mag.   Les extrêmes se touchent ; Zeiten fliehen so manches Jahr, mich doch niemand holen mag. (to the waitress) Du Luder, du unverschämtes Saumensch, kannst du darüber lachen, dass die guter Hoffnung ist, von Rose gesprochen, drum bist du Esel so grau.   Grau, teurer Freund, ist alle Theorie.   Stern, Blume so gern.   Der Grossherzog soll leben hoch.   Leberecht Hühnchen," and so on.

The want of connection here is not at all caused by over-flowing abundance of thought, but by deficient cultivation of guiding end-ideas.   The normal individual also may produce very similar series, when he lets go the reins of his thinking and says aloud whatever comes into his mind.   Nevertheless, in normal individuals, as the investigations of Stransky have shown, the manifold variety of ideas appears to be considerably less, in consequence of the involuntary persistence of end-ideas and the slighter distractibility which is caused by that.   In place of this variety there appear enumerations as well as variations and repetitions of the same thoughts.   The patients also often produce enumerations.   A female patient called out, " Straubing, Osterhofen, Vilshofen, Passau," and later, " Life, light, death, hell, eternity."

As a rule the conversation of the patients is considerably influenced by external impressions.   They weave in words which they have heard, connect up chance impressions, and make them serve as starting-points for utterances spun out by the flight of ideas.   But occasionally in jocular manner they directly evade all external stimulus, only laugh at every question, repeating it in a teasing way, and purposely give false or wittily elusive replies.   A female patient always replied with unrestrained laughter to everything that was said to her, the one word " Nixen " (nichts).   Another, on being asked her age, replied, " Amn't born at all " ; when asked what is seven times seven, " One doesn't count any more, one weighs, one measures."   Lastly, it also happens that the patients not only string together of themselves single words and incomplete sentences without connection, but also they pay no attention to the meaning of the questions directed to them ; they rather give utterance to completely unrelated, nonsensical remarks. Many patients remain mute, yet communicate with their surroundings by means of a very expressive and comical language of signs.

In the *writings* of the patients there is a tendency to use foreign words and to mix up different languages. The influence of clang-association on the sequence of ideas is here on obvious grounds much slighter than in speaking, especially in the case of patients, whose internal speech does not by preference wholly take the form of speech motives or clang-pictures. Instead of that it often comes to the enumerations of similar ideas described in detail by Aschaffenburg, while association according to external similarity, or according to contiguity, takes the place of a progressive train of thought. The increase of distractibility and excitability are usually seen in the circumstance that the first words or lines are for the most part quite connected, whereas the remainder consists of a confused sequence of enumerations, reminiscences, scraps of verse, assonances and rhymes.

The following fragment of a letter of condolence contains such derailments :—

"Ach ! gnädigste Frau ! Komm' ich auch spat zu Ihnen, meine innigste, wirklich aus meinem Herzen fliessende Teilnahme zu dem Heimgange à la Fidelio Thres teuren Florestan auszudrücken—niemals kommt man dann zu spät, wenn man sich frägt : Ach, wie ist's denn möglich wohl, dass mir so viele Schmerzen Dein Tod, Du treuer, lieber Seladon und Romeo Mir, Deiner einzigen ach ! der teuren Gattin naht die . . . Ja die Tränen ! ecc. Pamela Questenberg Neumann Gordon a la Vitzthum Magdalena o Terzky Struve Carola auch Du Graf von Lula o Leonore o Sollschwitz o Gitschin Generalmajor von Schmieden aussi bientot Hauptmann qu'est que la pardonnez . . ."

Here we first meet the series Fidelio—Florestan—Seladon—Romeo, which interrupts the original train of thought. Next comes the series Questenberg—Neumann—Gordon—Terzky, to which is added a number of other names, this series being probably suggested by the expression " spät komm ich " (I come late). At the end there follows the digression into French, and then in the further course of the letter fragments in English, Latin and Greek and a series of high-sounding verses.

The handwriting of the patients may at first be quite regular and correct. In consequence of the excitability, however, it usually becomes gradually always larger, more pretentious and more irregular. There is no more consideration for the reader ; the letters run through one another, are scribbled ; more words are underlined ; there are more marks of exclamation ; the flourishes become bolder. All those

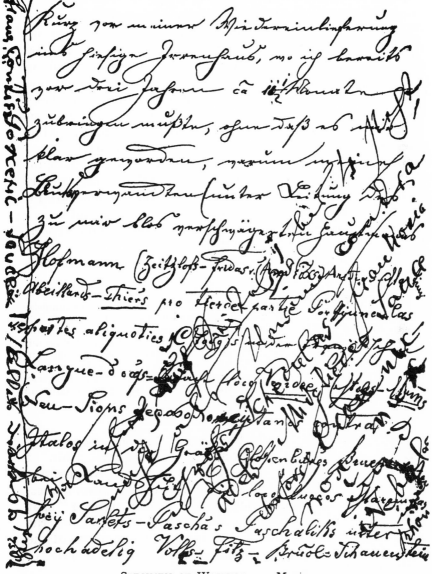

SPECIMEN OF WRITING.—1. Mania.

disorders, those of substance as well as those of form, are well shown in the accompanying specimen of writing. The number of documents produced by manic patients is sometimes astonishing, though certainly they themselves do not count on their being read ; the pleasure of writing itself is the only motive.

Inhibition.—In the states of *depression*, in place of pressure of activity inhibition of will, its complete antithesis, generally appears. The performance of actions is here made difficult, even impossible. The slighter degrees of the disorder are seen in the indecision of the patients. The emerging impulses are not strong enough to overcome the opposing inhibitions ; in spite of clear recognition of necessity, although all genuine motives to the contrary and reasons for doubt are absent, the patient is yet not able to rouse himself to carry out the simplest actions. He " has no longer any will of his own," " does not know how he is to manage " ; he must always ask advice about what he is to do ; he can no longer do any thing rightly, as he is never certain that it is the right thing. A patient said, " I'm a weak man, who doesn't know what he wants."

The activity also, which after much hesitation is at last begun, comes to a stop every moment, as the energy of vigourous decision is lacking. The patient no longer finishes anything, does everything the wrong way about, does not get any further on in spite of all the work which he performs with the greatest effort ; he has no right spring in him ; he is weighed down with gloom. A female patient said that she had dressed early intending to go out, and in the afternoon she was still at home. All isolated movements, so far as they require volitional impulse, are carried out with more or less reduced speed and without vigour ; hands and feet obey no longer. The patient can no longer take hold of anything or keep hold of it ; mouth and tongue are heavy as lead. His bearing is relaxed and weary ; his behaviour stiff and constrained ; his expression rigid and immobile.

In ergographic curves Gregor and Hänsel were able to demonstrate an abrupt and early fall of the curve, to which followed low, long drawn-out curves, a sign of rapid failure of volitional impulse in prolonged exertion of muscles. External influence, and especially pleasant excitement, may decrease the inhibition. With steady persuasion or in danger the patient is able to accomplish what otherwise would be impossible for him. Often no parrying movements at all follow pinpricks, or they only follow if very sensitive places are pricked. Waxy flexibility and echo-phenomena are not rare.

In the most severe *stuporous* forms every volitional expression of the patient may be arrested, so that he is only able to lie still and can scarcely open his eyes. He is unable to show his tongue, to take his meals, to give his hand, or even to leave his bed and relieve nature. Although he perhaps understands quite well what he is told to do, yet at most a few weak, trembling attempts at the required movements follow. The patient retains uncomfortable attitudes, because it is not possible for him to change his position; all objects, which are placed in his hand one after the other, he spasmodically tries to hold, as he is incapable of letting them go.

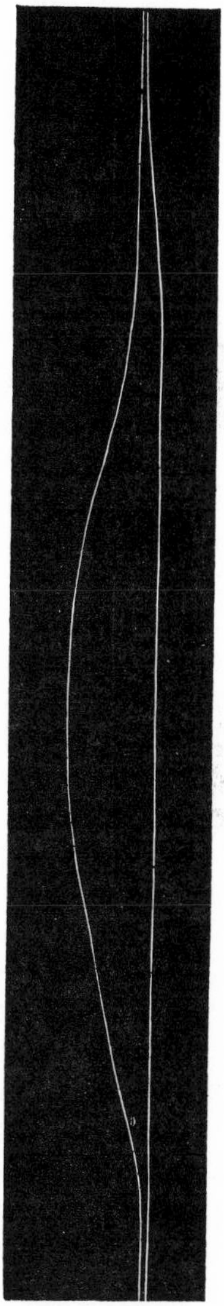

The extreme inhibition of even quite simple volitional actions appears very distinctly in the accompanying curve, Fig. 8, of a reaction movement, which Isserlin obtained from a depressed patient. It should be compared with the curves of normal individuals and of catatonics given elsewhere.[1] It shows conclusively the extremely slow flexion and extension of the finger and also the small extent of the movement.

The inhibition of will is usually felt as extremely painful by the patients. The feeling of "insufficiency," of incapacity, is frequently already present, when to outward observation no difficulty at all in volitional actions can be recognised. Very commonly the remission in their work is interpreted by the patients as a moral offence. They reproach themselves most bitterly with their inactivity; they will not remain in bed in order not to be thought lazy. Many patients develop a convulsive mania for work, and grudge themselves all rest in order to defend themselves from their own reproaches. "The spade had to be taken out of

FIG. 8.—Simple flexion and extension movement of a finger in an inhibited patient.

[1] Kraepelin, *Dementia Præcox and Paraphrenia.* Translation Edinburgh, p. 80 *et seq.* (Oct. 1919).

his hand for otherwise he did not stop," reported the relatives of a patient. It is possible, however, that in such cases a psychomotor excitement plays a part.

The difficulty in volitional discharge leads naturally to a more or less considerable restriction of activity. Even if the most necessary work is at first still performed, every spontaneous activity remains yet undone. The patients give up their leisure occupations, and posts of honour, withdraw themselves from society and continually feel the need of rest. Later they neglect themselves and become careless. In the end they give up every activity and take refuge in bed, where they remain lying motionless, and in certain circumstances even pass their motions there. Of practical importance is the circumstance that the inability of the patients to come to a decision lessens the danger of suicide in some degree, at least at the height of the malady. Although they cherish the fervent desire to put an end to their life, they yet have not the power to carry out this intention. One of my patients already stood in the water, but had not " the courage " to jump in completely.

The various domains of volitional expression may be influenced in very different degree by volitional inhibition. As primarily the *discharge of volitional resolves* appears to be made difficult, those actions which are habitual and require no interference of will are still done unhindered, while the inhibition makes itself very strongly felt in other domains. The patients are able to dress themselves without difficulty and to occupy themselves, while they are incapable of making any independent resolve ; they still perhaps accomplish easily and habitually the work of the day without special difficulty, but are alarmed at every new enterprise, at every special responsibility.

Movements of expression, as far as they should reflect psychic emotions, are usually attacked with special severity by the inhibition ; mimic gestures also and movements generally lose in vivacity. The patients speak in a low voice, slowly, hesitatingly, monotonously, sometimes stuttering, whispering, try several times before they bring out a word, become mute in the middle of a sentence. They become silent, monosyllabic, can no longer converse, although they are able to count with customary rapidity or read aloud. Sometimes they do not speak a word of their own accord, but readily give information when asked, or they speak in a whispering tone, but vehemently with vivacious gestures.

Pfersdorff has called attention to the fact, that many patients make gross mistakes in spelling, omissions, duplications, exchanges of letters ; here it can occasionally be recognized that associated clang-pictures influence the perception of the visual picture (*k* instead of *a* or *h*). Copying is done in certain circumstances unhindered, while the patients sit for hours before a letter, which they have begun, without bringing it to an end. The disorder meantime does not affect speech and writing at all in equal measure. There are patients who speak quite fluently but can scarcely write a few lines, and *vice versa* others write long passionate letters, while they become mute as soon as one wishes to converse with them.

In the place of volitional inhibition *anxious excitement* appears not very infrequently. The patients display a more or less lively restlessness, cannot sit still, do not remain in bed, run about, hide in corners, try to escape. They whimper, groan, sigh, scream, wring their hands, tear out their hair, beat their head, pluck at themselves and scratch themselves, cling to people, pray, kneel, slide about on the floor, beg for mercy, for forgiveness. In severe cases it comes to senseless screaming, lamenting, screeching, turning and dancing about, snatching, twisting and twitching of the hands and the trunk, rubbing and wobbling. Frequently monotonous, rhythmical repetition is conspicuous.

Specht, Thalbitzer, and also Dreyfus are inclined to interpret that kind of anxious excitement from the point of view of mixed states. It is said to be a case here of a conjunction of depression with the manic morbid symptom of volitional excitement. Taking the contrary view, Westphal and Kölpin have pointed out that the excitement represents an immediate outflow of anxiety, and therefore cannot be regarded as a manic component of the morbid state. To this is may be replied that the anxiety in itself may produce inhibition just as well as excitement of volition ; it would be therefore possible that the transformation of inward tension, as we find it in many states of depressive stupor, into anxious excitement, is facilitated or even caused by the appearance of a volitional excitement in the sense of mania. It, however, appears to me hazardous to approach circumstances, which are certainly very involved, with such simple conceptions. We shall later meet with experiences which give evidence that the peculiar, anxious colouring of the states of depression, which completely differs from those of the manic states, has a certain relation to *age*, a circumstance which Specht, in fact, has made use of for his view. I consider it, however, in the meantime very doubtful whether that anxious excitement which occurs solely in the form of movements of expression, though they may be of a very violent and nonsensical kind, may without hesitation be conceived as a mixture of anxious mood and manic pressure of activity But on the other hand, as we shall later see, there are without doubt states which are to be interpreted in this sense, and it must be conceded that in certain circumstances the distinction will be difficult, that perhaps, indeed, transition forms also may come under observation.

Pressure in Writing.—A good idea of the peculiarities of the psychomotor disorders in manic-depressive insanity is afforded by the accompanying curves, Fig. 9. They represent the pressure-oscillations in the writing of 1 and 10 in a continuous series of figures. They were obtained with the aid of a writing balance. The spaces on the horizontal lines give an idea of the time taken by the writing ; the height of the curves represents on an enlarged scale the pressure exercised each moment on the writing-table. Under the individual curves there are accurate copies of the figures themselves, as they were made in the experiments. Fig. A comes from a healthy nurse. The remission of pressure during the turning of the movement of writing and the rise in the down-stroke are seen in the first 1 and still better in the second ; in the 0, also, a small pressure-oscillation corresponds to the turning. The small curves at the end are caused by after-oscillations of the pen on its being rapidly removed.

Fig. C was furnished by a female manic patient. The psychomotor excitement appears here in the large ' pretentious figures. The pressure is considerably raised and also the speed of writing, if we take into account the different length traversed by the pen. In the second 1 both pressure and speed are raised very considerably, a phenomenon, which also occurs in normal individuals everywhere, but which in them is not nearly so marked. As it indicates to us the increased facility of production during work, it may be regarded as an expression of increased psychomotor excitability. The rapidly increasing number of after-oscillations in the course of the writing points to the greater abruptness of the pressure-oscillations in the violent movements of writing.

A wholly different picture is presented by Fig. B, which

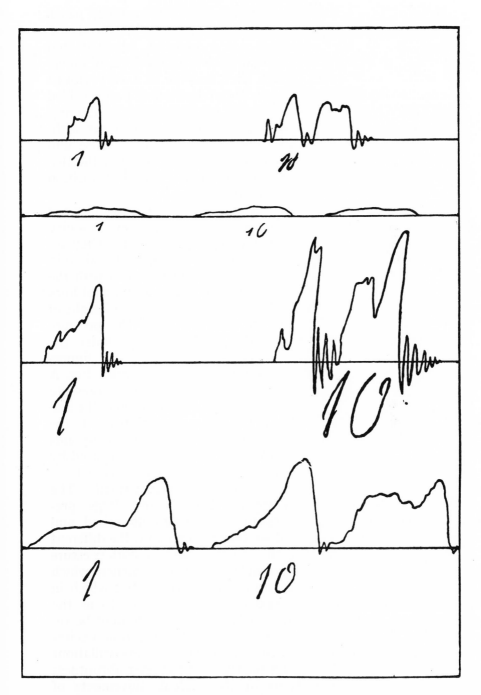

FIG. 9.—Pressure curves in writing in manic-depressive insanity.

was obtained from a patient in a state of depression. The figures are remarkably small, in spite of which they required considerably longer time than Fig. A; the speed was, therefore, much less. At the same time the pressure is extraordinarily low; it does not even amount to 50 g., and the oscillations are very slightly marked. After-oscillations are absent; the pressure of the writing therefore did not stop abruptly but very gradually. Here also, moreover, a slight increase of speed is seen in the second i. Between it and the following o there is a disproportionately long pause. Accordingly, as we found in the manic patient violent movements very much accelerated with rapid and considerable increase of excitability, so here we meet with hesitating commencement and discontinuance, little vigour, and significant decrease in the speed of writing, signs which clearly indicate the existence of a psychomotor inhibition.

But the two states of the instrument of our volition, which are here distinguished from each other, are scarcely so opposed to each other as might appear at first sight. We see them at least in the course of the disease frequently enough abruptly pass over the one into the other. Inhibition and facilitation of volitional impulses may accordingly be only *nearly related* phenomena of a common fundamental disorder. That becomes still more evident, when we see that the symptoms of both the morbid changes not at all infrequently *are mixed*. The special clinical forms of this mixture we shall later have to examine more in detail.

Here I should like merely to refer to Fig D in the page of curves. It is written by the same patient as Fig. C, only she was then in a state, in which for a few days during a severe attack of mania, the pressure of activity had completely disappeared. The figures are now smaller and the pressure curve shows a slight decrease of pressure with slow ascent and decline, and a very considerable decrease of speed, thus an extremely peculiar mixture of the changes which we have already learned to recognise in manic excitement and in inhibition.

Certainly we do not by any means find everywhere such marked changes of the pressure lines in writing. In especial the investigations carried out hitherto to a somewhat greater extent in states of depression have taught that here we find the most manifold gradations of the forms of Fig. B to approximately normal forms. Vigour, speed, and extent of movement in writing may not suffer any essential change while the patients otherwise distinctly display the signs of volitional inhibition. It must for the present be left undecided whether the more severe disorders of writing are peculiar to specially characteristic states, or are dependent on the content of what is written, or on the greater or less significance of the volitional impulses for the movement of writing in individual persons.

CHAPTER III.

BODILY SYMPTOMS.

THE attacks of manic-depressive insanity are invariably accompanied by all kinds of *bodily changes*. By far the most striking are the disorders of *sleep* and of *general nourishment*. In mania sleep is in the more severe states of excitement always considerably encroached upon; sometimes there is even almost complete sleeplessness, at most interrupted for a few hours, which may last for weeks, even for months. In the slighter states of excitement the patients go late to bed and are also very early wide awake, but their sleep appears to be extraordinarily deep. In the states of depression in spite of great need for sleep, it is for the most part sensibly encroached upon; the patients lie for hours, sleepless in bed, tormented by painful ideas, and after confused, anxious dreams awake the next morning dazed, worn out and weary. They get up for the most part very late; they also perhaps remain in bed for days or weeks, although even in bed they find no refreshment.

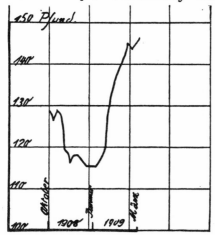

FIG. 10.—Body-weight during a manic attack.

Appetite is in manic patients frequently increased, but the taking of nourishment is nevertheless irregular in consequence of haste and restlessness. In more severe morbid states the patients frequently devour all possible indigestible and disgusting things; they bolt their food without due mastication, throw away the food that is offered them, smear it about, spill it. Depressed patients have as a rule little inclination to eat, and usually take nourishment only with reluctance and with much persuasion. Their tongue is coated and they suffer from constipation. Wilmanns and Dreyfus have put forward the view, within certain limits probably quite rightly, that so-called " nervous dyspepsia " frequently represents merely an expression of the slightest

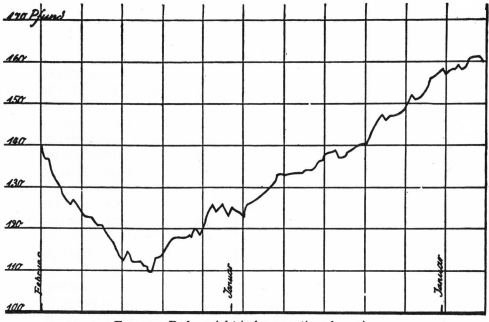

FIG. 11.—Body-weight in long-continued mania.

states of depression. Individual patients complain from time to time, or else continuously, of ravenous appetite, which appears to be a manifestation of anxiety.

The **Body-weight** always falls very considerably in acute mania, while in hypomanic attacks it rises as a rule. An example of the course of the body-weight during an attack of severe manic excitement, which

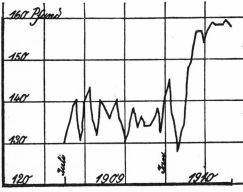

FIG. 12.—Great fluctuation of body-weight in mania

lasted about six months, is given in Fig. 10 up to recovery. With the advent of tranquillity the weight here rises with very surprising rapidity, in one week 5 kg.

Fig. 11 shows a course extending over more than two

years. It is seen here that the lowest weight was already reached in about six months. Although the manic excitement from that time onwards lasted nearly a year in its former severity, the weight yet rose with small fluctuations steadily, and only in the last weeks remained constant, when an irregular fluctuation between slight manic and depressive moods had developed.

An essentially different picture is given by the curve represented in Fig. 12. It comes from a manic patient, who was discharged cured, perhaps a little depressed, after treatment for ten months in the hospital; he had already before that been some months ill. We observe here before the last rapid and considerable rise of the curve quite a number of smaller oscillations of the weight, some of them fairly regular, the highest points of which, however, remain far under the height which was later reached. In general the fluctuations of the psychic state corresponded to these oscillations, yet the alternation of more excited and quieter periods appeared to clinical observation far more irregular. The impression is made here as though the whole attack had been composed of a series of shorter single attacks, a phenomenon which is met with not so very rarely. It cannot indeed specially surprise us considering the frequent inclusion of variously coloured attacks in one series, an occurrence which has given circular insanity its name.

A somewhat divergent, but still for all that a similar picture is seen in Fig. 13. Here it was a case of manic excitement, at first slight, then rapidly becoming more severe,

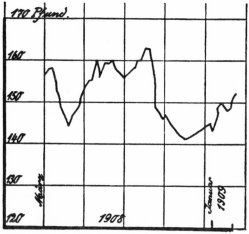

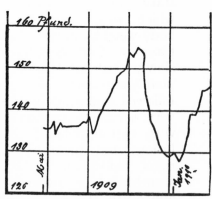

Fig. 13.—Body-weight during a compound attack.

Fig. 14.—Body-weight in depression.

after which tranquillity and transition to slight depression soon followed. To this period of the disease the first fall and renewed rise of the curve correspond. The small descents which now follow, and which certainly are always again compensated, must render it doubtful whether the attack had already reached a close, and indeed the commencement of a severe depressive state of stupor appeared very suddenly with a very rapid fall of the body-weight, which then was followed by recovery. We gather from this, that in states of depression also the body-weight usually falls, and this happens as a rule, in contrast to mania, in the slightest forms.

A peculiar example of this is presented in Fig. 14. Here there was at first a slight, simple state of depression, which, with rise of the body-weight, in about three or four months slowly but not completely improved. Then followed immediately a very severe depression with extraordinary delusions and hallucinations, which in five months led to complete recovery. To this attack, which apparently at the time of discharge was not yet quite at an end, the second large fluctuation of the curve corresponds.

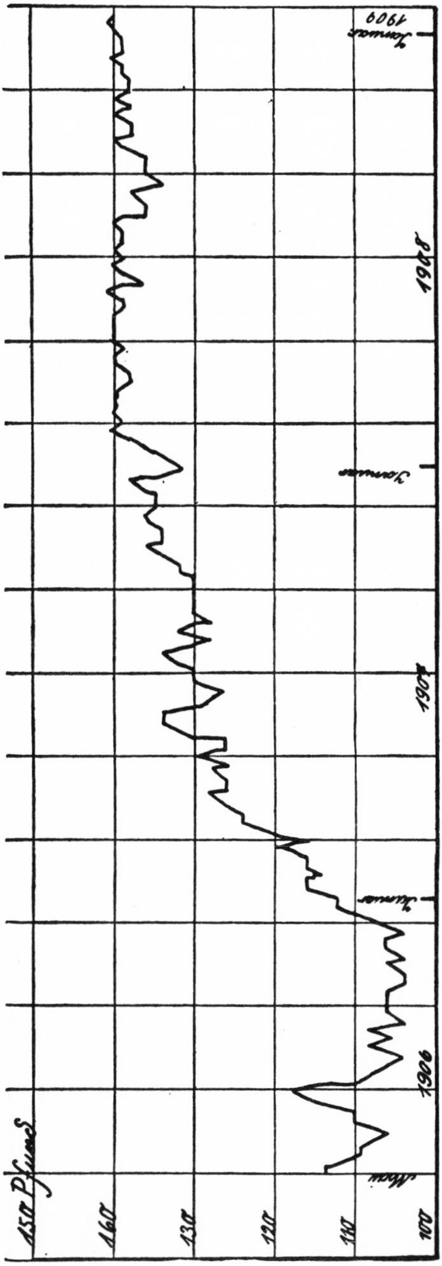

FIG. 15.—Body-weight in protracted depression.

In a very protracted course of states of depression, extending over a series of years I have repeatedly seen great rise of the body-weight without any considerable improvement of the psychic state. Recovery then followed much later, occasionally after the weight had again fallen not inconsiderably and without a manic state being conjoined. An indication of this behaviour can be recognised in Fig. 15, where, in spite of very great increase of body-weight which constantly remained high, there was yet no recovery. Much rather was the psychic state of the patient during this time essentially worse than at the time of his discharge, which happened later, when he weighed 4.5 kg. less.

General State.—Corresponding to the course of the body-weight the general state of the patients usually experiences striking changes. In the hypomanic periods the skin acquires a fresh colour and tension ; the movements become elastic and vigorous ; the scanty hair grows afresh, even with renewed colour. In states of depression on the contrary, the skin becomes pale, wrinkled, withered, dry, rough ; the eye becomes dull ; the growth of the nails stops and becomes irregular, as Falcida has demonstrated ; the menses become scanty or intermittent ; the secretion of tears dries up ; the whole being appears prematurely old.

All these changes indicate that in manic-depressive insanity marked *disorders of metabolism* must take place. Unfortunately the results of investigations carried out in regard to this have been up till now still rather unsatisfactory. Mendel found in mania a decrease of phosphorus in the urine, while Guérin and Aimé found the excretion of lime and magnesia increased ; in states of depression that is said to be diminished. On the other hand Seige was not able to demonstrate any abnormality in the metabolism of minerals. He observed in melancholia a strong tendency to the storage of nitrogen, which then is suddenly excreted in increased quantity. The endogenous excretion of uric acid, according to his statements, remains in depressive patients at the lower limits of the normal, whereas in manics it is reduced. Here it appeared to be a case of abnormally rapid breaking down of the purin bodies to still lower stages of disintegration. Lange has arrived at the opinion, that increased formation of uric acid may be regarded as the essential cause of states of depression. Raimann was able to establish that in states of depression alimentary glycosuria could be produced. Schultze and Knauer likewise were able to demonstrate that, as in other forms of psychic disease so also in the states of manic-depressive insanity, alimentary glycosuria appeared, probably as a consequence of anxiety ; it was found with special frequency in depression (67%), more rarely in mixed states (53%), and in mania (19%). Now and then diabetes insipidus is observed ; in older patients I often saw continuous excretion of sugar. The reducing power of the urine was found by Pini raised in general, especially in mania, on the other hand lowered in long-continuing states of excitement.

Alberti investigated the toxicity of the urine and blood-serum, without obtaining any useful results. Pilcz was able fairly frequently to establish the appearance of all kinds of abnormal substances in the urine, acetone, diacetic acid, indican, albumose, which re-appeared in the attacks of the same patients, but without any definite relation to the colouring of the mood being recognised. Taubert found indican-uria in mania, often one or two days before the outbreak of excitement, while Seige observed indican disappear almost completely from the urine in excitement. On the other hand he observed in a depressed patient an unusually great excretion of indican, which began already two days before the transition from the former manic excitement and which was not accompanied by constipation. Townsend also was able to demonstrate an increased indoxyl excretion, which in states of depression was specially strongly marked, and which began to disappear shortly before the appearance of psychic improvement. Apparently it is here everywhere a case of the consequences of intestinal disorders which are so frequent in manic-depressive insanity. Hannard and Sergeant found in states of depression frequent cholæmia.

Blood - Picture.—The investigations of blood which Fischer carried out in five manic patients did not yield any characteristic change. The hæmoglobin content and the number of red blood corpuscles were frequently increased, the number of the white almost always, perhaps in consequence of the constant excitement. Dumas reports a decrease in the red blood corpuscles in the beginning of mania, an increase at the beginning of depression, changes which are said to be occasionally reversed in the further course of the attacks. The hæmolytic resistance of the red blood corpuscles in the presence of the serum of other patients or of normal individuals was found by Alberti to be weakened in mania, fluctuating in states of depression. Parhon and

Urechie in both periods of the disease observed increase of the mononuclear leucocytes.

Circu ation.—The changes in the behaviour of the circulatory organs are often specially striking. Fairly frequently there are found murmurs at the heart, extension of cardiac dulness, increased excitability of the heart, tendency to congestion, erythemata, great perspiration, dermography. In manic patients the face is often flushed, the conjunctivæ injected. I once saw, in consequence of continued screaming, extreme swelling and tortuosity of the superficial veins of the neck. In states of depression the complexion is usually pale and grey ; the lips often appear slightly cyanotic, the hands and feet cold, pale or livid. Not very infrequently one observes indications of Basèdow's phenomena, a soft *swelling of the thyroid* gland with acceleration of the pulse, tremor and abundant perspiration, now and then also occasional exophthalmos. Not at all infrequently and in comparative youth arteriosclerosis is present.

About the behaviour of the *pulse-rate* and the *blood-pressure* statements are very divergent. It is usually assumed that in mania the pulse is accelerated, in melancholia retarded. The investigations carried out by Weber in our hospital gave on the contrary a raised pulse-rate in states of depression, especially in those with excitement ; in lively manic excitement a similar result was found, while in quieter manic patients the frequency of the heart-beat was frequently shown to be normal and even somewhat retarded. The blood-pressure was found by Pilcz to be lowered in mania, raised in melancholia, while Falcioli observed it fall in states of depression and only rise on the appearance of anxiety. In mania, in consequence of the rapid and extensive widening of the vessel, one observes at each heart-beat pulse waves with rapidly rising, sharp, steeply-falling summit and distinctly marked dicrotism. In depressed patients, on the other hand, because of the raised tension there are low and sluggish pulse waves with slightly raised or rounded summit and feeble dicrotism.

The investigations of Weber carried out with newer and more perfect instruments confirmed the rise of blood-pressure in states of depression ; it was greatest in depressive excitement. On the other hand it was shown that also in mania, especially in more severe excitement and in manic stupor, it is frequently raised. The behaviour of pulse and blood-pressure at the same time usually corresponds fairly closely to the changes in the psychic state. A picture of this is given in Fig. 16, in which besides pulse-rate and blood-pressure,

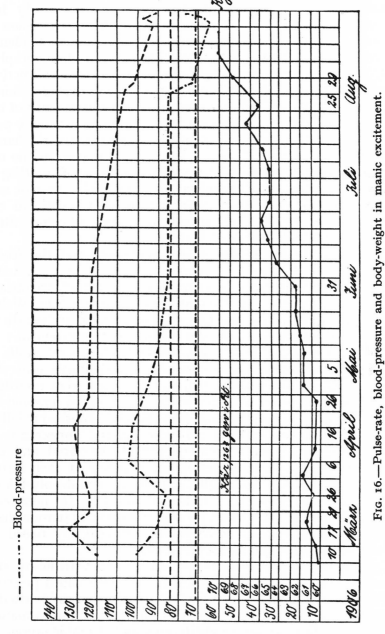

FIG. 16.—Pulse-rate, blood-pressure and body-weight in manic excitement.

which at the times indicated below were investigated by means of the Recklinghaus method, together with the horizontal lines indicating the normal average values, the course of the body-weight is also reproduced. It is seen how pulse and blood-pressure, after fluctuations at the beginning, gradually return to normal with the rise of body-weight, which accompanies the improvement in the general state.

Respiration is accelerated in states of excitement, retarded in simple depression and in stupor ; in great anxiety interrupted or jerky breathing is occasionally observed. Vogt found the fluctuations of respiration on the plethysmograph curve specially marked in manic patients ; in more severe depression they were also invariably present.

Temperature is occasionally high-normal in violent excitement, and often lowered in severe states of depression.

The **Menses** at the beginning of the attack frequently stop for some time, especially in depressed patients, and return on the approach of recovery, occasionally as the first sign of it. Not infrequently during the menses aggravation of the morbid phenomena is observed.

" **Nervous** " **Disorders** of all kinds usually appear, especially in depressed patients. Apart from the headaches already mentioned and the manifold dysæsthesiæ, the patients complain about tiredness, feelings of oppression, noises in their ears, palpitation, shivering in the back, heaviness in the limbs. The *tendon reflexes* are frequently increased. Weiler found in general a steeper rise of the reflex curve, shortening of the reflex time, and powerful brake-action of the fall. In deep depression and in states of stupor the extent of the reflex decreased ; in the latter the reflex time was lengthened. The *pupils* are, according to Weiler's statements, somewhat frequently dilated, but otherwise show no deviations worth mentioning.

In many patients special sensitiveness to the *influence of weather* seemed to me to exist ; they felt lively discomfort for a considerable time on the approach of thunder-storms.

Of special importance is the fact that in our patients disorders are extraordinarily often observed, which we usually call *hysterical*. Here belong above everything fainting fits and attacks of giddiness, as well as fully developed hysterical convulsions, further, choreiform clonic convulsions, psychogenic tremor, singultus, convulsive weeping, somnambulism, abasia. Decrease in the pharyngeal and conjunctival reflexes, disorders of sensation of various nature, namely analgesia, patella and ankle clonus are also found. Many delirious states, which run a rapid course with dulling of consciousness, appear to have an hysterical colouring, as Imboden has emphasised. A female patient, who became manic after the death of her lover, wandered aimlessly about for some days in order to look for her dead " Toni," and had only a very dim recollection of this journey. Another asserted that she had been surprised and overpowered, but then stated that she could not say definitely whether it had not been a dream. In spite of the very imperfect information which was forthcoming about these morbid symptoms, they were proved in 13-14% of the men, and in about 22% of the women, by preference at the younger ages.

In a few cases also attacks of *epileptic* nature were noted, some of them being observed by ourselves. Lastly *organic disorders* appeared now and then especially among the men and at a more advanced age, apoplectic attacks with or without subsequent paralysis, transient loss of speech, cortical epileptic attacks. For the most part it was here a case of a conjunction with *arteriosclerosis*, often also with *lues*.

CHAPTER IV.

MANIC STATES.

The presentation of the individual clinical states, in which manic-depressive insanity usually appears, will in the first place have to begin with the conspicuous contrasts between *manic* and *depressive* attacks. With these are associated, as third form, the *mixed states* which are composed of states apparently the opposite of each other. Lastly, we shall have to consider the inconspicuous changes in the psychic life which continue even in the intervals between the marked attacks, changes in which the *general psychopathic foundation* of manic-depressive insanity comes to expression. It must, however, be emphasised beforehand that the delimitation of the individual clinical forms of the malady is in many, respects wholly artificial and arbitrary. Observation not only reveals the occurrence of gradual transitions between all the various states, but it also shows that within the shortest space of time the same morbid case may pass through most manifold transformations. The doctrine of form given here may accordingly be regarded as an attempt to set in order quite generally with some degree of lucidity the mass of material gathered by experience.

HYPOMANIA.

The slightest forms of manic excitement are usually called "hypomania," mania mitis, mitissima, also, but inappropriately, mania *sine delirio*. The French have spoken of a "folie raisonnante," an insanity without disorder of intellect. Indeed the sense, the power of perception, the memory of the patients, appear in general not disordered. Psychic activity, mobility of attention, are not infrequently even increased ; the patients may appear livelier, more capable than formerly. In especial the ability to perceive distant resemblances often surprises the hearer, because it enables the patient to produce witty remarks and fancies, puns, startling comparisons, although usually not very valid when examined more minutely, and similar products of the imagination. Nevertheless even in the slightest degrees of the disorder the following features are extraordinarily characteristic, *the lack of inner unity in the course of ideas*, the incapacity to carry out consistently a definite series of thoughts, to work out steadily and logically and to set in order given ideas, also the fickleness of interest and the sudden and abrupt jumping from one subject to another. Certainly the patients are not infrequently able with some effort to overcome temporarily these phenomena and to gain the mastery again for some time yet over the course of their ideas which have become unbridled. In writing and especially in rhyming, which is often diligently indulged in, a slight flight of ideas usually makes a distinct appearance. But even in these slight forms fairly severe excitement and confusion may temporarily be present.

Recollection of recent events is not always exact, but is often coloured and supplemented by original additions. The patient is easily led away in his narrations to exaggerations and distortions, which arise partly from mistaken perception, but partly also from subsequent misinterpretation without the arbitrariness of it coming clearly into his consciousness. Although genuine delusions are absent we invariably meet with a very much exaggerated opinion of *self*. The patient boasts about his aristocratic acquaintances, his prospects of marriage, gives himself out as a count, as a " doctor because of his services to the state," wants " to have everything magnificent," speaks of inheritances which he may expect, has visiting cards printed with a crown on them. A lady signed her letters " Athene ". A lay-sister narrated that a miracle happened at her birth, that she had supernatural gifts and would reform the order. In eloquent words the patient boasts of his performances and capabilities ; he understands everything best ; he ridicules the doings of others with aristocratic contempt, and desires special recognition for his own person. He is an " excellent poet, orator, jester, and man of business ", a " jolly fellow " ; he can work like a nigger, can take the place of many a proprofessor or diplomatist. A patient, who was charged with begging, declared proudly, " The beggar is the true king."

Insight.—Of this there is as a rule no question ; even by a reminder of former attacks, of which during depression the patient perhaps formed a quite correct opinion, he cannot for a moment be convinced of the real nature of his state. On the contrary he feels himself healthier and more capable than ever, has "a colossal energy for work", is "awfully merry", at most is somewhat excited by the unworthy treatment. The restriction of his freedom he regards as a bad joke, or as an unpardonable injustice, which he connects with the perverse ongoings of his relatives or of persons otherwise inimical to him, and he threatens to take legal measures for their removal and punishment. Those, not he, are mentally afflicted, who did not know how to appreciate his intellectual superiority and his gifts, and who tried to excite him by irritating and provoking him. This behaviour reminds one of the experiences so frequently encountered of the self-deceptions of drunkards.

Mood is predominantly exalted and cheerful, influenced by the feeling of heightened capacity for work. The patient is in imperturbable good temper, sure of success, "courageous," feels happy and merry, not rarely overflowingly so, wakes up every morning "in excellent humour". He sees himself surrounded by pleasant and aristocratic people, finds complete satisfaction in the enjoyment of friendship, of art, of humanity ; he will make everyone happy, abolish social wretchedness, convert all in his surroundings. For the most part an exuberant, unrestrained mood inclined to practical jokes of all kinds is developed. Occasionally there is developed a markedly humorous trait, the tendency to look at everything and every occurrence from the jocular side, to invent nicknames, to make fun of himself and others. A patient called himself a "thoroughbred professional fool" ; another declared the hospital was a "nerve-ruining institution" ; a third stated that he was a "poet, cattle-driver, author, tinker, teacher, popular reformer, chief anarchist and detective". On the other hand there often enough exists a great emotional irritability. The patient is dissatisfied, intolerant, fault-finding, especially in intercourse with his immediate surroundings, where he lets himself go ; he becomes pretentious, positive, regardless, impertinent and even rough, when he comes up against opposition to his wishes and inclinations ; trifling external occasions may bring about extremely violent outbursts of rage. In his fury he thrashes his wife and children, threatens to smash everything to smithereens, to run amuck, to set the house on fire, abuses the "tribe" of his relatives in the most violent language, especially when under the influence of alcohol. The internal equilibrium of the patient is lost ; he is led wholly by momentary impressions and emotions which immediately obtain mastery over his mood and his excited volition. His actions accordingly often bear the stamp of impulsiveness, lack of forethought, and—because of the slight disorder of intellect—of immorality.

Increased Busyness is the most striking feature. The patient feels the need to get out of himself, to be on more intimate terms with his surroundings, to play a part. As he is a stranger to fatigue, his activity goes on day and night ; work becomes very easy to him ; ideas flow to him. He cannot stay long in bed ; early in the morning, even at four o'clock he gets up, he clears out lumber rooms, discharges business that was in arrears, undertakes morning walks, excursions. He begins to take part in social entertainments, to write many long letters, to keep a diary, to go in a great deal for music and authorship. Especially the tendency to rhyming (letters !) is usually very conspicuous. A simple peasant published his rhymes made up of flights of ideas himself. A young lady on her departure from the institution composed a humorous testament in doggerel and had it printed.

His pressure of activity causes the patient to change about his furniture, to visit distant acquaintances, to take himself up with all possible things and circumstances, which formerly he never thought about. Politics, the universal language, æronautics, the women's question, public affairs of all kinds and their need of improvement, give him employment. A physician advertised lectures about " original sin, Genesis, natural selection and breeding." Another patient drove about in a cab and distributed pictures of the saints. The patient enters into numerous engagements, suddenly pays all his business debts without its being necessary, makes magnificent presents, builds all kinds of castles in the air, and with swift enthusiasm precipitates himself in daring undertakings much beyond his powers. He has 16,000 picture post-cards of his little village printed, tries to adopt a negro boy from the Cameroons. A patient made a sudden offer to the police to produce on the spot immediately a political criminal who had been long sought for, at the same time lending the official a fancy uniform as a joke, and by an advertisement in the newspaper he invited " the whole Hautevolée " to a ball in a little outlook tower.

At the same time the real capacity for work invariably suffers a considerable loss. The patient no longer has any perseverance, leaves what he begins half finished, is slovenly and careless in the execution of anything, only does what he likes, neglects his real duties. A patient spent his whole time in plans for marriage, reading the newspapers, going walks, and playing bowls. " He is over-busy," was said of another, " but accomplishes less than formerly." Just as it occurs to him, the patient undertakes unnecessary journeys, wanders about, takes drives, pawns his watch, borrows money, makes useless purchases and exchanges, even when he has not a penny in his pocket, because every new object stimulates his desire. Even occasional theft and fraud are sometimes committed in this morbid lust for possession in order to obtain what is desired. A patient emphatically demanded a rise of salary, and at the same time threatened to give the alarm to the fire brigade in order to draw people's attention to his condition. A female patient gave over-weight in business ; another drank other people's glasses empty.

External Behaviour.—*Exalted self-consciousness*, the passion to come to the front, is conspicuous, and also restlessness and changeableness. The patient dresses contrary to his usual custom, according to the newest fashion, though perhaps negligently, wears " a hat like Bismarck," sticks flowers in his button-hole, uses perfume galore. A female patient had her hair dressed eleven times in succession. The patient everywhere leads the conversation, interferes, forces his way to the front at every opportunity, in spite of deep mourning takes part in noisy entertainments, recites in public, subscribes largely to collections, tries to turn all eyes to himself, to make an impression, indulges in peculiarities. A patient described himself as " a conglomerate of all passions, sadist, masochist, fetishist, onanist ".

He often makes himself conspicuous by all sorts of disorderly conduct ; he serenades with trumpets, spends the night on benches out of doors, promenades in a dress coat wearing an order made by himself, takes a bath with his clothes on, performs military exercises with a broom, goes about the streets distributing blessings, pays a visit to the archbishop without any occasion. A female patient imitated an hysterical attack ; another acted a little scene from a drama, apparently gave all sorts of domestic directions, telephoned for meat, quarrelled with the telephone girl, expressed herself very indignantly about the girl's alleged negligence ; a third read aloud from the newspapers all sorts of invented nonsensical things.

In company the patient behaves without ceremony, is guilty of offences against decency and morality, tells risky jokes before ladies, carries on boastful conversations, in wanton merriment behaves with unsuitable familiarity towards strangers or his superiors, is friends with the first person he meets and calls him by his first name. A peasant girl began to charge the people in her surroundings with all their "wrong-doings," especially her companions, with illegitimate children. In consequence of his petulance and irritability the patient frequently comes into conflict with his surroundings and with the authorities ; he insults officials, demands from the physician satisfaction as a cavalier, runs up debts in public houses, is called to account by his superiors and brought to order. A school-boy, who had a quarrel with some peasants, challenged them with pistols, handed them his card, and then fired a shot in the air ; he threatened to shoot his headmaster, who had inflicted a punishment on him. Many patients become involved in law-suits which they carry on with great passionateness in the most correct forms through the highest courts of appeal. Because of their comprehensive petitions teeming with self-consciousness, affronts, and bold assertions, they are easily taken for litigants, till with the appearance of tranquillity or even the transition to depression, they repentantly beat a retreat.

The tendency to debauchery usually becomes especially fatal to the patients. He begins to get drunk frequently, to gamble foolishly, to remain out at night, to frequent brothels and doubtful taverns, to smoke and snuff excessively, to eat strongly-seasoned food. When such states of excitement occur frequently, and are of short duration, a picture very similar to dipsomania may arise.

Sexual Excitability experiences a considerable increase. An elderly father of a family, who otherwise lived a very retired life, began to drink champagne with the girl fencers from a circus. Another tried to force his way into the cook's room, and when he was found fault with, excused himself with his "midsummer madness." Women begin to dress conspicuously, to wear false hair, to put on style, to carry on equivocal conversations, to go to balls, to be frivolous, to enter into love-affairs regardlessly, to read indecent novels. A young girl pawned her clothes in order to procure a fancy dress and go to a ball with a gentleman who was a stranger to her. A woman handled the genitals of her sixteen-year-old son and threw back the coverings of the journeyman who was lying in bed. Another female patient, when in this state, invariably made proposals of marriage, which in the end had the result that, with the help of an agent, she actually did enter into marriage with a man not at all trustworthy. A married lady in each manic attack conceived a violent passion for any male person in her surroundings, finally with a man, thirty years her junior, and in every respect very much her inferior, and she overwhelmed her beloved with the most fervid declarations of love in spite of his unresponsive attitude. Another began to write bombastic verses about a teacher. A servant-girl harassed a captain in the army with numerous love-letters, which she signed "your fiancée," and she tried in every way to force herself into his presence. Incomprehensible engagements, also pregnancies, are not rare in these states. I know cases in which the commencement of excitement was repeatedly announced by a sudden engagement. "Each child has a different father," declared a female patient. From these proceedings serious matrimonial quarrels naturally arise. A woman declared that she was going to commit adultery in order to get a divorce from her husband. Others become jealous and assert that their husbands keep company with innumerable females, and on this account want to shut them up in the asylum.

Rationalisation by Patients. — With extraordinary acuteness the patient can find a reason for all his astonishing and nonsensical doings ; he is never at a loss for an excuse or explanation. The exertions of his relatives to quiet him are, therefore, not only ineffectual, but they only irritate him and easily lead to violent outbursts of rage. In the institution the patient usually presses for discharge from the first day, gives as exclusive cause of his violence the unjust deprivation of freedom, declares off hand that the physicians are "crazy," reproaches them with their incapacity, and demands to be examined by other authorities. One of my patients succeeded in persuading his wife to transfer him against my advice to another institution. On the journey, which was quite short, he himself took the lead, drove away from his wife, and went to Berlin to have himself examined by a physician who had obtained a certain reputation for certifying mentally unsound people as sane.

Movements of Expression are as a rule lively and passionate. The patients talk a great deal, hastily, in loud tones, with great verbosity and prolixity, jumping from one subject to another, using sought-out, bombastic expressions, speaking with peculiar intonation, and of themselves often in the third person in order to place themselves in the right light. Silly joking, puns, violent expressions, quotations, scraps of foreign languages play a large part, and occasionally violent abuse and swearing or emotional weeping intervenes. Their writing displays large, pretentious flourishes, many marks of exclamation and interrogation, underlining, besides negligence in the external form. Many patients compose bombastic or humorous documents full of flights of ideas and irritation, in which they narrate without reserve all their family affairs, beg for certificates of sanity, and call for the protection of public opinion.

The variety in detail of this state is, in spite of all the common features, very large. The more slightly the real morbid process affects the individual, the more conspicuous are his personal peculiarities in the form which the manifestations assume. The differences are noticeable especially in the kind and intensity of the emotions. While many patients at this time are amiable, good-natured, docile, sociable, and at most become disturbing to their surroundings by their restlessness, others because of their irritability, their imperiousness, and their regardless pressure of activity, are extraordinarily difficult and unpleasant. It is just the peculiar mixture of sense and maniacal activity, frequently also an extensive experience of institutions, which makes them extremely ingenious in finding out means to satisfy their numerous desires, to deceive their surroundings, to procure for themselves all kinds of advantages, to secure the property of others for themselves. They usually soon domineer completely over their fellow-patients, use them for profit, report about them to the physician in technical terms, act as guardian to them, and hold them in check.

ACUTE MANIA.

From the slighter forms of mania here described, imperceptible transitions gradually lead to the morbid state of actual acute mania. The beginning of the illness is always fairly sudden; at most headaches, weariness, lack of pleasure in work or a great busyness, irritability, sleeplessness, precede by some days or weeks the outbreak of the more violent manifestations, when a definite state of depression has not, as is very frequent, formed the prelude. The patients rapidly become restless, disconnected in their talk, and perpetrate all sorts of curious actions. They run out of the house in a shirt, go to church in a petticoat, spend the night in a field of corn, give away their property, disturb the service in church by screaming and singing, kneel and pray on the street, fire a pistol in a waiting-room, put soap and soda in the food, try to force their way into the palace, throw objects out at the window. A female patient jumped into the carriage of a prince for a joke. Another rang a chemist's bell at night, as she alleged that she had been poisoned. A third went to the physician at his consulting hour in her ball-dress, and to church similarly dressed. A male patient appropriated the property of others in taverns. Another appeared in the court of justice in order to catch a murderer. Yet another asserted that he was on the track of an anarchist plot.

As a rule, therefore, the patients must be brought to an institution in a few days. Here they show themselves sensible and approximately oriented, but extraordinarily distractible in perception and train of thought. Sometimes it is quite impossible to get into communication with them ; as a rule, however, they understand emphatic speech, and even give isolated suitable replies, but they are influenced by every new impression ; they digress, they go into endless details, in short, they display more or less developed flights of ideas, as we have already described minutely.

Delusions.—Very commonly fugitive delusions are expressed, usually more in a jocular way. The patient asserts that he is descended from a noble family, that he is a gentleman ; he calls himself a genius, the Emperor William, the Emperor of Russia, Christ ; he can drive out the devil. A patient suddenly cried out on the street that he was the Lord God ; the devil had left him. Female patients possess eighty genuine diamonds, are singers, leading violinists, Queen of Bavaria, daughter of the Regent, Maid of Orleans, a fairy ; they are pregnant, are going to be engaged to St Francis, are to give birth to the Redeemer of the Jews, the Messiah. St. Joseph lay beside them in bed ; the pope and the king came to them ; Christ lives in them again. A female patient asserted that she was the Christchild and was three years old. The patients are often disoriented about their own position and their place of residence ; they make mistakes about persons, often in a playful way. Now and then isolated *hallucinations* are reported. The patients see horsemen in the clouds, saints, a dead child ; they carry on a conversation with their father who is dead, with the Virgin Mary ; they feel themselves influenced by something external.

Occasionally the patients narrate all sorts of extraordinary adventures. A female patient asserted that she had been assaulted and abused, but then said that she could not swear that it had not been a dream. Many patients have a certain morbid feeling, and at times make fun of the ideas which they bring forward. Great wishes and plans are also developed. The patient wishes to invent something, to buy houses, to marry a professor's daughter with a large dowry, to go to the university ; he has already a doctor's degree. He hopes to get his whole breast covered with orders, wishes to cure patients by hypnosis, will see to it that everyone goes to heaven, and that the penal code will be reformed according to religious principles. A female patient desired to buy a bicycle " decorated with lilies " ; others demand diamond earrings, expensive clothes.

Mood is unrestrained, merry, exultant, occasionally visionary or pompous, but always subject to frequent variation, easily changing to irritability and irascibiltiy or even to lamentation and weeping. Such fluctuations of mood are very clearly seen in the following letter of a manic patient :—

" When I think of my rude behaviour towards you at the last visit, I do not know how I am to atone for it. I ask you for pardon from my heart ; as far as it lies in my power, such a thing will never occur again. As I now understand, I should have given you an answer and I did not do so. O God, how discourteous ! |

" So gern möcht ich nun offen sein,
Doch längst hab' ich's gefühlt,
Dass niemand mich versteht, allein,
Nur ich empfind', wie's wühlt.
Das Leiden, das ich hab' in mir,
O Gott, ich frag', warum,
Das weisst Du nicht, ich gab es Dir.

" And you still ask so stupidly. Whom the Lord loveth, he chasteneth. Thy will be done. | And when the Lord chasteneth ! Then he pierces ! But I must stop.— | The sky is blue ! The weather is beautiful ! Professor, I should like to take a walk. If it is not good for me, I shall obey."

At the places marked a new page began ; of the contents of the first about the half has been left out as unessential. One notices how the penitent contrition, which appeared after a violent state of excitement, is on the second page diverted by the interruption made by turning the leaf to another depressive circle of ideas, but how immediately now, in the rhyme and also in the self-derision at the end, manic excitement is conspicuous. From here onwards the calligraphy begins to be fantastic, large and pretentious, so that the few following words with their frequent marks of exclamation and interrogation cover the whole side. At the same time the train of ideas vacillates from religious ideas to the blue sky and in rhyming to taking a walk. [Several of the words rhyme in German.] The concluding words are obviously quieter and are added in smaller writing.

At the most trifling affront it may come to outbursts of rage of extraordinary violence, to veritable high-tides of clamorous abuse and bellowing, to dangerous threats with shooting and stabbing, to blind destruction and actual attacks. The female sex has a much greater tendency to such outbursts than the male sex. Sexual excitement finds an outlet in obscene talk, forcible approach to youthful patients, shameless masturbation ; among the female patients in calling the physicians by their first names, dressing up, taking down their hair, anointing themselves with saliva, frequent spitting, using indecent and abusive language, as well as in sexual calumniation of the nursing staff. A female patient made signs to the soldiers from the window.

Conduct.—The behaviour of the patients is, as a rule, free and easy, self-conscious, unmannerly or confiding, importunate. They run after the physician, are always interrupting, let themselves be diverted or influenced by persuasion, imitate other patients, and not rarely display indications of automatic obedience ; they do not defend themselves from pricks. But often enough they are repellent, pert, unapproachable ; they resist, hide in corners, close their eyes, hold their fingers before their face in order to blink through them. Many patients obey no directions, act on purpose the wrong way about. A female patient in greeting gave her index finger, another gave her foot instead of her hand. The morbid picture is dominated by the rapidly increasing *volitional excitement*, which in its impulsiveness and suggestibility may remind one of alcoholic poisoning. A female patient behaved herself according to the description given by her neighbours. " like a drunken man ".

The patient cannot sit or lie still for long, jumps out of bed, runs about, hops, dances, mounts on tables and benches, takes down pictures. He forces his way out, takes off his clothes, teases his fellow-patients, dives, splashes and squirts in the bath, romps, beats on the table, bites, spits, chirps and clicks. These volitional utterances in general usually exhibit the stamp of natural activities and movements of expression, although frequently mutilated and over-hasty. Among these, however, are frequently interpolated movements which can only be regarded as discharges of inner restlessness, shaking of the upper part of the body, waltzing about, waving and flourishing the arms, distorting the limbs, rubbing the head, bouncing up and down, stroking, wiping, twitching, clapping and drumming. Sometimes these movements are conspicuously clumsy and inelegant, or affected and peculiar. Not at all infrequently they are carried out rhythmically, also perhaps for a considerable time they are continued monotonously. Similarly the patients are heard now and then repeating for hours the same phrases and laughing to themselves. Not rarely they are dirty, pass their motions under them, and smear things with their evacuations.

Many patients display a great tendency to be destructive. They slit up their suits and bed-clothes in order to use the rags knotted and twisted in a hundred ways for extraordinary decorations. All objects in any way attainable are broken up into their component parts, in order to be put together again as new structures of various kinds, according to the inspiration of the moment. Buttons are twisted off, pockets torn out, the coat is turned inside out, the trousers are stuck in the stockings, the ends of the shirt are knotted together, rings made of remnants of yarn or destroyed shirt buttons are forced on to the fingers, cuffs and collars are manufactured from paper. Whatever falls into the hands of the patient, stones, little bits of wood, broken pieces of glass, nails, he collects in order by means of them to scratch walls, furniture, and windows and to cover these in all directions with paintings or writing. Remains of cigars and withered leaves are wrapped in paper and smoked ; scraps of paper are used for writing, nails for filling pipes, and shards for sharpening lead-pencils. Other things found are used for barter in order to obtain small advantages from fellow-patients. Occasionally all sorts of things are stuck in the nose and ears ; the lobes of the ears are pierced with matches or little bits of wire ; ashes and dust are used as snuff ; the beard is partially singed with the cigar.

Movements of Expression are for the most part very vivacious. The patient makes faces, rolls his eyes, assumes theatrical attitudes, stands erect, salutes in military fashion. He usually produces in the shortest interval of time an enormous flood of words with changing intonation, makes jokes, is quick at repartee, swears, scolds, suddenly makes a noise, recites, preaches, mutters to himself, and now and again screams out loud. He bellows, sings music-hall songs, hymns, often for hours the same, prays, imitates the sounds of animals, calls out hallelujah ; among these are interpolated roaring, whistling, yodeling, shouting, uncontrollable laughter. But at times, even in spite of lively excitement, the patients may be taciturn ; they do not reply to questions or they give short and evasive answers ; they perhaps only make a few expressive gestures and then suddenly break out with the greatest vivacity. Jocular speaking past the subject also occurs now and then, right instead of left, six instead of five. A female patient always repeated the question directed to her ; another persistently replied, " How ? " ; a third, " I don't know that ". Associations with external impressions and rhyming frequently occur in the conversation of the patients. A female patient called out to the physician, " Du bist allerhand—Kraut und Rüben durcheinand ". In more severe excitement the utterances may become quite. disconnected as the following notes show :—

" On the most real of all grave—1, 2, 3, and always, always in the greatest of all row—in the pancake—Elsie—by the grace and mercy of God, by all reality might one 17 incomprehensible little graves of thought —taken from the highest of all slender little grave—no Provisor believes that — and always again for a Siegfried or assessor — Professor in an extended—So was it and not otherwise—I can't help it—1, 2, 3 Francisca B. it was—no, that one must no longer of a Professor—a, b, c—in all reality —most real first of all state trumpet . . ."

No thought whatever can be recognised here. Isolated words return ever again in various connections and transformations : " most real of all—highest of all—first of all," " most real—reality," " and always, always—always again," " grave—little graves of thoughts—little grave," " 1, 2, 3," " Professor—Provisor." In " Gedankengrüftchen—schlanken Grüftchen," and in " Provisor—Assessor—Professor " clang-associations may be surmised ; and " 1, 2, 3,"—" a, b, c " linguistic practice due to co-ordination might have been the connecting link.

Many patients develop a veritable passion for *writing*, cover innumerable sheets with very large fantastic calligraphy, the words crossing one another in all directions. An example of this is given in the specimen of writing No. 2, with its confused array of words, which in the most various kinds of calligraphy run pell-mell hither and thither. It shows at the same time in high degree the tendency to endless enumerations, which sometimes appears in the writings of manic patients, in so far as it is a case here of almost only

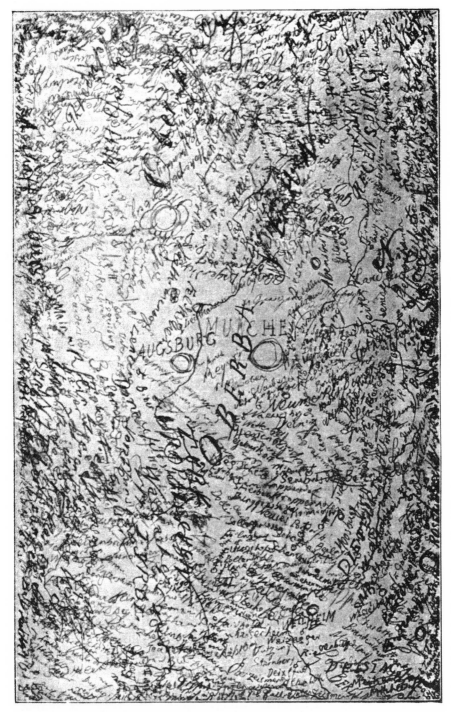

SPECIMEN OF WRITING 2.—Manic Scribbling.

geographical names. It is remarkable that there are no re-petitions as there are in catatonic documents which have a similar appearance. The patients are also very fond of composing poems, letters, petitions to highly placed person-ages. In these the connection may be completely lost, as in the following fragment of a rather long petition :—

" Rottach Waalberg (Rodel) Lorenz Tarok Katzenjammer Gautsch Handelsrichter abgesägt 2 Grad (Celsius) 5000 Lire Kriegsentschädigung zu bezahlen von Guadagnini für Übernahme (Reich Dein III) schwarz weiss 4/5 Bovril Annaberger Schlüssel gelb 10 Pf. gehisst Chardonnerstag Westnerday unwohl Gallo Hohenzollern Kirche Vikar Bari Sprung Biringer Meisterspringer Zobel Max Arnulf 15. Febbrajo geboren bei Plinio Neapel Appel Sänger I an Paralyse—Analyse—Stolze—Freytag Crispi bei Riva Cavour bei Roosevelt . . ."

Only a few associations dependent partly on meaning, partly on clang, can perhaps be found here : Rottach (beside Tegernsee) — Waalberg (Wallberg) — Rodel," " Gautsch—Handelsrichter (minister ?)—abgesägt," " Chardonnerstag —Westnerday (Wednesday ?)," " Bari—Biringer," " Sprung —Meisterspringer," " Neapel — Appel," " Paralyse — An-alyse," " Stolze — Freytag (Stolze — Schrey)," " Crispi—Cavour—Roosevelt," " Plinio—Neapel," · " Crispi—Riva—Cavour ".

DELUSIONAL MANIA.

The **Delusions and Hallucinations,** which in the morbid states hitherto described are fugitive or merely in-dicated, acquire in a series of cases an elaboration which calls to mind paranoid attacks. His surroundings appear to the patient to be changed ; he sees St Augustine, Joseph with the shepherd's crook, the angel Gabriel, apostles, the Kaiser, spirits, God, the Virgin Mary. Statues salute him by nodding ; the moon falls down from the sky ; the trumpets of the day of judgment are sounding. He hears the voice of Jesus, speaks with God and the poor souls, is called by God dear son. There are voices in his ears ; the creaking of the floor, the sound of the bells take on the form of words. The patient has telepathic connection with an aristocratic fiancée, feels the electric current in the walls, feels himself hypnotized ; transference of thought takes place.

The delusions, which forthwith emerge, move very fre-quently on religious territory. The patient is a prophet, John II, is enlightened by God, is no longer a sinner, is some-thing supernatural ; he fights for Jesus, has to fulfil a divine mission, is a spirit, hides the world-soul in himself, intends to ascend to heaven, possesses secret power over mentally afflicted people. He preaches in the name of the holy God, will reveal great things to the world, gives commands according to the divine will. Female patients are queen of heaven and of earth, the immaculate conception, female clergyman, mother of the heathen children ; they have a child by God, are going to heaven to the bridegroom of their soul ; Christ has restored their innocence to them. The devil is done away with ; the patient has taken all the suffering of the world on himself ; it is a wonderful world.

Other patients are descended from a royal house, are princes, German and Austrian Emperors, Royal Highness, destined to a higher life ; they possess millions, are to marry a princess, a rich widow. They have already died a thousand times, always come again, can practise magic, can help people by prayer, can make themselves invisible. A patient had " the feeling as if he would get money from somewhere " ; another declared that he was the most distinguished private detective ; a third called himself the " sanitary physician of all the natural sciences and natural medical science " ; a fourth said that he would be the most famous man in Europe ; a fifth stated that he had found a female 193 cm. in height and would get for her 40,000 marks. Female patients boast that they are related to the royal house, are fourfold queens, earthly somnambulists, have a beautiful voice, are going to place the imperial crown on their husband. A female patient declared that she was the Sleeping Beauty, had pricked herself with the spindle, and was now waiting for the Prince. The patients often narrate all sorts of journeys and adventures, secret experiences ; they have encountered men who made assaults ; they were received in the capital with honour. Many patients complain of persecutions, they have been illused having been struck with the fist 130 to 150 times ; they are fired at, whipped with rods.

Occasionally the delusions of the patients call to mind those of the paralytic. They possess millions, diamond cups, get a golden crown, have created mountains, built whole cities. A patient wrote that he would offer his fiancée a life such as no princess in the world had. " In Munich I shall build for myself Castle Miramare, in Feldafing the Castle of King Max formerly planned, make Munich the most beautiful city in the world ; I have already designed three hundred magnificent buildings, the most beautiful in the world. I shall construct railways and gain millions by that."

These delusions are produced by the patients sometimes in a theatrical manner, sometimes more in play. Sometimes they are fleeting and changing ; but as a rule they are for a considerable time adhered to and defended although with very varying emphasis. The same ideas often appear again in later attacks. The consciousness of the patients appears as a rule to be slightly dulled. They perceive imperfectly, have no complete understanding of what happens in their surroundings, are not clear about time-relations, possibly also make mistakes about individual people. Judgment about their own condition is frequently led astray by hallucinations and delusions. Their mood is cheerful, self-conscious, visionary; a patient "wept tears of joy". But at a time the patients are also pretentious, high-flown and abusive in all keys, or they break out suddenly in passionate weeping.

Excitement is not usually very severe. In their conduct the patients may appear approximately well ordered, but they display a certain restlessness, meddle with everything, sing, versify, preach, and work mischief. They want to buy houses, distribute their money " among distressed children," throw everything into the collecting-box, make speeches from the railway-train, give the benediction in public. A patient declared war on France ; others make attempts to cure their fellow-patients, practise enchantment on them by solemn movements of the arms.

DELIRIOUS MANIA.

A **Delirious State** fills up the picture in a further group of cases, which is not very large. This state is accompanied by a dreamy and profound clouding of consciousness, and extraordinary and confused hallucinations and delusions. The attack usually begins very suddenly ; only sleeplessness, restlessness or anxious moodiness may already be conspicuous one or two days, more rarely a few weeks, beforehand. Consciousness rapidly becomes clouded ; the patients become stupefied, confused, bewildered, and completely lose orientation for time and place. Everything appears to them changed ; they think that they are in heaven, in Herod's palace, in the " Christchild Hospital." Mistakes are made about the people in their surroundings ; their fellow-patients are near relatives ; the physician is a Royal Highness, an ecclesiastic, a black devil. A female patient, who in numerous similar attacks always fancied that she was surrounded by historical celebrities, Louis XIV, Cæsar, Elizabeth, called that her " historical delusion ".

At the same time numerous hallucinations appear. Something is burning ; birds are flying about in the air ; angels appear ; spirits throw snakes in the face of the patient ; shadows come and go on the walls. The patient sees heaven open, full of camels and elephants, the King, his guardian-angel, the Holy Ghost ; the devil has assumed the form of the Virgin Mary. The ringing of bells is heard, shooting, the rushing of water, a confused noise ; Lucifer is speaking ; the voice of God announces to him the day of judgment, redemption from all sins. The patient carries on dialogues with absent people, receives revelations ; his thoughts are borne from one voice to another. The coffee smells of dead bodies, his hands as if rotten ; in the house there is a smell of burning ; the food tastes of goat-flesh or of human flesh, the water of sulphur. His head is very giddy, full of fever-heat. The patients think that they are lifted and thrown into an abyss ; they swim with the king in the ocean ; everything is falling to pieces round them.

At the same time dreamy, incoherent delusions are developed. A terrible misfortune is coming suddenly ; the patient feels the devil in his breast, has had a scuffle with him, prides himself on his strength; he must die, go through terrible struggles ; he is going to be poisoned, beheaded, is lost, accursed, rotten, quite alone in the world. Everything is annihilated ; God has shot himself ; all his relatives have died. He has won the first prize in the lottery, is proclaimed emperor, is the promised hero who is to redeem the world, would like to go with his children to heaven. The millennium has begun ; King Ludwig will rise from the dead ; the great battle with the Antichrist is being fought.

Mood during this delirium is very changing, sometimes anxiously despairing ("thoughts of death"), timid and lachrymose, distracted, sometimes unrestrainedly merry, erotic or ecstatic, sometimes irritable or unsympathetic and indifferent. At the beginning the patients frequently display the signs of senseless raving mania, dance about, perform peculiar movements, shake their head, throw the bedclothes pell-mell, are destructive, pass their motions under them, smear everything, make impulsive attempts at suicide, take off their clothes. A patient was found completely naked in a public park. Another ran half-clothed into the corridor and then into the street, in one hand a revolver in the other a crucifix.

The patients do not trouble themselves at all about their surroundings ; they do not listen, they give no information, obey no requests, are resistive, strike out. Their linguistic utterances alternate between inarticulate sounds, praying, abusing, entreating, stammering, disconnected talk, in which clang-associations, senseless rhyming, diversion by external impressions, persistence of individual phrases, are recognised. Other patients only display a slight restlessness, whisper flights of ideas to themselves, when addressed look up astonished and without comprehension, obey simple requests, give irrelevant answers, smile, weep, cling to people, suddenly begin to sing a song or scream. A female patient called out abruptly, " I am justice ; do not touch me ; I am omniscient ; away from me ! " Waxy flexibility, echolalia, or echopraxis can be demonstrated frequently.

As a rule the state is subject to manifold fluctuations. The patients become at times quite quiet, but at first they are not clear ; they remain incapable of thought and confused. They then perhaps complain themselves that they cannot collect their thoughts, are not in their right mind, that every-thing is mixed, that they have so many thoughts in their head. Often there can be observed repeated change between excitement and stupor. The disappearance of morbid pheno-mena takes place now and then fairly suddenly, much more often gradually. Frequently there remain for some time isolated delusions or remnants of them, and especially fluctuations of mood, after the excitement and confusion have already disappeared. The patients are at first still distrustful, without insight, discontented, irritable ; perhaps also they easily give way to flights of ideas, especially in writing ; they are talkative or inaccessible ; they force their way out. Little by little the last morbid symptoms dis-appear. Recollection of the delirious time is mostly rather dim ; frequently there even exists almost complete amnesia.

The **Course** of manic attacks is very variable. The commencement is almost always a period of anxious or mournful mood, either marked depression lasting for months or even years, or a prodromal stage of a few days or weeks. Much more rarely and perhaps only when there is frequent repetition, mania begins quite suddenly. A patient became severely maniacal in the cemetery at his daughter's funeral. without any change having been noticed in him before that,

The height of the morbid phenomena is usually reached fairly quickly, occasionally even within a few days. From then onwards the state may just as quickly approach the normal, though that occurs almost only in delirious forms, much more rarely in simple mania, most rarely in hypomania. As a rule, manic excitement is maintained for a considerable time with approximately the same severity, though always with manifold fluctuations. Very frequently there are periods interpolated of mournful moodiness and even passing stupor, a phenomenon which opens the way for the understanding of the mixed forms to be discussed later.

The final quieting down usually appears very gradually after somewhat long duration of the disease, while improvements in the condition become always more distinctly marked. The patients become clearer about their surroundings, more accessible, more attentive, but they still fall very easily into the former flight of ideas. Even when the more violent disorders have already gone into the background, there usually still remains behind for sometime an increased emotional irritability, heightened self-consciousness, as well as a certain restlessness. Sudden outbursts of rage of surprising violence may occur on trifling occasions, even after apparently complete quiet has for long been present, especially in the later attacks with a protracted course. One often sees also manic excitement flare up again if the patients get into unfavourable circumstances or begin to drink.

The **Duration** of manic excitement is also subject to great fluctuations. While occasionally attacks run their course within a few weeks or even a few days, the great majority extend over many months. Attacks of two or three years' duration are very frequent ; isolated cases may last considerably longer, for ten years and more. Especially the forms with delusions and moderate excitement, increasing only from time to time, appear readily to run a lingering course ; also in hypomanic attacks one will frequently have to reckon with a fairly long duration. Now and then, as already formerly indicated, I have got the impression from the course of the body-weight and the other phenomena, as if it were a case of *several attacks* following close on one another.

Very frequently after the disappearance of manic excitement a more or less marked condition of weakness and despondency appears, which is generally regarded as exhaustion after the severe illness ; it is obviously only a case, however, of the transition to depression peculiar to the disease. The patients are extremely susceptible to fatigue, incapable of any mental or bodily exertion, monosyllabic, dull, irresolute ; they reproach themselves with their manic actions, and are anxious about their future. These disorders usually clear up gradually as the body-weight continues to increase.

CHAPTER V.

DEPRESSIVE STATES.

MELANCHOLIA SIMPLEX.

The slightest depressive states are characterised by the appearance of a *simple psychic inhibition without hallucinations and without marked delusions.* Thinking is difficult to the patient, a disorder, which he describes in the most varied phrases. He cannot collect his thoughts or pull himself together ; his thoughts are as if paralysed, they are immobile. His head feels heavy, quite stupid, as if a board were pushed in front of it, everything is confused. He is no longer able to perceive, or to follow the train of thought of a book or a conversation, he feels weary, enervated, inattentive, inwardly empty ; he has no memory, he has no longer command of knowledge formerly familiar to him, he must consider a long time about simple things, he calculates wrongly, makes contradictory statements, does not find words, cannot construct sentences correctly. At the same time complaints are heard that the patient must meditate so much, that fresh thoughts are always coming to him, that he has too much in his head, that he finds no rest, is confused.

The patients frequently describe that change of their inward state, which is usually called " depersonalisation." Their presentations lack sensuous colouring. The impressions of the external world appear strange, as though from a great distance, awake no response in them ; their own body feels as if not belonging to them ; their features stare quite changed from the mirror ; their voice sounds leaden. Thinking and acting go on without the co-operation of the patient ; he appears to himself to be an automatic machine. Heilbronner has pointed out that Goethe has described similar disorders in Werther, when he says :—

" O, when this glorious nature lies before me so rigid, like a little varnished picture, and all the joy of it cannot pump a drop of bliss from my heart up to my brain," and " I stand as though in front of a cabinet of curiosities, and I see little men and little horses moving about in front of me, and I often ask myself whether it is not an optical delusion. I play with them, or rather I am played like a marionette, and I sometimes take hold of my neighbour by his wooden hand and start back shuddering."

Mood is sometimes dominated by a profound inward dejection and gloomy hopelessness, sometimes more by indefinite anxiety and restlessness. The patient's heart is heavy, nothing can permanently rouse his interest, nothing gives him pleasure. He has no longer any humour or any religious feeling,—he is unsatisfied with himself, has become indifferent to his relatives and to whatever he formerly liked best. Gloomy thoughts arise, his past and even his future appear to him in a uniformly dim light. He feels that he is worth nothing, neither physically nor mentally, he is no longer of any use, appears to himself " like a murderer ". His life has been a blunder, he is not suited for his calling, wants to take up a new occupation, should have arranged his life differently, should have pulled himself together more. " I have always given advice, and then things have gone wrong," said a patient.

He feels solitary, indescribably unhappy, as " a creature disinherited of fate " ; he is sceptical about God, and with a certain dull submission, which shuts out every comfort and every gleam of light, he drags himself with difficulty from one day to another. Everything has become disagreeable to him ; everything wearies him, company, music, travel, his. professional work. Everywhere he sees only the dark side and difficulties ; the people round him are not so good and unselfish as he had thought ; one disappointment and disillusionment follows another. Life appears to him aimless, he thinks that he is superfluous in the world, he cannot restrain himself any longer, the thought occurs to him to take his life without his knowing why. He has a feeling as if something had cracked in him, he fears that he may become crazy, insane, paralytic, the end is coming near. Others have the impression as though something terrible had happened, something is rising in their breast, everything trembles in them, they have nothing good to expect, something is happening.

Imperative Ideas of all kinds occasionally emerge in these states, agoraphobia, mysophobia, the fear of having been pricked by a splinter and having to die of blood-poisoning, the fear of having vicious or " unclean " thoughts, the idea of throwing people into water, the fear of having stolen bread or money, of having removed landmarks, of having committed all the crimes mentioned in the newspapers. A patient was tormented by the idea of having murdered people with his thoughts, and of having been guilty of the death of King Ludwig. A female patient, who in a former attack had thought that she was an empress with a court of dogs and cats, made convulsive efforts to get rid of the word empress which always forced itself upon her, the effort consisting in rubbing her teeth rhythmically with her hand. Another was very greatly tormented by being compelled to connect obscene sexual ideas with religious representations (crucifixes). A third patient wrote the following in a note :—

> " It is really so, that I have now become unclean with what I always played with ; from negligence and clumsiness I often do not now go at the right time to the closet and I pass something into my chemise, into my bed, and into my clothes, and, as I always put on the clothes again, it so happens that the petticoat is drawn on over the night-jacket, something on there and on to my head, from the petticoat on to the bodice, on to the hair and so on."

She was afraid also that something would fall out of her nose into a book ; she often destroyed things supposed to be dirty ; she would not sit down on a chair or give her hand in order not to soil anything. All these ideas she herself called " on-goings," in order to make herself interesting. The fear of knives, with the idea of being obliged to kill someone, occurs occasionally also. A patient went to bed in order not to do anything of that kind. One of my patients impulsively stole all sorts of things which had no value for herself and of which she made no further use. She stated that she could not help it, it was an impulse, just as if she had been thirsty, she was uneasy if she did not yield to it. Gross by means of " psychoanalysis " has arrived at the result here, that the theft-impulse, being forced to do secretly what is forbidden, to take " something secretly into the hand," signifies a transference of sexual desires unsatisfied by the impotent lover, which has been further influenced by the question of a priest at confession whether she herself had introduced the organ in sexual intercourse. On other grounds also we may perhaps regard these imperative fears and impulses as the expression of a certain relationship between manic-depressive insanity and the insanity of degeneration.

The **Total Absence of Energy** is very specially conspicuous. The patient lacks spirit and will-power, like a wheel on a car, which simply runs but in itself has no movement or driving power. He cannot rouse himself, cannot come to any decision, cannot work any longer, does everything the wrong way about, he has to force himself to everything, does not know what to do. A patient declared that he did not know what he wanted, went from one thing to another. The smallest bit of work costs him an unheard-of effort ; even the most everyday arrangements, household work, getting up in the morning, dressing, washing, are only accomplished with the greatest difficulty and in the end indeed are left undone. Work, visits, important letters, business affairs are like a mountain in front of the patient and are just left, because he does not find the power to overcome the opposing inhibitions. If he takes a walk, he remains standing at the house door or at the nearest corner, undecided as to what direction he shall take ; he is afraid of every person whom he meets, of every conversation ; he becomes shy and retiring, because he cannot any longer look at any one or go among people.

Everything new appears uncomfortable and unbearable. One of my patients insisted on leaving a post which he had been very anxious to get, but he was alarmed at the removal to a new residence, and importuned the authorities with contradictory requests, as his new position immediately appeared to him much worse than the former one. Finally the patient gives up every activity, sits all day long doing nothing with his hands in his lap, brooding to himself in utter dulness. His sorrowful features show no play of emotion ; the scanty linguistic utterances are laboured, low, monotonous and monosyllabic, and even the addition of a simple greeting on a postcard is not attainable or only after much urging.

Sometimes a veritable passion for lying in bed is developed ; the patients ever again promise to rise to-morrow, but have always new excuses to remain in bed. Just because of this severe volitional disorder it relatively seldom comes to more serious attempts at suicide, although the wish to die very frequently occurs. It is only when with the disappearance of inhibition energy returns while the depression still continues, that the attempts at suicide become more frequent and more dangerous. A patient with very slight moodiness hanged himself a few days before his discharge on a free pass when he already appeared quite cheerful.

Insight.—Sense and orientation are in spite of the great difficulty in perception and thinking completely retained. Generally a very vivid morbid feeling also exists, not infrequently even a certain morbid insight, in as far as the patients express their regret for former improprieties, and their fear lest they might again let themselves be carried away by excitement. Others, however, think that they are not ill, only destitute of will-power, that they could indeed pull themselves together, only will not ; that they are simulating. Frequently the return of moodiness is connected with external accidents, unpleasant experiences, changes in circumstances and such things. To the unprejudiced observer it is clear that the psychic working of those influences has been produced by the morbid clouding of disposition. A good picture of the thinking and feeling of such patients is given in the following letter :—

" Louisa, the whole truth ! It is all a squandering of money. I dare not go home, I dare not stay here ; shut me up in a cell and give me only bread and milk ; I am no longer ill ; they will not believe me ; I am loathsome to myself and wholly weary of life, I may not further be a burden to good people. I cannot write any more to my children, because I cannot say to them, that they are no interest to me ; I am a horror and am hounded by furies, the longer I am here, the wilder. You saw my lifeless expression, Louisa ; you are a human being—have human compassion with me. Give me only so much—to cover my nakedness ; everything else is torment to me. Life itself is a frightful torment ; I must go to a house of correction ; I must be forced to work. Here I cannot work, because anxiety worries me about my condition. No medicine takes effect, because anxiety consumes me. Here I had to pull myself together under such strict control, but life is extinguished—how shall I manage among strangers, as I cannot keep my things in order ? I go about with worn-out boots and cannot provide myself with new ; money does not help me. My life is comfortless and only bearable so long as I am complaining of my distress. Then I hope for help. You will despise me instead of your former love. Louisa, don't speak further of my misery."

The deep depression, the feeling of inward desolation and indifference, the irresolution, the delusion of sin, the weariness of life, lastly, the slight hope of help, appear distinctly here.

STUPOR.

In the highest grades the psychic inhibition described may go on to the development of marked stupor. The patients are deeply apathetic, are no longer able to perceive the impressions of the surroundings and to assimilate them, do not understand questions, have no conception of their position. A female patient who was made to leave her bed and go into the one beside it, said quite without understanding, " That is too complicated for me." Occasionally, it can be recognized that the inhibition of thought is slighter than the volitional disorder. A patient was able to give the result of complicated problems in arithmetic in the same time, certainly considerably prolonged, as that of the simplest addition.

Sometimes the occasional, detached utterances of the patients contain indications of confused, delusional ideas, that they are quite away from the world, have a crack through the brain, are being sold ; down below there is an uproar. A definite affect is at the same time mostly not recognisable, yet in the astonished expression of the patients their helplessness in regard to their own perceptions, and further a certain anxious feeling of insecurity on attempting anything can usually be seen.

Volitional utterances are extremely scanty. As a rule, the patients lie mute in bed, give no answer of any sort, at most withdraw themselves timidly from approaches, but often do not defend themselves from pinpricks. Sometimes they display catalepsy and lack of will-power, sometimes aimless resistance to external interference. They sit helpless

FIG. 17.—Depressive Stupor.

before their food ; perhaps, however, they let themselves be spoon-fed without making any difficulty. They hold fast what is pressed into their hand, turn it slowly about without knowing how to get rid of it. They are, therefore, wholly unable to care for their bodily needs, and not infrequently they become dirty. Now and then periods of excitement may be interpolated. The patients get out of bed, break out in confused abuse, sing a folk-song. Of the peculiarly strained, disturbed expression of such patients, Figs. 17 and 18 give a good idea. After the return of consciousness, which usually appears rather abruptly, memory is very much clouded and often quite extinguished.

MELANCHOLIA GRAVIS.

The picture of simple depression corresponding perhaps to the former " *melancholia simplex*," experiences very varied elaboration through the development of hallucinations and delusions, which frequently follows ; one might here perhaps speak of a " *melancholia gravis*." The patients see figures, spirits, the corpses of their relatives ;

something is falsely represented to them, " all sorts of devil's work." Green rags fall from the walls ; a coloured spot on the wall is a snapping mouth which bites the heads off children ; everything looks black. The patients hear abusive language (" lazy pig," " wicked creature," " deceiver," " you are guilty, you are guilty "), voices, which invite them to suicide ; they feel sand, sulphur vapour in their mouth, electric currents in the walls. A patient, who

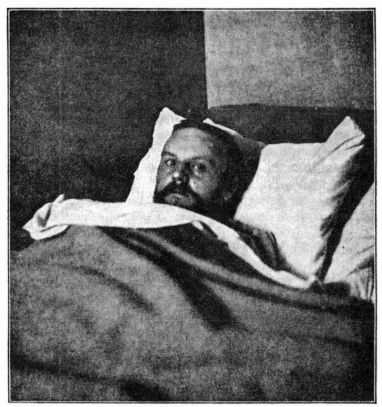

FIG. 18.—Depressive Stupor.

reproached himself with having had connection with a cow, felt a cow's tail flicking his face.

Ideas of Sin usually play the largest part. The patient has been from youth up the most wicked being, an abomination, filled with malice, has led a horrible life, as far as possible has let others do his work, has not put his full strength into his calling, has sworn falsely in taking the military oath, has defrauded the sick fund. He has offended everyone, has borne false witness, has overreached some one in making a purchase, has sinned against the seventh commandment. He cannot work any more, has no more feeling, no more tears ; he is so rough ; something is lacking in his disposition. Frequently the self-accusations are connected with harmless occurrences which have often happened long before. The patient, when a child, communicated unworthily, did not obey his mother, told a lie before he was twelve years old. He has not paid for his beer and on this account will be imprisoned for ten years. A patient, fifty-nine years of age, alleged that as a boy he had stolen " apples and nuts," and " played with the genitals " of a cow. Conscience is roused. " Certainly it would have been better, if it had been roused sooner," he said in answer to the objection that up till then he had not been troubled about the supposed sin. Others have once turned away a beggar unkindly, have skimmed the cream from the milk. By renting a house, by undertaking some building, by a thoughtless purchase, a suicidal attempt, they have brought their family to misery ; they should not have entered the institution ; then it would all have come differently. Female patients have put too much water into the milk of their dead children, have not brought up their boys well, have neglected them in religion, have procured the abortion of a child, have not had patience in their confinements, have not kept their house properly ; they do not put things in order, they are lazy. A female patient, because of this, would not stay in bed. When it was represented to another that it was a delusion, she replied, " It is only conscience ; when I was at school it once came like this." Obviously she was speaking of a former depression.

The domain of *religion* is a peculiarly favourable soil for self-accusation. The patient is a great sinner, cannot pray any more, has forgotten the ten commandments, the creed, the benediction, has lost eternal bliss, has committed the sin against the Holy Ghost, has trafficked in divine things, has not offered enough candles. He has apostatized from God, is gripped firmly by Satan, must do penance. The spirit of God has left him ; he feels that he dare not enter church any more. He is going to Hell, has only two hours to live ; then the devil will fetch him ; he must enter eternity with transgression, and redeem poor souls.

The following extract from a letter of a married peasant woman to her sister affords a glimpse into the spiritual state of such patients :—

" I wish to inform you that I have received the cake. Many thanks, but I am not worthy. You sent it on the anniversary of my child's death, for I am not worthy of my birthday ; I must weep myself to death ; I cannot live and I cannot die, because I have failed so much, I shall bring my husband and children to hell. We are all lost ; we won't see each other any more ; I shall go to the convict prison and my two girls as well, if they do not make away with themselves, because they were borne in my body. If I had only remained single ! I shall bring all my children into damnation, five children ! Not far enough cut in my throat, nothing but unworthy confessions and communion ; I have fallen and it never in my life occurred to me ; I am to blame that my husband died and many others. God caused the fire in our village on my account; I shall bring many people into the institution. My good, honest John was so pious and has to take his life ; he got nineteen marks on Low Sunday, and at the age of nineteen his life came to an end. My two girls are there, no father, no mother, no brother, and no one will take them because of their wicked mother. God puts everything into my mind ; I can write to you a whole sheet full of nothing but significance ; you have not seen it, what signs it has made. I have heard that we need nothing more, we are lost."

Besides the marked ideas of sin there is to be noted the delusional conviction, that her husband is dead and her son must take his life, but especially the tendency to find " signs " and " significance," which God sends (nineteen marks and nineteen years), the regret about the failure of an attempt at suicide by cutting her throat, lastly, the remark that her many sins have only now occurred to the patient.

His present activities also frequently give the patient the opportunity for continual self-reproach. He notices that he always commits fresh faults, talks at random so stupidly, says things which he does not wish to say, offends everyone. " What I do, is the wrong way about ; I must always retract everything that I say," said a patient. He causes so much trouble, is to blame that the others are so distressed, that they are being taken away. " I have probably done all this," said a patient. He has brought in all his fellow-patients, must care for them all, is responsible for them, complains that he is really not able to feed the others, to do the work of the head-waiter, to pay for them all. Everyone must go hungry when he eats. A patient reported as follows about his " offences against the doctors " :—

" The patient F. is very often vexed with himself when at the visit of the physicians he does not greet relatively thank in a more friendly way, he very often says : " I have the honour," which expression may be mis-interpreted. The better and more usual responses to greetings, as " Good morning," and expressions of gratitude, as " Many thanks for the kind visit," are often omitted. Then the patient must take offence at his position, that is the position and attitude of his body. Very often he does not assume the requisite demeanour towards such highly placed gentlemen. Just made another offence ; I have omitted to rise from my seat when the chief physician went past. At the washstand I omitted to show a boy how to fill the basin. He of course might have asked me. But those who were near will certainly have blamed my conduct and not the boy's. Once I omitted to hand the water to a patient, when he asked for it. It is true that he did not apply directly to me ; he only called into the room ; others were much nearer to him, but it would have been my duty to fulfil his request at once."

Ideas of Persecution frequently exist in the closest connection with the delusion of sin. Disgrace and scorn await the patient everywhere ; he is dishonourable, cannot let himself be seen anywhere any more. People look at him, put their heads together, clear their throats, spit in front of him. They disapprove of his presence, feel it as an insult, cannot tolerate him any longer among them ; he is a thorn in the side to all. Speeches in the club have reference to him ; there is secret talking of stories about females ; he is a bully, should hang himself, because he has no character. Everywhere he notices signs. The writer of the letter quoted above said that her twisted knot of hair signified that her husband had hanged himself, the scarfs of her fellow-patients that her children were drowned at home. A patient concluded from the remark, " Still waters run deep," that he should drown himself. The patient therefore asks for an explanation ; he did not know that such was his state. " What is being done with me ? " he asks anxiously. Things are so put before him as if every step in his life had been wrong. He defends himself, therefore, in despair against the supposed accusations and declares his innocence. But I have not done anything wrong, have stolen nothing, have not betrayed my country, such patients are heard to lament. They are afraid that on the death of a relative they may be suspected of poisoning (" Has poison been found ? "), that they may be called to account for lese-majesty, or for a planned assault.

Everywhere danger threatens the patient. The girls read his letters ; strange people are in the house ; a suspicious motor-car drives past. People mock him, are going to thrash him, to chase him from his post in a shameful way, incarcerate him, bring him to justice, expose him publicly, deport him, take his orders from him, throw him into the fire, drown him. The people are already standing outside ; the bill of indictment is already written ; the scaffold is being put up ; he must wander about naked and miserable, is quite forsaken, is shut out of human society, is lost body and soul. His relatives also are being tortured, must suffer ; " I do hope they are still at home." His family is imprisoned ; his wife has drowned herself ; his parents are murdered ; his daughter wanders about in the snow without any clothes on. Everything goes the wrong way; the household is going to ruin; there is nothing more there but rags; the clothes have been changed at the laundry. Things have been pawned; the money is not sufficient, is false; everything costs too much; everyone must starve. A woman said that her husband did not like her any longer; he wanted to kill her. Others release their husband, invite him to get a divorce.

His bodily state also appears to the patient to be frequently in a very dangerous condition, which may be connected with the dysæsthesiæ formerly described. He is incurably ill, half-dead, no longer a right human being, has lung-disease, a tapeworm, cancer in his throat, cannot swallow, does not retain his food, passes such thin and such frequent stools. Face and figure have changed; there is no longer blood in his brain; he does not see any longer, must become crazy, remain his whole lifetime in the institution, die, has already died. He has become impotent by onanism, has had a chancre from birth, has incurable blood-poisoning, infects everyone, he must not be touched. On this account a woman no longer had

FIG. 19.—Depression.

the bread baked in the house. The people in his surroundings become ill and yellow through the nasty exhalation of the patient, are already mentally disordered and weary of life. Female patients feel themselves pregnant, have been sexually ill used. Such a patient with a deeply troubled expression is represented in Fig. 19.

PARANOID MELANCHOLIA.

When ideas of persecution and hallucinations of hearing are frequently present and sense remains preserved, morbid states may occasionally arise, which readily call to mind alcoholic insanity, without alcohol having any causal significance ("paranoid melancholia"). The patients feel themselves watched, are pursued by spies and threatened by masked murderers; they catch sight of a dagger in their neighbour's hand. On the street, in the restaurant from the neighbouring table, they hear isolated remarks about themselves. In the next room a court of justice is deliberating on their case; intriguing is going on; experiments are made on them; they are threatened with secret words and with suspicious gestures. Delusional mistakes are made about people. One of my patients tried to escape from his persecutors by taking a journey, but noticed already in the station that they were accompanying him, and he walked only in the middle of the street because the voices threatened him with shooting as soon as he turned aside either to the right or to the left.

In the course of the forms here described consciousness is mostly clear, and sense and orientation are preserved. The patients perceive correctly the conversations and occurrences in their surroundings and then frequently misinterpret them in a delusional way. They think perhaps that they are not in the proper institution with proper physicians, but in the convict prison, that fellow-patients are acquaintances or members of their family; they address the physician as if he were the public prosecutor; their letters are falsified; what is said in the surroundings has a hidden meaning. Their train of thought is orderly and connected, although mostly very monotonous; the patients always move in the same circle of ideas; on an attempt being made to divert them, they return again immediately to the old track. All mental activity is as a rule made difficult. The patients are absent-minded, forgetful, are easily tired, progress slowly or not at all, and at the same time are sometimes most painfully precise in details. Often a certain morbid feeling exists. The head is darkened; the patient speaks of his chimeras; "I have something just like a mental disorder"; "understanding, reason, and the five senses are lacking." There is no question, however, of genuine morbid insight. Even if his attention is called to earlier similar attacks of which the patient had formed a correct opinion, it makes no impression on him. At that time everything was still quite different; now things are much worse; now every possibility of being saved is excluded.

Mood is gloomy, despondent, despairing. By persuasion or visits from relatives it may usually be somewhat influenced ; sometimes on such an occasion lively excitement follows. On the other hand unpleasant news often makes little impression. What happens in the surroundings also usually affects the patients only slightly. " The noise does not annoy me, but the unrest in myself," said a female patient, when it was proposed that she should be transferred to another part of the building on account of the disturbing surroundings. The patients very frequently complain about the great inward excitement in spite of outwardly quiet behaviour ; they may then give vent to it at times in violent outbursts of anxiety. Not infrequently it takes the form of an unquenchable home-sickness which drives the patients perpetually to try to get away, deaf to all reason. If one gives in to this, their state of mind deteriorates rapidly at home, as a rule. Many patients in regard to their delusions appear remarkably dull and indifferent, occasionally also perhaps good-humoured and even cheerful.

In the **Activities** of the patients their *volitional inhibition* on the one hand makes itself felt, on the other the influence of their *delusions* and *moods*. They feel tired, in need of rest, are no longer able to take care of themselves, neglect themselves, spend no more money, take no nourishment, wear very shabby clothes, refuse to sign the receipt for their salary, as indeed they have not done any work. They shut themselves up, go to bed, lie there rigidly with a troubled expression in a constrained attitude, sometimes with closed eyes, or sit timidly on the edge of the bed, because they do not venture to lie down. Indications of automatic obedience are not rare. In other patients anxious restlessness is predominant. They run off in a shirt, remain for days in the forest, beg for forgiveness, entreat for mercy, kneel, pray, pluck at their clothes, arrange their hair, rub their hands restlessly, give utterance to inarticulate cries. Their utterances are, as a rule, monosyllabic ; it is very difficult to get anything out of them. They do not give information on their own initative, are immediately silent again, but, at the same time, occasionally display in their writings a fluent and skilful diction. Speech is mostly low, monotonous, hesitating and even stuttering. Calligraphy is often indistinct and sprawling. There are also occasional omissions and doubling of letters.

Suicide.—The extraordinarily strong tendency to suicide is of the greatest practical significance. Sometimes it continually accompanies the whole course of the disease, without coming to a serious attempt owing to the incapacity of the patients to arrive at a decision. The patient buys a revolver, carries it about with him, brings it with him to the institution. He would like to die, begs that he may be beheaded, that he may be provided with poison ; he ties a scarf round his neck, goes to the forest to search for a tree on which to hang himself ; he scratches his wrist with his pocket-knife or strikes his head against the corner of the table. One of my female patients bought strychnine wheat and phosphorus paste, but luckily only took the first, because the phosphorus " smelt too filthy." Another stepped on to the window-sill in the second storey in order to throw herself down, but returned to the room, when a policeman, who by chance was passing, threatened her with his finger.

Nevertheless the danger of suicide is in all circumstances extremely serious, as the volitional inhibition may disappear abruptly or be interrupted by violent emotion. Sometimes the impulse to suicide emerges very suddenly without the patients being able to explain the motives to themselves. One of my female patients was occupied with household work, when the impulse came to her quite abruptly to hang herself ; she at once did so and was only saved with difficulty. Subsequently she was not able to give any explanation of her deed, and had only a dim recollection of the whole occurrence.

Occasionally after indefinite prodromata the first distinct morbid symptom is a suicidal attempt. Only too often the patients know how to conceal their suicidal intentions behind an apparently cheerful behaviour, and then carefully prepare for the execution of their intention at a suitable moment. The possibilities at their command are numerous. They may, while deceiving the vigilance of the people round them, drown themselves in the bath, hang themselves on the latch of the door, or on any projecting corner in the water-closet, indeed even strangle themselves in bed under the cover with a handkerchief or strips of linen. They may swallow needles, nails, bits of broken glass, even spoons, drink up any medicine, save up sleeping-powder and take it all at one time, throw themselves downstairs, smash their skull with a heavy object and so on. A female patient by sticking in pieces of paper managed to prevent the upper part of a window, where there was no grating, being properly shut, and then threw herself down from the second storey in an unwatched moment. Another who was shortly to have been discharged, was alone for a few minutes in the scullery ; she took a little bottle of spirit and a match from the cupboard, which had been left open through negligence, and having poured the spirit over herself set herself on fire. Not at all infrequently the idea occurs to the patients to do away with the family also, because it would be better if none of them were alive. They then try to strangle their wife, to cut their children's throats, they go with them into the water, in order that they may not also be so unhappy, that they may not get step-parents.

Fantastic Melancholia.

A further, fairly comprehensive group of cases is distinguished by a still greater development of *delusions*. We may perhaps call it " fantastic melancholia." Abundant *hallucinations* appear. The patients see evil spirits, death, heads of animals, smoke in the house, black men on the roofs, crowds of monsters, lions' cubs, a grey head with sharp teeth, angels, saints, dead relatives, the Trinity in the firmament, a head rising in the air. Especially at night extraordinary things happen. A dead friend sits on the pillow and tells the patient stories. The patient thinks that he is on a voyage ; God stands beside the bed and writes down everything ; the devil lies in wait behind the bed ; Satan and the Virgin Mary come up out of the floor. God speaks in words of thunder ; the devil speaks in church ; something is moving in the wall. The patient hears his tortured relatives screaming and lamenting ; the birds whistle his name ; call out that he should be taken up. " There's a black one, a sozi," it is said, " a vagabond," " Do away with him, do away with him," " Look, that's the masturbator," " Now she's coming, now there'll be blood again," " Now we've caught her nicely," " You have nothing more," " You're going to hell." A woman is standing at the door and is giving information to the persecutors ; there is a voice in his stomach, " You must still wait a long time till you are arrested ; you are going to purgatory when the bells ring." The patient is electrified by the telephone, is illuminated at night by Röntgen-rays, pulled along by his hair ; someone is lying in his bed ; his food tastes of soapy water or excrement, of corpses and mildew.

Besides those genuine hallucinations there are also multifarious delusional interpretations of real perceptions. The patient hears murderers come ; some one is slinking about the bed ; a man is lying under the bed with a loaded gun ; an electro-magnet crackles. People with green hats or black spectacles follow him on the street ; in the opposite house someone is bowing conspicuously ; the motor-cars are making a very peculiar noise ; in the next room knives are being sharpened ; the conversations on the telephone refer to him. Plays in the theatre, the serial story in the newspaper, are occupied with him ; there is gross abuse written on a post-card ; a female patient found her hat portrayed in a fashion paper for mockery. There is a great deal of talk, another said, and she imagined that it refererd to her. What is said in the surroundings has a hidden meaning. Another one asserted that the physicians spoke a "universal language," in which they expressed all thoughts in a quite different form not understood by her. The most extra-ordinary conclusions are drawn from every perception ; ravens flying signify that the daughter is being cut to pieces in the cellar ; the son when he made his visit was wearing a black tie, so the youngest child must be dead. Everything is "so fateful," comedy and illusion. "Everything simu-lates, everything is talmi-gold," said a patient. The food is flesh and blood of their own relatives, the light is a funeral-light, the bed is an enchanted bed, the clattering cart out-side is a hearse. It is quite another world, not the right town, quite another century. The clocks strike wrong ; the letters are as if from strangers ; the mortgages are exchanged ; the savings-bank book is not valid. The trees in the forest, the rocks, appear unnatural, as if they were artificial, as if they had been built up specially for the patient, in fact, even the sun, the moon, the weather, are not as they used to be. One of my patients thought that the sun was artificial electric illumination, and he complained about the weakness of his eyes because he could not see the real sun (in the night).

The people, who visit the patient, are not the right people, are only false show. The physicians are only "figures" ; he thinks that he is surrounded "by elemental spirits" ; the children appear changed. The nurse is a disguised empress ; a fellow patient (female) thinks that the patient (also female) is her husband ; the attendants have false names. The wife is a witch, the child is a wild cat, a dog. A patient noticed that her husband looked black, and on this account attacked him with a bottle.

The numerous delusions are very extraordinary. The patient has committed mortal sins, has caused a derailment, has killed many people, has brought on himself a primeval sin, has murdered many souls ; he has forged documents, been a legacy hunter, caused an epidemic. Because of sins of his youth he is in detention ; he has committed bestiality ; he is poisoning the whole world by his onanism. He has torn down the firmament, drunk up the fountain of grace, tormented the Trinity ; cities and countries are on his account laid waste. The other patients are there by his fault, are be-headed on his account ; every time that he eats or turns round in bed, someone is executed ; the devil's mill is work-ing over there ; they are being killed there, Female patients have committed abortion, have been extravagant, have not been good housewives, must be the devil's whore.

Because he is to blame for all misfortune, the patient is going to hell. The devil slipped down the chimney to take him away, has him by the nape of the neck, sits in his bosom as a black beast with sharp claws, speaks in his heart ; he himself is changed into the devil ; neither will his dead son come into heaven. His baseness is revealed in his expression ; everyone knows of his crime. No one likes him any longer ; he is surrounded by spies, is watched by the police, is con-tinually followed by suspicious people ; detectives wait for him ; the judge is already there. He is dragged off to Siberia, to the convict prison ; he is being electrocuted, stabbed, shot, is having petroleum poured over him, is being tied to a corpse, run over by the motor car, hacked to pieces, cut up into a thousand bits, flayed, devoured by mice ; naked in the wild forest he is being torn to pieces by wolves. His fingers are being chopped off, his eyes dug out, his sexual parts, his entrails cut off, his nails torn out ; women have their womb drawn out. The last judgment is coming ; the vengeance of God is at hand. To-day is the death-day, the last meal before execution ; the bed is a scaffold ; the patient wishes to confess once more. Over his family also misfortune is poured out. His relatives are crucified by the mob ; his daughter is in the convict prison ; his son-in-law has hanged himself ; parents and brothers and sisters are dead, his children are burned up. The husbands of female patients have been murdered. The sister was cut to pieces, sent away in a box ; the son's corpse was sold for dissection,

At home the patient is teased by everyone, regarded as a fool, cheated ; people have no respect for him, spit in his face ; the servants take everything from him with their finger tips, because they think that he is syphilitic. All are in alliance together and vent their anger on him ; many dogs are the death of the hare. The telephone conversations were listened to ; the house was searched ; the things sent to the laundry were lost ; false keys were found on the ring ; at night the children were rendered insensible by gas. The patient is surrounded by an international gang of robbers ; his house is going to be blown up into the air. People knew his career and his thoughts. At night he is sent to sleep, taken away and made to carry out practical jokes, for which he is later held responsible. A female patient aged sixty-five complained of improper assaults, thought that she had been brought to a house of ill-fame and was pregnant. Another of the same age fancied that she was exposed to the persecutions of old bachelors, who lay down beside her in bed. A young girl asked if she would get a child. A woman forty-eight years of age declared that she was pregnant and that she had impregnated herself. An elderly man thought that he was dragged about every night in brothels and there infected with syphilis. " I am here again," said a female patient everytime she was visited, as she thought that she was always being taken away each hour to a different place.

Hypochondriacal delusions usually reach a considerable development ; they often completely resemble those of the paralytic. In the patient everything is dead, rotten, burnt, petrified, hollow ; there is a kind of putrefaction in him. He has syphilis of the fourth stage ; his breath is poisonous ; he has infected his children, the whole town. His head is changing in shape, is as large as Palestine ; his hands and feet are no longer as they were ; the bones have become thicker, have slipped lower down ; all his limbs are out of joint ; his body is no longer compact ; it stretches out and is shrivelled up. In his skull there is filth ; his brain is melting ; the devil has displaced it backwards by a discharge of blood. His heart no longer cooks any blood, is a dead piece of flesh ; his blood-vessels are dried up, filled with poison ; no circulation goes on any longer ; the juices are gone. Everything is closed ; in his throat a bone is sticking, a stone ; stomach and bowel are no longer there. There is a worm in his body, a hairy animal in his stomach ; his food falls down between his intestines into his scrotum ; neither urine nor fæces are passed ; his entrails are corroded. His testicles are crushed, have disappeared ; his genitals are becoming smaller. His mucous glands have risen up ; his life is lacerated ; rolling about is going on at the navel. There is a hole in his nose ; there is pus in his jaw, in all his limbs, and it passes away in great quantity with his motions and with hawking ; his palate stinks. His skin is too narrow over the shoulders ; worms are lying under it and are creeping about. A patient declared that for eleven years he had been a spirit, and had only the internal organs left ; when some one died, death passed through him and took away his entrails ; he still had the scar. A female patient asserted that there was iron in her and the bedstead attracted her. Another said that she would get a child with a cat's head. Many patients believe that they are bewitched inwardly, changed into a wild animal, that they must bark, howl and rage. Others cannot sit, cannot eat, cannot go a step, or give their hand.

The ideas of *annihilation*, already frequently indicated in the foregoing pages, may experience a further, wholly non-sensical elaboration. The patient has no longer a name, a home, is not born, does not belong at all to the world any more, is no longer a human being, is no longer here, is a spirit, an abortion, a picture, a ghost, " just only a sort of shape." He cannot live and he cannot die ; he must hover about so, remain in the world eternally, is as old as the world, has been already a hundred years here. If he is beaten with an axe on his head, if his breast is cut open, if he is thrown into the fire, he still cannot be killed. " I cannot be buried any more," said a patient, " when I sit down on the weighing-machine, it shows zero ! " The world has perished ; there are no longer railways, towns, money, beds, doctors ; the sea runs out. All human beings are dead, " poisoned with antitoxic serium," burned, dead of starvation, because there is nothing more to eat, because the patient has stuffed every-thing down into his enormous stomach, and has drunk the water-pipes empty. No one eats or sleeps any more ; the patient is the only being of flesh and blood, is alone in the world. A female patient declared that there was no blood in her internal organs, therefore the electric light caught fire from her, so that the whole human race and the firmament were consumed. Another thought that a thunderstorm would destroy the whole world.

Consciousness is in this form frequently somewhat clouded. The patients perceive badly, do not understand what goes on, are not able to form clear ideas. They com-plain that they cannot lay hold of any proper thought, that they are beastly " stupid," confused in their head, do not find their way, also perhaps that they have so many thoughts in their head, that everything goes pell-mell. Many patients say that they have been made confused by medicines and much eating, that they have been hypnotized, that they continually talk nonsense, must profess sometimes one thing, sometimes another, that they have become crazy. But at the same time, when their delusions come into play, they are incapable of recognising the grossest contradictions or of correcting them; they assert that they cannot take a bite more while they are chewing with full cheeks. "This is my last," said a patient every time the contradiction was pointed out to her. Others beg to be sent out of the world by poison, although they assert that they cannot die at all.

Yet the train of thought is usually in general reasonable. They are frequently also able to give appropriate and connected information about their personal circumstances and more remote things, though certainly they are for the most part little inclined to engage in such conversations, but return immediately to their delusions again.

Mood is sometimes characterised by dull despondency, sometimes by anxious tension or excitement; at times the patients are also repellent, irritated, angry, inclined to violence. But not altogether infrequently we meet in the patients slight self-irony; they try to describe their sins and torments in excessively obtrusive colours, use the language of students, enter into a joke, allow themselves to smile; erotic moods also may be conspicuous. Especially in the last periods of the attack a grumbling, insufferable, perverse mood is developed, which only with complete recovery gradually disappears. A patient declared that she was envious of the other children of God.

The **Volitional Disorders** are also not quite uniform. The activity of the patients is frequently dominated by volitional inhibition; they are taciturn, even mute, cataleptic; they lie with vacant or strained expression of countenance in bed, often with closed eyes, do not ward off pricks, do not do what they are bidden, are resistive when taking nourishment, hide themselves under the cover, are occasionally unclean. The inward tension is, perhaps, only revealed by isolated whispered utterances ("Entreat for me," "What's the matter?"), convulsive grasping of the rosary, imploring looks, excitement during the visits of relatives. Many patients feel themselves not free, but under the influence of a higher power. A patient declared that people had him in their power, he had lost his will completely, and was a broken man. A female patient was obliged to kiss the floor and altar in church.

Anxious restlessness, however, seems to me to be more frequent, occasionally alternating with slight stuporous states. The patients do not remain in bed; they wander about, bewail and lament, often in rhythmical cadence, "Sinful creature, wicked creature." They beg for forbearance as they have not committed any fault; people want to kill them, to bury them alive, to throw them into the outermost darkness, into the river, into the fire, to poison them and then have them dissected, to chase them out naked into the forest, for choice when it is freezing hard. A patient begged to be let down for execution. They refuse nourishment, as they are not worthy of food, do not want to deprive others of nourishment, cannot pay, observe poison or filth in the dishes; they would like to nourish themselves on refuse and to sleep on bare boards. A patient ran about bare-footed in order to be accustomed to the cold when people chased him out into the snow.

At times more violent states of excitement may be interpolated. The patients scream, throw themselves on the floor, force their way senselessly out, beat their heads, hide away under the bed, make desperate attacks on the surroundings. A female patient knelt down in a public warehouse in front of religious pictures and tried to destroy secular ones. Another made herself conspicuous in the tramway car by her loud self-accusations. A third in great anxiety seized the full spittoon and emptied it. A patient, who was wholly disordered, suddenly proposed the health of the Prince Regent. Serious attempts at suicide are in these states extremely frequent. God commanded a female patient to kill her relatives.

DELIRIOUS MELANCHOLIA.

From the form here described, which essentially corresponds to the "melancholia with delusions" of Griesinger, partly also to the "depressive insanity" of many investigators, gradual transitions lead to a last, delirious group of states of depression, which is characterized by *profound visionary clouding of conscience*. Here also numerous, terrifying hallucinations, changing variously, and confused delusions are developed. The appearance of people is changed; faces are distorted; it is like a "wandering of souls." His wife appears "queer" to the patient; mistakes are made about the nearest relatives ; a stranger is mistaken for the loved one, a woman believed that her husband was mad. The patient sees the Virgin Mary, the Christ-child, spirits, devils, men, who wish to kill poor souls with the sword. Every one is in mourning ; someone must have died. Clouds sink down ; fire and flames rise upwards ; buildings with wounded men are burning ; cannon are being brought up ; the windows are turning round ; the sky is falling down. The room stretches itself out into infinity, becomes heaven, in which God sits on his throne, or it becomes the narrow grave, in which the patient is suffocated, while outside prayers for the dead are muttered. On a high mountain sits a little manikin with an umbrella, who is always being blown down again by the wind. The patient hears shooting, the devil speaking, screams, terrifying voices ; twenty-seven times it is said, " You are to die like a beast ! " Outside the scaffold is being erected ; a numerous company is watching him and scoffing at him ; the stove makes snappish remarks ; the patient is ordered to hang himself in order to bury his shame ; he feels burning about his body.

He is in a wrong house, in the law-courts, in a house of ill-fame, in prison, in purgatory, on a rolling ship, attends the solemn burial of a prince with funeral music and a large retinue, flies about in the universe. The people round him have a secret significance, are historical celebrities, divinities ; the Empress, disguised as a maid-servant, cleans the boots. The patient himself has become of another sex, is swollen like a barrel, suffers from ulcers in his mouth and cancer ; he is of high descent, guardian-angel, the redeemer of the world, a war-horse. An action is brought against him ; he is to blame for all misfortune, has committed treason, set the house on fire, is damned, forsworn, and accursed ; it penetrates through his whole body. His lungs are to be torn out of him ; wild beasts will devour him ; he is made to wander about naked on the street, is exhibited publicly as a Siamese twin. A patient called from the window, " The devil is taking me away ! " A female patient asked, " Am I allowed to die in open death ? " The patient feels quite forsaken, does not know what wrong he has committed, cries aloud, " That is not true ! " The children have been shot by their father ; the husband wants to marry the sister, the father-in-law to kill the daughter ; the brother is threatening murder. Everyone is lost ; all is ruined ; everything is falling to pieces ; everything is undermined. Seething and burning are going on ; there is revolution, murder, and war ; in the house there is an infernal machine ; the justice of God exists no longer. The whole world is burnt up and then again becomes frozen ; the patient is the last man, the wandering Jew, alone in desolation, immured in Siberia.

During these changing visionary experiences the patients are outwardly for the most part strongly inhibited ; they are scarcely capable of saying a word. They feel confused and perplexed ; they cannot collect their thoughts, know absolutely nothing any longer, give contradictory, incomprehensible, unconnected answers, weave in words which they have heard into their detached, slow utterances which they produce as though astonished. The following transcript distinctly shows the great confusion.

" One voice has choked the other—No, it wasn't so—It is something peculiar—It was quite different—The house is athwart—Everyone has poison—No, those ones cried out that—No, I've written it extra—Yes, now I eat nothing more—If you had only done it otherwise, then it would have been better—You would have written nothing at all—She alarmed everyone —It isn't really a right sentry up there—Now it will never be better—."

For the most part the patients lie in bed taking no interest in anything. They betray no pronounced emotion ; they are mute, inaccessible ; they pass their motions under them ; they stare straight in front with vacant expression of countenance like a mask and with wide open eyes. Automatic obedience alternates with anxious resistance ; at times the patients assume peculiar attitudes and make curious movements. Temporarily they become restless, get out of bed, wander slowly to and fro, force their way out, search round about, want to pull other people out of bed, wring their hands, cling to people, cry out, beg for pardon, protest their innocence. Suicidal attempts also occur. A female patient went with her children into the water and declared, " The devil and lightning and electricity were in me." The taking of food is frequently made very difficult owing to the resistance of the patients.

The **Course** of states of depression is in general fairly protracted, especially in more advanced age. Not infrequently their development is preceded by fluctuating, nervous disorders and slight irritable or depressive moodiness for years before the more marked morbid phenomena begin. Sometimes they appear only as an increase of a slight morbid state which had always existed.

The **Duration** of the attack is usually longer than in mania ; but it may likewise fluctuate between a few days and more than a decade. The remission of the morbid phenomena invariably takes place with many fluctuations ; not infrequently there is developed at the same time an impatient, grumbling, discontented behaviour, with restlessness and continual attempts to get away, which probably should be connected with the admixture of slight manic disorders.

When the depression disappears with remarkable rapidity, one must be prepared for a manic attack. The improvement of the physical state is for the observer already very conspicuous, while the patient feels himself not at all easier, indeed worse, than formerly. That is perhaps related to the fact that he is more distinctly aware of the disorder when the natural emotional stresses have returned, than at the height of the malady. Later an increased feeling of well-being may take the place of depression ; this we must perhaps regard as a manic indication even when it acquires no real morbid extent. A female patient wrote as follows in a letter of thanks shortly after recovery from a rather long period of depression :—

" I am now such a happy human being, as I never was before in my whole life ; I simply feel that this illness, even though quite insane to endure, had to come. Now at last, after a hard struggle, I may look forward to a quiet future. My spirit is so fresh ; I absolutely don't need to be trained, I cook with the greatest calmness . . . at the same time I keep my ideals, which, God be thanked, life has left to me in spite of all that is dreadful. And so my soul is in the greatest peace."

In other cases dejection, lassitude, lack of pleasure in work, sensitiveness still persist for a long time after the more conspicuous morbid phenomena have disappeared. Occasionally also one sees hallucinations, which have arisen at the height of the attack, diasppear very gradually although the patients otherwise are perfectly unconstrained psychically and have acquired clear insight into the morbidity of the disorder. A female patient, after recovery from a severe, confused depression still for a number of weeks heard in decreasing strength " her brain chatter," and she made the following notes about it :—

" I have nothing more, I do nothing more, I like no one any longer, you submissive thing, you ; I have no intention—must come here—they must come here ; I know no one any longer—O God, O God, what shall I do, when you have offended all here, in here, you impudent female, you . . ."

The content of these auditory hallucinations, which betray a certain rhythm, is partly changing and disconnected, but on the whole lets the trains of thought be recognised, by which the patient was dominated in her depression.

CHAPTER VI.

MIXED STATES.[1]

IF one follows more closely a considerable number of cases, which belong to the different forms of manic-depressive insanity, one soon observes that numerous *transitions* exist between the fundamemtal forns of manic excitement and depression, hitherto kept apart. Firstly, it has to be pointed out that the individual attacks of the disease have by no means permanently a uniform colouring. Manic patients may transitorily appear not only sad and despairing, but also quiet and inhibited ; depressive patients begin to smile, to sing a song, to run about. Such sudden reversals lasting for hours or for whole days are extremely frequent in both directions. A patient perhaps goes to bed moody and inhibited, suddenly wakes up with the feeling as if a veil had been drawn away from his brain, passes the day in manic delight in work, and next morning, exhausted and with heavy head, he again finds in himself the whole misery of his state. Or the hypomanic exultant patient quite unexpectedly makes a serious attempt at suicide.

But then very often we meet temporarily with states which do not exactly correspond either to manic excitement or to depression, but represent a *mixture* of morbid symptoms of both forms of manic-depressive insanity. This relationship becomes most clear in the transition periods from one state to another, which often extends over weeks or months. At the same time we do not see the phenomena of the one state always disappearing at the same time in all the realms of psychic life, and being replaced after a time of colourless equilibrium by disorders of other kinds, which gradually develop. Rather do some morbid symptoms of the earlier period vanish more quickly, others more slowly, and at the same time some or other phenomena of the state, which is now developing are already emerging. If one examines more precisely those transition periods, one is astonished at the

[1] Weygandt, Uber die Mischzustände des manisch-depressiven Irreseins. Habilitationsschrift, 1899.

multiplicity of the states which appear; some of them scarcely seem compatible with the orthodox attacks. Nevertheless I believe that we can understand these states better, if we assume that they proceed from a mixture of different kinds of fundamental disorders of manic-depressive insanity.

If we begin with the cases which develop in the orthodox manner, in which purely manic and purely depressive states appear one after the other, we find at the height of the attack combinations of definite symptoms which on the whole may be regarded as psychological opposites. On the one hand we meet with distractibility, flight of ideas, exalted ideas, cheerful mood, volitional excitement; on the other sluggishness of attention and of thinking, ideas of sin and of persecution, mournful or anxious mood, volitional inhibition. In other domains certainly, as that of perception, of mental work, of judgment, there are no such contrasts; they may ,therefore, be left out of consideration for the characterization of the mixed states. In order to simplify, as far as possible, the discussion based purely on principles, we will even restrict ourselves to the consideration of the disorders of the train of thought, of mood, and of volition, and at the same time for the present make the assumption, that these three domains of the psychic life form a unity and are similarly changed in their totality by every disorder. In orthodox mania and depression then all the three groups of psychic processes would display deviations in the same direction, which roughly might be contrasted as excitement and inhibition. It appears meanwhile that besides such similar influences, dissimilar influences of the individual domains also occur owing to the morbid process, with the mixed states as result. We ought not to be surprised at this, as in normal psychic life also the changes in the train of thought, in disposition and in will are frequently divergent. Anxiety may paralyse thought and action but also incite; ·along with loud joyful excitement we meet moods of quiet enjoyment, and along with rigid, gloomy, painful depression wild outbursts of despair.

In order to explain first the frequent occurrence of mixed states in the transition periods, it would only require the assumption, that the transformation of the individual partial disorders into their opposites does not begin simultaneously but one after the other. According to this hypothesis *one* disorder will already be transformed into its opposite, while in *other* domains the former state still continues to exist. The two following illustrations (Fig. 20) explain more clearly the

possibilities arising here with limitation to the three domains
mentioned above. They represent the transition from manic
excitement to depression and again to mania. The parts of
the curves above the horizontal line signify according to the
usual custom the partial disorders of mania, while the parts

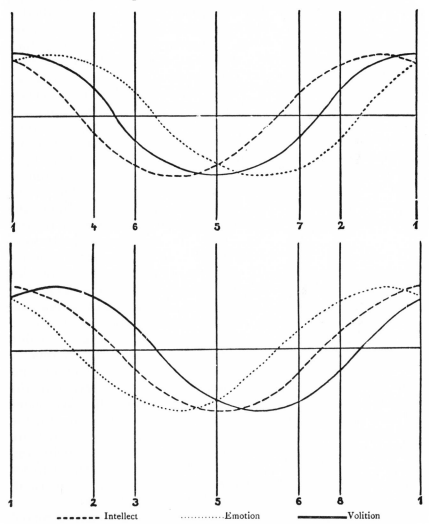

FIG. 20.—Comparison of the mixed states of manic-depressive insanity.

below the line indicate the transition to depression. The
disorders of thought are represented by broken lines, changes
in mood by dotted lines, volitional disorders by continuous
lines. In the first case illustrated, the disorder of thought is
transformed to its opposite earlier, the change of mood later

than the volitional disorder, while in the second case thought and mood precede volition. In a similar way one may, of course, demonstrate also various other possibilities, early transformation of volitional disorder, simultaneous course of two disorders before or after the third. As, however, here it only concerns elucidation of the point of view, which has led to the doctrine of mixed states, it suffices to consider the examples reproduced.

If we examine the first curve, the initial state would correspond to that of manic excitement. At line 4 the flight of ideas has made way for inhibition of thought, while the cheerful mood and pressure of activity still continue ; at line 6 volitional inhibition has also developed. As now mood is also transformed, we find at line 5 the picture of circular depression at its height ; it dominates the situation for a considerable time, although in somewhat changing combination. At line 7 we have before us flight of ideas along with mournful moodiness and volitional inhibition, while a short time afterwards at line 2 the volitional disorder has also changed and only the depressive mood still persists. The further course then again leads to the development of mania which lasts for a considerable time.

In the second curve, which begins in a similar way to the first, we have at line 2 the same state, which was developed in the first curve before the fresh manic attack. But further on at line 3 it comes to a combination of inhibition of thought and depressive mood with excitement. After the complete development of depression at line 5 there next follows again a state already known to us from the first curve, inhibition of thought and volition with cheerful mood, but then at line 8 volitional inhibition with flight of ideas and exalted mood.

If the transitions between the opposed states of manic-depressive insanity ran their course similarly to the way here described, we should in the first place infer that the transition states have hitherto, in comparison with the two principal forms, had relatively little attention paid to them, since they, as a rule, are of very short duration. Moreover there may be only a limited number of cases, in which the temporary divergence of the changes from each other on the different domains is at all strongly marked. And further we must picture to ourselves that the individual curves do not at all run their course smoothly, but display manifold sudden oscillations, so that the changing pictures become still more blurred. But, on the other hand, the conception described here would make it appear comprehensible that even in the pure pictures of mania and of depression the relation of the partial disorders to one another may change within wide limits. Volitional inhibition may be extremely severe, while moodiness is comparatively little marked, and *vice versa*; manic patients may have great flights of ideas but, at the same time, not be much excited; they may display extremely exalted mood with slight distractibility and so on. Even in the course of the same attack we not infrequently meet with a quantitative change in states of the same kind.

We must now, however, put the question, whether then clinical experience actually shows us morbid states which correspond to the hypotheses laid down here. Although our resources for the analysis of the individual phenomena are still very incomplete and a really systematic investigation of the mixed states and the conditions of their development has till now scarcely been attempted, I still think that I may reply to that question in the affirmative. As soon as one's eye is trained to these observations, one very soon recognises that in truth the orthodox descripton of mania and of circular depression is only to some extent appropriate for certain of the principal forms. Round these are grouped a multiplicity of states of various kinds, which, meanwhile, as far as we are able to judge, appear to be composed of quite the same fundamental disorders. Those which are immediately derived from the above considerations, we shall here discuss shortly.

1. **Mania.**—We begin with the picture of mania with flight of ideas, exalted mood, and pressure of activity.

2. **Depressive or Anxious Mania.**—If in the picture depression takes the place of cheerful mood, a morbid state arises, which is composed of flight of ideas, excitement, and anxiety, The patients are distractible, absent-minded, enter into whatever goes on round them, take themselves up with everything, catch up words and continue spinning out the ideas stirred up by these; they do not acquire a clear picture of their position, because they are incapable of systematic observation, and their attention is claimed by every new impression. They complain that they must think so much, their thoughts come of themselves, they have a great need of communicating their thoughts, but easily lose the thread, they can be brought out of the connection by every interpolated question, suddenly break off and pass to quite other trains of thought. Many patients display a veritable passion for writing, and scrawl over sheets and sheets of paper with

disorderly effusions. At the same time ideas of sin and persecution are usually present, frequently also hypochondriacal delusions, as we have formerly described them.

Mood is anxiously despairing ; it gives itself vent in great restlessness, which partly assumes the form of movements of expression and practical activity, but partly also passes over into a wholly senseless pressure of activity. The patients run about, hide away, force their way out, make movements of defence or attack ; they lament, scream, screech, wring or fold their hands, beat them together above their head, tear out their hair, cross themselves, slide about kneeling on the floor. With these are associated rhythmical, rubbing, flourishing, snatching, turning, twitching movements, snapping with the jaw, blowing, barking, growling. If one will, one might here speak of a " depressive " or " anxious " mania.

3. **Excited Depression.**—If in the state described the flight of ideas is replaced by inhibition of thought, there arises the picture of excited depression. It is here a case of patients who display, on the one hand, extraordinary poverty of thought but, on the other hand, great restlessness. They are communicative, need the doctor, have a great store of words, but are extraordinarily monotonous in their utterances. To questions they give short answers to the point, and then immediately return to their complaints again, which are brought forth in endless repetition, mostly in the same phrases. About their position in general they are clear ; they perceive fairly well, understand what goes on, apart from delusional interpretation. Nevertheless they trouble themselves little about their surroundings, they are only occupied with themselves.

Mood is anxious, despondent, lachrymose, irritable, occasionally mixed with a certain self-irony. Sometimes one hears from the patients witty or snappish remarks. Delusions are frequently present, but they are usually scantier and less extraordinarily spun out than in the form just described. The excitement of the patients also is usually not so stormy or protean. They run hither and thither, up and down, wring their hands, pluck at things, speak loud out straight in front of them, give utterance to rhythmic cries and torment themselves as well as their surroundings often to the uttermost by continuous, monotonous lamenting.

4. **Mania with Poverty of Thought.**—Again another picture is developed, when now depression is transformed to cheerfulness. We have then before us a manic state without

flight of ideas, an unproductive mania with poverty of thought. This state is very frequent. The patients perceive slowly and inaccurately, often only understand questions on repeated, impressive repetition, pay no attention at all, frequently give perverse, evasive answers, cannot immediately call things to mind. Nothing at all occurs to them ; their conversation is, therefore, very monotonous and empty ; the same students' phrase, jocular or vigorous, is produced ever again with sniggering laughter. The patients, therefore, not infrequently make a definite impression of weakmindedness, while later they may even prove themselves to be specially gifted. The state is subject to great fluctuation, so that the patients temporarily are quick and clever at repartee, while at other times they are incapable of saying anything at all.

Mood is cheerful, pleased, unrestrained ; the patients laugh with and without occasion, are delighted with every trifle. Now and then they are somewhat irritated, repellent, or deliberately coarse, immediately afterwards breaking out into a merry laugh. Excitement is often limited to making faces, occasional dancing about, wanton throwing things here and there, changes in dress and coiffure, without any display of busyness, such as is otherwise peculiar to mania. The patients are, however, very excitable, and quickly becomes noisy and clamorous, as soon as they find themselves in unrestful surroundings. While they in general do not speak either with special haste or very much, and often for a considerable time behave quite quietly, it may happen that in the course of a conversation an increasing flow of talk develops. Many of these patients conduct themselves in general so quietly and methodically, that to superficial observation excitement does not appear at all. Others sit about in idleness, and when addressed burst out laughing, but give utterance to nothing except a pert remark. Invariably one also notices that they are incapable of any regular occupation, but rather display a tendency to all sorts of mischievous tricks and silly jokes ; they make collections, steal and tear up things, make knots, stop up key-holes, stick scraps of paper on to the wall, are wantonly destructive. At times it comes also to very abrupt, short-lived, impulsive outbursts of great violence, Such a patient without cause suddenly jumped out of the bath, knocked down the attendant with a chair, smashed several window-panes, and slipped out completely naked into the snow-covered garden, where he quietly let himself be caught, as if nothing at all had happened ; he was also incapable of giving any motive whatsoever for his action.

5. **Orthodox Depression** with inhibition of thought, mournful moodiness and irresoluteness.

6. **Manic Stupor.**—If here mournful mood is replaced by cheerful mood, that form arises which first instigated me to investigate the mixed states, and which we usually call " manic stupor." The patients are usually quite inaccessible, do not trouble themselves about their surroundings, give no answer, at most speak in a low voice straight in front, smile without recognizable cause, lie perfectly quiet in bed or tidy about at their clothes and bed-clothes, decorate themselves in an extraordinary way, and all this without any sign of outward restlessness or emotional excitement. Not infrequently catalepsy can be demonstrated.

Occasionally isolated *delusions* of changing content find utterance. The patients feel cold in their brain, have an iron tongue, are devoured by polar bears, are the exchanged child of a prince, Eleonora von Halberstadt. But for the most part they prove themselves fairly sensible and oriented. Quite unexpectedly, however, they become lively, give utterance to loud and violent abuse, make a pert, telling remark amidst unrestrained laughter, jump out of bed, throw their food about the room, suddenly take off their clothes, run in double quick time through several rooms, tear up a garment or ill-use a fellow-patient without external cause, and immediately sink back again into their former inaccessibility.

At other times one finds them perhaps even quiet, sensible and intelligent, for the most part certainly only quite temporarily. Many patients wander with measured step about the ward, scarcely speak at all, but occasionally make a joke, call the physician by his first name, force their way erotically to him, smile. One night such a patient stole the keys from the nurse who was asleep, and escaped into the room of one of the physicians ; she enjoyed the successful trick very much but never spoke a word.

The patients often have a quite accurate recollection of the time that has elapsed, but are totally unable to explain their singular behaviour. " I wanted to have no will," one of these patients said to me. He had refused food in order to be lighter and so attain to health, but felt himself caused by hunger to sip a large quantity of milk through his nose and to smell a roll passionately. In carrying out these singular arrangements he smiled himself, but did not speak a word and did not let himself be dissuaded from it.

A certain idea of this state is perhaps given by Fig. 21. In the rigid expression of countenance of the patient who always remains standing on the same spot, the constraint can be distinctly recognised, which for many months has dominated her and made her dumb. But, at the same time, there appeared in the almost invincible tendency to destructiveness and filthy habits, the fundamental manic feature of the disorder, which in the adornment of torn-off leaves and twigs is recognisable also in the picture. In other patients the expression is more cheerful, sportive, erotic. This state is often interpolated, only temporarily, in a pronounced manic attack. Still more frequently it forms the transition between depressive stupor and the mania which goes along with it, as was assumed in our second curve. One may then follow step by step the various intermediate stages, the yielding of the mournful moodiness, the appearance of the first smile, the movements becoming freer, the development of a certain restlessness with low whispering, and lastly, the disappearance of inhibition in the domain of speech also, with the bursting forth of pressure of speech and flight of ideas.

FIG. 21.—Manic stupor.

7. **Depression with Flight of Ideas**—In the usual picture of depression inhibition of thought may be replaced by flight of ideas. These patients are incited by their delusions to vivid associations of ideas, they read much, show interest in, and understanding of what goes on in their surroundings, perhaps even sheer curiosity, although they are almost mute, and are rigid in their whole conduct and are of cast-down and hopeless mood. We then hear from them as soon as they again begin to speak about their state, that they cannot hold fast their thoughts at all, that constantly

things come crowding into their head, about which they had never thought. Regard being had to the other experiences in the mixture of morbid symptoms, the assumption is easy, that in such cases we have to do with the appearance of a flight of ideas which only on account of the inhibition of external movements of speech is not recognizable. A female patient connected plays on words with what she heard. When a rose was given to her, she said that meant that she was guilty (Rose-reo sei). In spite of great moodiness she used peculiar slang expressions ; she spoke of the superintendent of the institution as the " chief bonze," " the Lord of hosts."

Occasionally the patients, who cannot give utterance to anything at all in speech, are capable of writing, and then compose to our astonishment comprehensive documents, often desultory, full of ideas of sin and delusional fears. A sad, moody, taciturn patient with distinct volitional inhibition, when he felt himself offended by a fellow-patient, whom, he thought, he had himself injured before, wrote as follows :—

" Now one might regard this conduct as retaliation, as equivalent, as a sweet revenge, well yes, but the Christian forgives, does not bear a grudge, forgets the wrong that has been done to him, does not abuse in return, when he is abused. If any one strikes you on the right cheek, turn to him the other also, says the Lord and Saviour and diverges here from the precepts of the Old Testament, where it says, " An eye for an eye, and a tooth for a tooth." Do not reward evil with evil or with abuse. Forgive one another as Christ has forgiven you."

The heaping up of synonymous phrases, the jumping off to side thoughts, show here distinctly the flight of ideas, which certainly was only recognizable in his writings. The patient felt it himself, while he wrote :—

" I am again becoming prolix ; I therefore consider it better to hasten to a conclusion, for long-winded explanations weary the reader, and are at the least felt as want of consideration . . ." " I also in writing repeat words which mean the same, as lack of energy and lack of will ; both expressions mean the same. . . ."

At the same time the patient spoke " of his over-great anxiety, of his lack of energy, in consequence of which, activity, the coming out of oneself, the firm will, the strong will-power are absent."

To this kind those cases may perhaps also be reckoned, the sad and moody patients, in whom the tendency to imaginative composition appears. One might perhaps call this picture " depression with flight of ideas." Not infrequently, as our first curve also indicates, manic excitement is developed with disappearance of volitional inhibition and transformation of mood.

8. **Inhibited Mania.**—Finally, I have also repeatedly come across states which would correspond with the last combination assumed by us, flight of ideas with cheerful mood and psychomotor inhibition. The patients of this kind are of more exultant mood, occasionally somewhat irritable, distractible, inclined to jokes ; when addressed they easily fall into chattering talk with flight of ideas and numerous clang associations, but remain in outward behaviour conspicuously quiet, lie still in bed, only now and then throw out a remark or laugh to themselves. It appears, however, as if a great inward tension, as a rule, existed, as the patients may suddenly become very violent. Formerly I classified this " inhibited mania " with manic stupor ; I think, however, that it may be separated from that on the ground of the flight of ideas which here appears distinctly.

Perhaps we may, as Stransky indicates, regard as the slightest form of these states the " *shamefaced mania* " which he mentions. In this the patients behave quite quietly in the presence of the physician, are perhaps even taciturn and motionless, although cheerful, while among their equals they may be fairly lively and high-spirited. It appears that here the inhibitions of embarrassment are by themselves sufficient to suppress the manic pressure of activity.

The doctrine of the *mixed states* is still too incomplete for a more thorough characterization of the individual forms to be advisable at present. Nevertheless attention may be directed here to some points of view which may be of significance for the further development of our knowledge in this domain, indeed, to a certain extent have already been so.

Partial Inhibition and Exataltion.—The idea of " partial inhibition," as it has been introduced into the doctrine of the mixed states by Dreyfus, Pfersdorff and Goldstein, finds without doubt its justification in the fact, that the classification of the psychic life, which forms the foundation of our arguments, naturally only reflects the very roughest outlines. First, it must be remarked that at the same time a whole series of psychic processes, which certainly might underlie independent disorders, have received no consideration at all, as the behaviour of attention, perception, impression, psychic work, the formation of judgments and inferences and so on. It would be conceivable that through more accurate consideration of the varying changes which appear in individual cases in these and many other domains, the multiplicity of forms would be still considerably enriched.

Here I will only bring forward a single experience, the frequent contradiction between the content of the delusions and the colouring of mood. A patient told me with laughing that his nerves were dried up and his blood circulated only as far as his neck. A depressed female patient spoke of the inward voice, which she heard, as of a " grace " ; others state with an air of secrecy that they are considered to be the Virgin Mary, that they are to be confined with Christ, that it is believed of them that they could work miracles, make gold, cure all diseases. Many patients speak cheerfully of their approaching death. In this domain also there are mixtures which do not correspond to ordinary behaviour. Moreover, there are manic patients who, as has already been partially indicated above, are not distractible, at least not by external impressions, and depressive patients whose attention may be excited with extraordinary ease.

Possibly more important than these phenomena, which are perhaps quite unessential, is the fact, that the three great domains of the psychic life, which we have laid as the foundation of our discussion are, in reality, nothing less than unities. Inhibition and excitement may attack partial domains separately, and so exist beside each other in the same territory. The pairs of opposites, which we have taken, are, therefore, only valid for the general grouping of the states, but in detail are frequently not sufficient. So in the domain of thought, there may apparently be a separation between conceptual thought, the emergence of sensuous memory pictures, and the occurrence of linguistic presentations. As already mentioned, there are patients who, without any difficulty worth speaking about, can think conceptually, but who feel most painfully the colourlessness of the presentations which emerge.

But then we occasionally observe beside each other inhibition of thought and flight of ideas.[1] The patients display great psychic dulness, but at the same time desultoriness of the train of thought and a tendency to linguistic clang associations. From this it appears that inhibition of thought and flight of ideas are by no means the kind of opposites which they might appear according to ordinary clinical epxerience.

[1] Schröder, Zeitschr. f.d. ges. Neurol. u. Psych., II, 57.

In fact we may likewise artificially produce by bodily exertion or by the use of alcohol states in which difficulty in thinking is combined with flight of ideas. Perhaps we may assume that there are various forms of inhibition of thought, according to whether conceptional, sensuous and linguistic thought are simultaneously or only partly disordered. When the domain of linguistic presentations is not affected by the inhibition or even is itself in a state of excitement, flight of ideas might exist along with difficulty in thought. I should like merely to indicate that probably we should also differentiate between inhibition of thought and monotony of thought ; likewise increased activity of imagination, as we observe it in the slighter forms of manic excitement, must be separated from flight of ideas.

In the other domains of psychic life things are very similar. The cheerful and the mournful or anxious mood are not simple opposites which are mutually exclusive, but they may mix with each other in the most different ways. Not at all infrequently we observe in our patients, as already mentioned, a kind of grim humour, which is compounded of despair and amused self-derision. The angry irritation also, which we meet so often in the most different states, is, as Specht [1] has rightly emphasized, to be regarded as a mixture of heightened self-consciousness with unpleasant moods. By the continued predominance of such a mixture of moods that state is characterized before everything, which is usually called " *acute delirious mania*," raving mania. This includes cases of pronounced manic excitement, in which the patients on the slightest occasion fall into outbursts of furious anger, overwhelm their surroundings with abuse, and become senselessly violent. To this group those manic patients probably belong, who are constantly peevish, repellent, inaccessible, who give pert answers, make scornful remarks, torment and ill-use their fellow-patients. If with that is compared the imperturbable cheerfulness and amiability of other patients who are just as excited, it becomes clear that peculiar mixtures of moods must here be present.

If in these cases the excitement is moderated, the *grumbling* forms of mania perhaps arise, to the slightest phases of which Hecker has specially drawn attention. The patients, indeed, display exalted self-consciousness, are pretentious and high-flown, but by no means of cheerful mood ; they rather appear dissatisfied, insufferable, perhaps even a

[1] Specht, Zentralblatt f. Nervenheilk., 1907, 529 ; 1908, 449.

little anxious. They have something to find fault with in everything, feel themselves on every occasion badly treated, get wretched food, cannot hold out in the dreadful surroundings, cannot sleep in the miserable beds, cannot have social intercourse with the other patients. Along with perfect sense they have a great tendency and capacity to offend and to hurt others, to stir them up, to incite them, everywhere to find out the unpleasant and place it in the foreground. Every day they bring forward fresh complaints, act as guardian to the people round them, are irritated, when, in their opinion, sufficient attention is not paid to them. The manic foundation is indicated in talkativeness, slight flight of ideas, great unsteadiness and restlessness, which drives the patients to wander about a great deal, to begin all possible cures without carrying through a single one, to smoke and to drink excessively.

Partial Mixtures.—If in the description of the clinical states we place the *colouring of mood* in the foreground, there is no doubt at all, that the firmness also with which an emotion persists, and the strength of the emotional stress which the occurrences of life call forth, must be of essential significance for the formation of the state. In general much more pronounced fluctuations of mood are observed in manic patients, but here also displacements occur, manias with imperturbable unchanging cheerfulness and depressions with frequent fluctuations of mood. The peculiar weakening of the emotional response, which is felt so painfully by many sad and moody patients, apparently does not occur equally in all forms of depression ; it may for example be absent in states of great anxiety. On the other hand we often enough miss the great vivacity of emotional stress, which distinguishes many slightly manic patients, in other manic states.

The *colouring of delusions* in general stands in close connection with mood, although here also, as already mentioned, contradictions appear to occur, which meanwhile might possibly be connected with the existence of mixtures of moods. But further a remarkable mixture of depressive and exalted ideas is often observed. The immeasurableness of the persecutions, to which the patients are exposed, might well be interpreted in this sense. A patient asserted that he had got cantharidin by the hundredweight. Another declared that his relatives had to live among robbers for trillions of years. A third, who believed that all his inside was destroyed and lacerated, said that the doctor might be proud to be allowed to treat him, a case of the kind had not occurred for six hundred years. Others are fetched away by "millions of devils," dragged to an "extra scaffold," persecuted by Kaiser and King, taken to America by the Kaiser in order to be shot there. Certain theatrical features in the depressive ideas probably also belong here. A female patient in despair described her approaching execution, and added with a satisfied sidelong glance at her neighbour, "and Gretchen must crack the whip." Another wished to die a "romantic death," wished to confess her sins openly. A third desired to be allowed as a martyr to embrace lions and leopards in their cage.

Perhaps the fact of limited inhibitions and excitements is most distinctly seen in the domain of *volitional* processes. The experiments with the writing-balance have already shown that in the simple action of writing the force and the rapidity of the movement may be changed in different directions. In still much higher degree must that be valid for the intricate processes of which an independent volitional action is composed. The decision, the impulse, its force, the rapidity of its transformation into actual activity may independently of each other be subject to disorders, and these disorders may again extend to different distances over the individual domains of activity. In fact we know some experiences, which go to prove that the expressions "volitional inhibition" and "volitional excitement" represent large general conceptions which must often be analysed. Rapidity or sluggishness of decision may exist without the external volitional action being recognizably changed. Dreyfus has directed attention to the fact, that a feeling of inhibition, a "subjective" inhibition may be present even without recognizable sluggishness of the action ; certainly it will be a case here of finer disorders which do not yet lead to definite results. Juliusburger has described cases with only subjective inhibition and a vivid feeling of depersonalisation as "pseudo-melancholia."

We observe further great inward restlessness, therefore volitional excitement, while the making of decisions and the carrying out of voluntary actions is difficult, indeed, the restlessness may even discharge itself in lively movements of expression without the volitional inhibition disappearing. From this we recognize that the impulsive discharges of states of inward tension may be influenced by the morbid process in another way than purposeful volition and activity.

Movements of linguistic expression also take up a peculiar position. Excitement and inhibition in the domain of speech and writing are up to a certain degree independent of the behaviour of the remaining volitional activities. We know patients, who display great pressure of activity, but at the same time are almost wholly mute, and on the other hand those, in whom incapacity to make a decision is conjoined with great pressure of speech, certainly also, as a rule, though not always, with a certain restlessness. Moreover, we have to distinguish between *external* and *internal* speech. The observation, that taciturn patients make plays on words, such as otherwise accompany pressure of speech with flight of ideas, permits the conjecture, which is supported by the self-observation of the patients, that here internal speech is facilitated, while the transformation into movements of speech appears to be inhibited. But lastly, as already indicated, writing may be facilitated, speech made difficult, and *vice versa.*

If we take into account the fact, that the development of the partial disorders here indicated may pass through the most various degrees in the individual domains of the psychic life, the number of which might still be considerably augmented, we have before us a sheer immeasurable multiplicity of clinical pictures, which may be compounded of greater or less excitement or inhibition of one or other psychic faculty. It would certainly be tempting to follow these phases in detail. But, nevertheless I would emphasize the fact, that such an analysis should not be given any too great significance for clinical consideration. The overwhelming majority of the actual morbid states display a relatively simple structure, similar disorders in the larger domains of psychic life, and may, therefore, be approximately brought under the forms here delimited.

In the meantime it will be useful in the interpretation of the states to remember that in manic-depressive insanity there is a large number of further possibilities without our being obliged to assume morbid processes of other kinds. It might be that here it is a case not so much of varieties of the morbid processes as of personal peculiarities. We might, perhaps, represent it thus to ourselves, that a further division of work in the domain of the individual psychic faculties and the resulting greater independence of partial domains might also have as a consequence that these partial domains would share in a different way and, to a greater or less degree, in the general morbid process.

The mixed states here described are with by far the greatest frequency *temporary* phenomena in the course of the disease. They pass over easily and often one into the other, as one partial disorder is displaced by another. Most frequently we meet with them, as already stated, in the transition periods between the two principal forms of the disease, indeed, only from the history of their development, their transformations from and to the known morbid states, do we derive the justification to interpret them as mixed forms and as states of manic-depressive insanity.

Moreover, mixed states may appear as independent morbid attacks. And we see in the course of an attack of manic-depressive insanity besides the simple states, states occasionally attaining to development, which wholly, or at least predominantly, run their course in the form of mixed states. By this naturally our conception of the essential identity of all these clinical phases is confirmed. More often certainly the different attacks of a patient seem to display the same mixed state. When once such a state has appeared, there is a certain probability that similar states will follow later. The agreement of the individual morbid pictures, which in certain circumstances are separated by decades, is often extraordinary. In a case of manic stupor I was in the highest degree astonished, when I had the old history sent to me from another institution. Although the former attack had occurred twenty-two years previously, the description given at that time would have done just as well for the later attack even in the smallest detail ; still ten years earlier a simple depression had preceded.

The **Course** of mixed states occurring as independent attacks appears in general to be lingering ; they might be regarded as unfavourable forms of manic-depressive insanity. They frequently occur in the later periods of the malady, in which in any case the tendency to a prolongation of the attacks is commonly seen.

The more exact knowledge of the mixed states makes it possible for us to recognise the clinical significance of those morbid pictures also which do not correspond with the principal forms. Where the previous history presents orthodox manic attacks or states of depression, the placing of the divergent picture in circular insanity is naturally not difficult. On the other hand those cases, which only display mixed states, may cause very considerable diagnostic difficulties, especially at the first attack. I know very well that even now it is still often impossible to attain to a certain decision ; yet it succeeds, certainly not too infrequently, to recognise correctly from the fundamental disorders of manic-depressive insanity, the composition of a peculiar morbid state at first incomprehensible and so to acquire important data for the further course and issue.

CHAPTER VII.

FUNDAMENTAL STATES.

MANIC-DEPRESSIVE insanity runs its course in attacks, whose appearance is in general independent of external influences. This fact shows us that the real, the deeper cause of the malady is to be sought in a permanent morbid state which must also continue to exist in the intervals between the attacks. This assumption becomes specially illuminating when frequent attacks return with approximately regular intervals. But also when the disease appears only a few times or even only once in a lifetime, its root must be sought in a change of the psychic life, which is of long standing or which has existed from youth up. At the first glance only an exception is made by the cases in which the attack has its origin in an external cause ; we shall later have to discuss how this exception is only apparent, and why and how far.

The difference in frequency and violence of the attacks is evidence that the severity of the change, which we presuppose as the foundation of the whole morbid state, must fluctuate within wide limits. The same thing is taught by clinical observation. The great majority of manic-depressive patients, especially of those with fewer attacks, display in the intervals no divergence from average health ; although undoubtedly it might be possible that many peculiarities escape the notice of the people round them, which, without being exactly morbid, would yet to expert observation betray a certain relation to their malady. But in a large series of cases it is clear to the laity also and to the patient himself that permanently slighter disorders of the general psychic condition continue to exist, which in faint indications correspond to the morbid phenomena of manic-depressive insanity. Among almost a thousand cases observed in Munich such permanent peculiarities were reported in about 37 per cent. Occasionally the developed morbid attacks frankly appear only as an increase of disorders which have already been present in the whole former life ; more rarely they are conjoined with these as complete opposites.

It is seen further that the permanent changes mentioned, which essentially consist of *peculiarities in the emotional life*, are not limited to individuals who suffer from attacks of manic-depressive insanity. Their clinical significance would be essentially impaired by this fact, if experience did not teach that they are observed with special frequency as simple personal peculiarities in the families of manic-depressive patients. Even if that is not true for all cases, these relationships are yet so frequent, that there can scarcely be any doubt about their deeper significance. We are, therefore, led to the conclusion, that there are certain temperaments which may be regarded as *rudiments of manic-depressive insanity*. They may throughout the whole of life exist as peculiar forms of psychic personality without further development ; but they may also become the point of departure for a morbid process which develops under peculiar conditions and runs its course in isolated attacks. Not at all infrequently, moreover, the permanent divergencies are already in themselves so considerable that they also extend into the domain of the morbid without the appearance of more severe, delimited attacks.

Classification.—On the grounds stated we consider ourselves justified in incorporating in the group of the manic-depressive "*fundamental states*" of our description besides those morbid phenomena, which appear in the attacks, those disorders also which on the one hand frequently accompany the " free " intervals between the attacks, on the other hand characterize the manic-depressive temperament in such cases also in which the full development of the malady is absent. The clinical forms, which would here perhaps have to be kept separate, are principally the *depressive* temperament (" constitutional moodiness "), the *manic* temperament (" constitutional excitement "), and the *irritable* temperament ; along with these, mention would have to be made of those cases in which moodiness and excitement frequently and abruptly alternate with each other (*cyclothymic* temperament).

DEPRESSIVE TEMPERAMENT.

The depressive temperament is characterized by a *permanent gloomy emotional stress in all the experiences of life*. Within the range of intellectual activity there is usually for the most part no very striking disorder. A few patients are even highly gifted, while in other cases mental development has remained somewhat behind from youth up. Mental efficiency may be good, yet the patients, as a rule, have to struggle with all sorts of internal obstructions, which they only overcome with effort ; they, therefore, are easily fatigued. Moreover, they lack the right joy in work. Although they are often ambitious and strive upwards with success, they yet do not find complete, lasting satisfaction in their work, as they keep in view the mistakes and deficiencies of their achievements, as well as the approaching difficulties, rather than the value of the thing accomplished. Therefore, difficulties and doubts very easily press upon them, which make them uncertain in their activity and occasionally force them to repeat the same piece of work again and again. The tendency to fruitless, especially hypochondriacal speculation often exists. The patients "everywhere at once imagine something." Their consciousness is always completely clear, the connection of their thinking is in no wise disordered ; they have a good understanding of the nature of their malady, often also an extremely painful feeling of the difficulty caused by their own insufficiency.

Mood is predominantly depressed and despondent, "despairing." "I was on a small scale always melancholic," declared a patient, and a female patient said, "I brought melancholy with me into the world." From youth up there exists in the patients a special susceptibility for the cares, the difficulties, the disappointments of life. They take everything seriously, and in every occurrence feel the small disagreeables much more strongly than the elevating and satisfying aspects of untroubled and cheerful enjoyment, of regardless surrender to the present. Every moment of pleasure is embittered to them by the recollection of gloomy hours, by self-reproaches, and still more by glaringly portrayed fears for the future. They "have never had anything nice in the world," "I was always a child of ill luck," said a patient. Frequently, therefore, a capricious, irritable, unfriendly, repellent behaviour is developed. The patients are occupied only with themselves, do not trouble themselves about their surroundings, display no public spirit. Other patients may to outward appearance be even-tempered and may only reveal their unhappy emotional constitution, their self-tormenting, to their nearest relatives or to the physician ; when stimulated by external circumstances they are perhaps cheerful, charming, and amiable, and even high-spirited, but when left to themselves, they return again with a certain satisfaction to their own introspective meditations on the wretchedness of life.

Every task stands in front of them like a mountain ; life with its activity is a burden which they habitually bear with dutiful self-denial without being compensated by the pleasure of existence, the joy of work. " I have always had to keep myself together by force and not easily, and now it becomes always more difficult," said a patient. The patients have no confidence in their own strength, they have " very little vital energy " ; they despair at every task, and become anxious and despondent with extreme facility, they feel themselves of no use in the world, good for nothing, nervous, ill, they fear the onset of a serious illness, especially mental disorder, a disease of the brain. They are distrustful, regard themselves as nature's step-children, are not understood by their surroundings, and they like to occupy themselves with thoughts of death, even already in childhood's years.

Many patients are constantly tormented by a certain " *feeling of guilt*," as if they had done something wrong, as if they had something to reproach themselves with. Sometimes the things are real, but very remote or quite insignificant, with which this tormenting uncertainty is connected. One of my patients could not get quit of the thought of a sexual offence committed years before. Another was not able to get over the recollection of his landlady's having said that he would never pass his examination. Although he succeeded without special difficulty in passing, the thought constantly persecuted him, that he had been a silly fool to let such a thing be said to him ; everyone saw by the look of him that he was a poor lot to take such things sitting down. Ever again he was impelled to take steps in some way or other, even after many years, to procure satisfaction for himself and to restore again his honour, injured as he supposed.

The *sexual* domain in especial usually offers abundant food for moodiness. The sexual emotions are roused very early and lead to debauchery, but most frequently to onanism, the consequences of which appear to the patients in the blackest colours. A patient who by his inward excitement was ever again, in spite of all vows and oaths, forced to " necessary onanism," said of his state of dull hopelessness :—

" No human words can describe the suffering of soul, which this abominable vice has caused me, and after I had gone through it, the word hell with all its terrors lost all meaning for me, if it means anything else than the consequences of onanism. To wander about as a living corpse, and with that the consciousness of bearing the stamp of this vice, as it were, on the forehead and to hear the critical looks or even the cynical allusions of kind friends, till one becomes so shy that one avoids going out during the day and rather hides away in one's mouse-hole, till night begins ! By far the worst is the horror and disgust at oneself, the feeling of hopelessness, which becomes deeper at each fall, finally the cretinous resignation, the loss of self-confidence ; one has no longer courage with the enemy in the camp."

Other patients also feel sexual excitement, which forces itself on them in voluptuous pictures, most painfully, and all the more if, through psychic impotence, through shyness, or through moral considerations they are prevented from satisfying it. Here is a favourable soil for the development of all sorts of singular expedients for help in this difficulty. Several times I saw such fathers of families adopt measures for the restriction of sexual intercourse or for the prevention of conception, because they feared to injure themselves or shunned the responsibility of bringing still more nervous children into the world.

Not infrequently the emotional life is dominated by a *weak sentimentality*, often with pronounced artistic and belletristic inclination and ability. One of my patients could not bear to read anything about the circulation of blood ; he went to the slaughter-house in order to see what he did when he ate meat, and thereafter adopted by preference a vegetarian diet.

Conduct.—The whole conduct of life of the patients is considerably influenced by their malady. On the one hand appears their *anxiety*. " I may say that I was born in anxiety," said a patient. They are without initiative, uncertain ; they ask for advice on the slightest occasion. They shrink from every responsibility, are afraid of the most distant possibilities, weigh all details and consequences scrupulously, avoid strictly all unusual, and still more, dangerous matters. They must do everything themselves, because they think that otherwise they cannot bear the responsibility ; they use themselves up early and late in trivial activity far more than is necessary, carry out everything with tormenting precision and accuracy. A lady with a very small household invariably in the evening used the time from ten o'clock to half-past eleven to put in order her few accounts for the day and so satisfy her duties as a housewife. The fear not to be able to earn a living, to fall into want, causes many patients to practise exaggerated frugality. They restrict their wants to the uttermost, they do not eat enough and they let their clothes fall into disrepair.

In consequence of their anxiety the patients never come

to a rapid decision.   They consider endlessly without carrying out anything.   A lady had first to be induced by the summoning of a council of her whole family to consult a physician, which she herself ardently wished to do, and even then she could not make up her mind actually to follow the advice given.   The patients, therefore, continue at each task and gradually arrive at an always narrower limitation of their activity.   They give up reading and music, cycling and smoking, and do not go shopping any longer, because they cannot make a choice,   They cannot travel, because the preparations, the decision where to go, are too difficult for them.   In the end even the drawing up of the bill of fare, the oversight of the servants, the anxiety that everything in the household shall be ready at the right time, are a very great trouble.   Many women cannot endure a strange face about them, try to limit more and more the number of their domestics, give themselves trouble to the uttermost.   Finally others let everything go as it will.

Examinations especially form an almost insurmountable obstacle for our patients.   In spite of very ample qualifications many a one renounces the higher career which beckons him and contents himself with a modest little place in life, because his deficient self-confidence and irresolution do not allow him to take the necessary examination.   Very often caprices and peculiarities develop, which commonly have some relation to the moodiness, and indicate measures by which the patient tries to help himself over the inward difficulties.   The patients invariably have the inclination to withdraw from intercourse with other people.   They find no joy in social life and pleasures, feel most comfortable when they can commune with their own thoughts by themselves or follow their artistic inclinations.

But it is especially their *lack of self-confidence* which prevents them from cultivating personal relations.   Compared with other people who are perhaps otherwise far beneath them, they appear to themselves awkward, boorish, foolish ; they do not get rid of the tormenting feeling that they are continually exposing their weak spot, that the people round them look at them over the shoulder, that their presence is not desired.   A female patient said that she did not find time to continue her education and must, therefore, appear stupid to everyone.   In consequence they become quiet and shy, avoid their acquaintances on the street, live a solitary and secluded life.

Suicide.—Many patients constantly play with thoughts of suicide and are always prepared on the first occasion to throw away their life. Although utterances of that kind are not, as a rule, to be taken seriously, yet sudden suicides still occur often enough among those morbidly ill-tuned patients. A patient, when ten years old, ate verdigris, when thirteen and again when twenty tried to hang himself, when fourteen took strychnine, and when twenty-four shot himself in the left breast, each time on a most trifling occasion.

Nervous Complaints. — Frequently the patients are tormented with all kinds of nervous complaints. They feel tired, exhausted, complain of heaviness and dull pressure in their head, unpleasant sensations in the most different parts of their body, oppression, palpitation, congestion, pulsation, twitching, vibration ; attacks of migraine are not rare. In the sexual domain psychic impotence often exists and frequent nocturnal emissions. The phenomena of nervous dyspepsia are frequent ; digestion is usually sluggish. Sleep is, as a rule, defective ; the patients have great need of sleep, but fall asleep late, are frequently disturbed by starting and by terrifying dreams, do not feel refreshed in the morning but tired and unfit, and only in the course of the day do they gradually become less uncomfortable.

Course.—The morbid picture here described is usually perceptible already in *youth*, and may persist without essential change throughout the whole of life. In isolated cases a transformation of the disposition takes place first in the years of development about the seventeenth, eighteenth, or twentieth year, while up till then no specially conspicuous deviations have appeared. Fluctuations also are later not rare. Especially in connection with a violent emotion or a bodily illness, but also without recognizable occasion the state may become worse, and after a longer or shorter time again improve somewhat. In rare cases once in a way after a duration of decades a complete disappearance of the depression appears to occur, as was reported by C. F. Meyer. Now and then there are indications of a periodic course, but the attacks are only very imperfectly delimited, and show a tendency to run together in as far as the remissions become always more indistinct. Occasionally psychogenic features also appear, great need of comfort, reinforcement of the complaints in the presence of the physician. "She is quite happy, so long as she does not associate with those women who also think that they are ill," wrote the husband of a patient.

It is exactly the fluctuations of the state progressing imperceptibly to real attacks, which point to the inner relationship of the depressive temperament with manic-depressive insanity.[1] There is actually an uninterrupted series of transitions to " periodic melancholia," at the one end of which those cases stand in which the course is quite indefinite with irregular fluctuations and remissions, while at the other end there are the forms with sharply defined, completely developed morbid picture and definite remissions of long duration.

But further, the fact is of the greatest significance, that the depressive state may be very suddenly interrupted by manic attacks, indeed that it not very rarely forms the foundation on which the morbid state of " periodic mania " is developed ; still more frequently an alternation of manic and depressive attacks occurs. We found the depressive temperament in 12.1 per cent. of our manic-depressive cases, but this proportion is certainly considerably too low because of the incompleteness of our histories of the patients. Lastly, the great clinical similarity of the picture here drawn with the slightest forms of depressive attacks must be pointed out. The shyness, the lack of self-confidence, the dejection, but especially the feeling of inward obstruction in thought and will, the irresolution, the hypochondriacal fears and thoughts of suicide are found in both morbid forms in quite similar manner.

Both the agreement of the states and the close clinical relations of the depressive temperament to manic-depressive insanity, and its place in the inherited series scarcely leave any doubt, therefore, that we have here to do with a rudiment of the fully developed disease. To that must still be added the circumstance, that we shall immediately become acquainted with a manic temperament which completely corresponds. The possibility must, however, be left open, that not all forms of depressive temperament are to be interpreted in the same sense. Thus specially the cases with more definitely delimited states of anxiety and fear might not belong to this form, and here also there is not usually any lasting, unchanging depressive moodiness nor any general inhibition.

On the other hand it appears to me that with the states here delineated certain tender and gentle natures a little inclined to melancholy are inwardly related. These are often

[1] Reiss, Konstitutionelle Verstimmung und manisch - depressives Irresein, 1910.

found in families with manic-depressive disposition, and sometimes these individuals actually fall ill. There are people, especially women, who combine anxiety, scrupulous conscientiousness, and lack of self-confidence with good intellectual endowment, attractive, clinging amiability, and great goodness of heart, who shun every rough contact with life, who easily make cares for themselves, who understand well how to endure, indeed to sacrifice themselves, but not how to fight. Not infrequently they display deficiency of the sense of reality, unworldliness and a tendency to visionary moods, occasionally perhaps also a surprising violence.

MANIC TEMPERAMENT.

The manic temperament which I formerly described as *" constitutional excitement "* forms the antithesis of the depressive temperament ; more recently it has been described in greater detail, especially by Specht and Nitsche.[1] The intellectual endowment of the patients is for the most part mediocre, sometimes even fairly good, in isolated cases excellent. They acquire, however, as a rule, only scanty, and, in particular, very imperfect and unequal knowledge, because they show no perseverance in learning, do not like exerting themselves, are extraordinarily distractible, and seek to escape in every way from the constraint of a systematic mental training, and in place of that they pursue all possible side-occupations in variegated alternation. " She can do everything well when she likes," reported the relatives of a patient. Not infrequently they possess a very good faculty of perception and remember details without difficulty. But their understanding of life and the world remains superficial, the mental working up of their experiences bleared and indistinct, the remembrance of former events fleeting, coloured by partiality, and falsified by numerous personal additions. The train of thought is desultory, incoherent, aimless ; judgment is hasty and shallow. The patients are not concerned about their past, their surroundings, their position, their future, have in general no need to account for the circumstances of life or to form a general view of life.

Mood is permanently exalted, careless, confident. The patients have very marked self-confidence, put an extremely high value on their own capabilities and performances, boast

---

[1] Specht, Zentralblatt f. Nervenheilk., 1905, 590 ; Nitsche, Allgem. Zeitschr. f. Psych., lxvii, 36.

with the most obvious exaggeration. They wholly lack understanding for the morbid imperfection of their temperament. Rather are they convinced of their *superiority* to their surroundings, are proud of their ideal sentiments, their refined accent, their depth of feeling, and they confidently expect to make their fortune by their excellent endowment. Towards others they are haughty, positive, irritable, impertinent, stubborn. They show little sympathy with the sorrows of others; they enjoy deriding, teasing, and ill-using those who, they think, are their inferiors. When contradicted they may be extremely rough and coarse, but in certain circumstances accept even great reproaches and insults with surprising equanimity without understanding the mortification properly. They are usually ready for jokes, even for self-derision, for conversation and pastimes of all kinds and for all sorts of tricks. Now and then once in a way anxious or mournful moods also may temporarily be present.

In the **Conduct** and the **Activities** of the patients a certain *unsteadiness and restlessness* appear before everything. They are accessible, communicative, adapt themselves readily to new conditions, but soon they again long for change and variety. Many have belletristic inclinations, compose poems, paint, go in for music. A patient spoke of writing up the fortunes of his fellow-patients as novels. They like picturesque and conspicuous clothes, wear a fez, or they neglect themselves and run about in rags and dirt. Their mode of expression is clever and lively; they speak readily and much, are quick at repartee, never at a loss for an answer or an excuse, although often only a very threadbare one. " She can speak and read like a lawyer, when she likes," was said of a young girl.

In conversation the patients assume a free and easy tone, give pert or ironical answers, use choice poetical phrases, quotations, sought-out allusions, or they talk in forcible language, in coarse dialect; they weave in equivocations and poor jokes, which they accompany with roaring laughter. Whenever they are irritated, they usually make use of a very comprehensive " Dictionary of Abuse," to use Specht's expression. " She has an extraordinarily foul mouth," was the expression used to describe a patient. What they write is verbose, prolix, bombastic, full of personal remarks, witticisms, insulting sallies. Frequently they perform peculiar and conspicuous actions. A patient had " Pray and

work " printed on his card after his name. Another accosted
people on the street and asked them if there is a God, and if
they had ever thought of dying.

In making decisions the patients are desultory and uncertain. In consequence their life is invariably a chain of
thoughtless and extraordinary, not infrequently also nonsensical and doubtful activities. Already at school they are
insubordinate and disorderly, ring-leaders in all disturbances
of the peace ; they play truant, run away, do not get on anywhere, have to change their school, fail in examinations,
because of their aversion to thorough and persevering study.
They stand military discipline very badly, neglect cleanliness
and order, overstay their leave, are remiss in service, resist
authority, and are, as a rule, often punished, when it is not
recognized that they are ill. At the same time an important
part is frequently played by the *sexual instinct* which awakens
early and is very active, and which leads them to debauchery.
Female patients almost of necessity fall a prey to prostitution.
The influence of alcohol is usually still more unfavourable,
to which, in general, they yield themselves without resistance ; the patients spend in drinking and conviviality all
that they can get hold of. One of my patients became a
morphinist ; others are great smokers and snuffers.

Further, it now comes to the most varied attempts to
attain to some position in life, and the patients often go about
it not without ability, but without perseverance. Without
sufficient reason they change calling and position, are always
beginning something new, make large plans and after a short
time drop them again, and get into all kinds of low company.
A clergyman invented a new card-game and passed his time
in fishing and photography ; he overwhelmed his superiors
with suggestions for improvements in the church. Others
wish to become missionaries, or to go to America. Many
patients join new movements with fervent zeal which rapidly
flags, become ardent vegetarians, anti-vaccinators, anti-
Semites, sportsmen, bathe in the cold of winter ; others
become cheap jacks, professional jokers, town originals.
They often attempt tasks to which they are in no way equal,
make purchases far beyond their circumstances, decorate
themselves with high-sounding titles, to which they have not
the least claim, try to gain respect by boasting and swaggering. A patient had a crown printed on his visiting cards.

The *aimlessness* of their procedure is sometimes very
peculiar ; it distinctly shows how little the inner pressure of

activity is guided by sensible deliberation. One of my
patients had inflated advertisements of various chemical
products printed at great expense, sent them all over the
world, and entered into contracts for delivery of the goods,
although he, as a former dealer in fancy goods, knew nothing
at all of chemistry, concocted his materials on a common
kitchen-range, and was quite unable to manufacture the
large quantities ordered. He said that he had first just
wanted to see whether buyers would come at all, before he
really made arrangements for production. A few patients
have really good ideas, make useful inventions, display great
business ability, but yet on account of their unsteadiness and
unreliability and also on account of their scattering their
resources in all possible enterprises have never any success.

With their surroundings the patients often live in constant *feud*. They interfere in everything, overstep their
rights, make arrangements which they are not entitled to
make. As they do not fulfil their obligations, but at the
same time make great claims and behave arrogantly, they are
soon dismissed from their posts. They then become involved in legal processes for compensation and bring actions
for damages, but everywhere they put themselves in the
wrong by the immoderation of their procedure. Sometimes
they fall into a veritable entanglement of lawsuits, which
they pursue with ardour and with vigour through all the
courts of appeal. They show no respect to their superiors,
their manners are churlish, they will not be taught, they
respond to regulations with poor jokes or abuse. They have
no understanding whatsoever for the unseemliness of their
behaviour ; they do not comprehend at all why everything
they do is taken amiss, are astonished in the highest degree
at the complications which arise, but get over it with a few
jests. A clergyman who had called his opponent " Hansw."
[Hanswurst—Merry-Andrew] and " Rindv." [Rindvieh—
cattle] on a post card, asserted quite naively, when he
was prosecuted, that that meant " Hanswief " and
" Rindvögelein " ; no one had the right to read anything
else into it than what he had meant.

As everywhere they prove themselves useless, the patients
invariably fall into financial difficulties. When their means
are exhausted, they begin to borrow, to raise money on
credit, to run up bills at public-houses, to defraud. To raise
their credit they have at their service their great hopes for
the future, an almost completed invention, an appointment

which they have in view, their acquaintance with highly-placed individuals, an impending marriage which will bring them money, an assumed title. When rebuked, they assert indignantly that they are quite in the right, that they have not had the slightest intention to defraud, but that in a short time they will be able to satisfy all their obligations. Immediately after the reproof their former practices begin again, till at last, often only after decades, the morbid foundation of this extraordinary and incoherent conduct of life is recognized. " People, who do not know her, just call her gay," was what the very intelligent mother of a patient wrote to us.

The points of contact of this morbid picture with slight hypomanic states are, as I think, unmistakable. But the excitement here is still more slightly indicated, and it does not run its course in circumscribed attacks, but it is a *permanent personal peculiarity*. Certainly the clinical picture often develops more distinctly first in the years of development, in certain circumstances in the form of a transformation from a period of youth with a more depressive colouring. Further, not infrequently a certain progressive development is seen. Nitsche has described cases as " progressive manic constitution," in which a slighter manic predisposition develops towards the fiftieth year into a pronounced hypomania. Fluctuations of the state also are frequently observed ; in certain circumstances they may progress to the development of slighter or more severe manic attacks. Just as often does it come to the appearance of alternating manic-depressive states ; more rarely states of pure depression are interpolated. A slight, quickly passing transformation of mood is still fairly frequent ; occasionally it may come to a suicidal attempt. Of the manic-depressive patients observed in Munich about 9 per cent. showed a manic predisposition.

The slightest forms of the disorder lead us to certain personal predispositions still in the domain of the normal. It concerns here brilliant, but unevenly gifted personalities with artistic inclinations. They charm us by their intellectual mobility, their versatility, their wealth of ideas, their ready accessibility and their delight in adventure, their artistic capability, their good nature, their cheery, sunny mood. But at the same time they put us in an uncomfortable state of surprise by a certain restlessness, talkativeness, desultoriness in conversation, excessive need for social life, capricious temper and suggestibility, lack of reliability, steadiness, and perseverance in work, a tendency to building castles in the air and scheming, occasional unusual activities. Now and then one possibly hears also of periods of causeless depression or anxiety, which usually are traced back to external circumstances, over-work, disappointments. This experience, as also the further circumstance, that we very often see the parents, brothers and sisters, or children end in suicide, in mournful moodiness, or even fall ill of definite manic-depressive insanity, suggests to me that that kind of strongly developed sanguine temperament is to be regarded as a link in the long chain of manic-depressive predispositions.

IRRITABLE TEMPERAMENT.

The irritable temperament, a further form of manic-depressive predisposition, is perhaps best conceived as a *mixture of the fundamental states*, which have been described, in as much as in it manic and depressive features are associated. As it was demonstrable in about 12.4 per cent. of the patients here taken into account, it appears to be still a little more frequent than the depressive predisposition. The patients display from youth up extraordinarily great fluctuations in emotional equilibrium and are greatly moved by all experiences, frequently in an unpleasant way. While on the one hand they appear sensitive and inclined to sentimentality and exuberance, they display on the other hand great irritability and sensitiveness. They are easily offended and hot-tempered ; they flare up, and on the most trivial occasions fall into outbursts of boundless fury. " She had states in which she was nearly delirious," was said of one patient ; " Her rage is beyond all bounds," of another. It then comes to violent scenes with abuse, screaming and a tendency to rough behaviour. In such an attack of fury a female patient threw a whole pile of plates on the ground ; she flung a lighted lamp at her husband and she tried to attack him with the scissors. The patients are positive, always in the mood for a fight, endure no contradiction, and, therefore, easily fall into disputes with the people round them, which they carry on with great passion. A female patient who thought that she had been taken advantage of in the purchase of a house, threatened her opponent with a revolver, which, however, was unloaded. In consequence of their quarrelsomeness the patients are mostly very much disliked, have frequently to change their situations and places of residence, never come well out of anything. A patient who was an officer fought a series of duels with swords. In the family also they are insufferable, capricious, threaten their wives, thrash their children, have attacks of jealousy.

Mood.—The colouring of mood is subject to frequent change. In general the patients are perhaps cheerful, self-conscious, unrestrained ; but periods are interpolated in which they are irritable and ill-humoured, also perhaps sad, spiritless, anxious ; they shed tears without cause, give expression to thoughts of suicide, bring forward hypochondriacal complaints, go to bed. At the time of the menses the irritability is usually increased.

Intellectual endowment is often very good ; many patients display great mental activity, and they feel keenly the necessity for further culture. But they are mostly very distractible and unsteady in their endeavours. Sometimes they are considered to be liars and slanderers, because their power of imagination is usually very much influenced by moods and feelings. It, therefore, comes easily to delusional interpretations of the events of life. The patients think that they are tricked by the people round them, irritated on purpose and taken advantage of ; occasionally they imagine there is poison in their food. On the other hand they build castles in the air, take themselves up with impracticable plans.

Capacity for work may not show any disorder worth mentioning ; many patients are very diligent, indeed over busy, over zealous, but yet accomplish relatively little. In conversation the patients are talkative, quick at repartee, pert. In consequence of their irritability and their changing moods their conduct of life is subject to the most multifarious incidents, they make sudden resolves, and carry them out on the spot, run off abruptly, go travelling, enter a cloister. A female patient " became engaged, before she realized what was happening." Psychogenic disorders are often conspicuous, convulsive weeping, fainting fits, cramps.

CYCLOTHYMIC TEMPERAMENT.

The cyclothymic temperament must still be shortly considered. It is characterized by *frequent, more or less regular fluctuations of the psychic state to the manic or to the depressive side.* It was found only in 3 to 4 per cent. of our patients, but without doubt in reality is much more frequent, as it is the invariable introduction to the slightest forms of manic-depressive insanity which run their course outside of institutions, and frequently leads to them by gradual transitions. These are the people who constantly oscillate hither and thither between the two opposite poles of mood, sometimes "rejoicing to the skies," sometimes "sad as death." To-day lively, sparkling, beaming, full of the joy of life, the pleasure of enterprise, and pressure of activity, after some time they meet us depressed, enervated, ill-humoured, in need of rest, and again a few months later they display the old freshness and elasticity.

"I have always throughout life imagined something," explained a patient, "one time I thought that everything was soaring, another time it appeared to me as if the sky were falling in." Another stated that she had times, in which "everything got on so well from herself outwards," and other times, in which "again everything was so frightfully diffi-cult." A third said that she was "like a barometer, one time so, another time different." A patient described how sometimes at his work "each grip was difficult," and how then a "lightening of the brain" came over him.

Wilmanns draws attention to artists, who are only at certain times happy in creating and productive, and in the intervals in spite of all efforts do not get beyond unsatisfying attempts. At first these deviations from the middle line are only occasionally perceptible once in a way and as rapidly passing attacks ; but for the most part they have the tendency to return more frequently and to last always longer, indeed finally to fill up the whole life.

CHAPTER VIII.

FREQUENCY OF THE INDIVIDUAL FORMS—GENERAL COURSE.

THE frequency, with which the different clinical forms of manic-depressive insanity here described occur in a fairly large series of observations, is naturally very various. The slight forms are excluded from such a view, as they only rarely come to institutions, but are usually treated in the family or in all possible sanatoria. Their number is extraordinarily large. There is no " Nursing Home for Nervous Cases," which has not constantly had a whole series of them as inmates, certainly for the most part under the terms, over work, nervousness, neurasthenia, hysteria, and so on. Among the patients who came to our hospital 48.9 per cent presented states of depression only, 16.6 per cent. manic attacks only, and 34.5 per cent. a combination of manic and depressive morbid phenomena, sometimes one after the other sometimes alongside each other. Then it has, of course, to be taken into account that the course of the disease in the very great majority of cases was certainly not nearly at an end. If only cases were taken into account, which died in advanced age, the number of the combined forms would without doubt be very considerably increased.

Among the simple forms states of depression in the form of melancholia simplex and gravis with 23.5 per cent. are the largest group ; in a further 13.5 per cent. there were extraordinary delusions, and in still other 6.1 per cent states of anxiety were present. Slight manic excitement was present in 4 per cent of the cases, acute mania in 9.8 per cent. States of confusion and stupor of various colouring occurred in 8.2 per cent., compulsive ideas in 1 per cent. Among the combined forms the slighter forms predominated with 10.6 per cent. against the more severe with 9.1 per cent. States of stupor and clouding of consciousness were seen in 4.9 per cent ; more definite delusions likewise in 4.9 per cent. A comparison, which Walker[1] gives, is drawn up, indeed, from

[1] Walker, Archiv f. Psychiatrie, xlii. 788.

other points of view, but in the main is not very divergent. He found among 674 cases in men 55.7 per cent melancholias, 11 per cent. manias, and 33.3 per cent. circular cases, in the women 70.2 per cent., 6.2 per cent., and 23.6 per cent.

The individual attacks of manic-depressive insanity, as already appears from the clinical description, are not all the same, but may have very different forms. If one wishes to classify, one may first separate out those forms, in which all the attacks exhibit the same colouring and those in which an alternation of states takes place. To these last the mixed states would be added, in as much as they come to development by far the most frequently in transitions of that kind.

Here it must meanwhile be emphasized, that this classification, apparently so simple, really encounters manifold difficulties. Firstly, it will always be doubtful in the case of patients still living, whether a series of similar attacks even after a duration of decades will yet not be unexpectedly interrupted by a state of quite a different kind. But then also the characterization of individual attacks is very often by no means simple. In the enormous majority of manias, as soon as attention is directed to it, states of depression either at the beginning or the end are observed, which certainly last only a few days and may be little marked. In the course of excitement also hours or days of opposite colouring are interpolated with extreme frequency, and finally it turns out often enough that slight moodiness has been present in the intervals between the manic attacks. On the other hand the states of depression which belong to this class are often followed by a remarkable " reactionary " cheerfulness which by physicians and patients is generally regarded as an expression of pleasure at recovery, as the reactionary " melancholia " after mania is regarded as exhaustion or as sorrow about the mental disease which has been passed through. During the depression we observe states of sudden excitement, transitory merriment, or we learn that the patients have either formerly or afterwards decorated themselves in a conspicuous way, have contrary to their usual custom visited places of pleasure, have been irritable and excited.

If, therefore, for the sake of having a general view we classify the attacks according to their colouring, we must at the same time not forget that here it does not at all concern fundamental distinctions. But rather, just as in the states of excitement and depression in paralysis or dementia præcox, all the pictures only represent the changing phenomena of one and the same fundamental morbid process, which may be connected with each other in the most multifarious ways and pass over one into the other.

A first survey over the general course of manic-depressive insanity gives the following classification in which 899 cases are arranged first according to the colouring, then according to the frequency of attacks. With regard to the former, three groups were made, according to whether the cases ran their course as depression, or as mania, or lastly, in both forms or in mixed forms. Next the cases were classified with only one attack, with two attacks, or with three or more attacks. As the observations were naturally, as regards the greatest number of them, not concluded, it would be expected that still considerable displacements with regard to the number of the cases would take place, yet even so perhaps a comparison between the different forms is not without value :—

	Depression.	Mania.	Combined Forms.
One attack . . .	263	102	106
Two attacks . . .	120	24	89
Three and more attacks	57	23	115

This summary shows first that in a fairly large series of observations depression occurring once has a great preponderance. Here the fact has to be noted, that the majority of all cases of manic-depressive insanity, about 60 to 70 per cent., begin with a state of depression. This first attack, which, as a rule, runs a mild course, is followed in about two-thirds of the cases by a free interval, which in certain circumstances may last throughout life. In about one-third of the patients, however, manic excitement immediately follows depression, and in most cases leads on to temporary recovery. Only in a small number of cases depression now begins again immediately, and again gives place to excitement and so on.

The number of the attacks, which are repeated in similar form, is in the first group comparatively small; three and more depressive attacks were about four to five times more rare than single attacks. The cause of that is obviously that a great number of patients only fell ill once or at the time of observation had only their first attack behind them. Proably, however, many of the single attacks of depression would in the course of time turn out to be the introduction to combined forms. At least the circumstance is in favour of this, that among the patients, in whom three and more attacks were recorded, the combined forms were by far the most often represented.

When the disease begins with a manic attack, a remission appears next, likewise in approximately two-thirds of the cases ; in the remaining cases moodiness or stupor immediately follows excitement. Here a similar repetition of the attack at first appears still considerably less frequent than in states of depression ; on the other hand, if it does follow, one may reckon with greater probability than in depression that still more similar attacks will follow. But on the whole with an increasing number of attacks the tendency evidently becomes greater to a change of colouring or to an admixture of morbid phenomena of other kinds. Generally speaking one certainly observes that the individual attacks in a patient present a certain similarity with each other, which may now and then rise to " photographic " similarity. But there is very frequently the opportunity in the course of the same disease of seeing quite a number of the states described here appear one after the other from slight depression and stupor through the most multifarious mixed states to hypomania and to acute mania. Up to now I have not succeeded in finding any rule to which they conform. In particular a quite regular alternation between manic and depressive morbid periods, of the kind to which the attention of alienists has been mainly drawn, belongs to the rarer exceptions. The grouping is mostly irregular, as we shall see later in more detail in some examples. Often enough it also occurs that in a whole series of similar attacks a single one of opposite colouring is interpolated. Frequently a more regular alternation is developed after a somewhat long duration of the disease, when in the first part of the disease one kind of attack predominated or was alone present. The mixed forms also, especially manic stupor, come to development, as it appears, usually first after repeated attacks.

The duration of individual attacks is extremely varied. There are some which last only eight to fourteen days, indeed we sometimes see that states of moodiness or excitement, undoubtedly morbid, do not continue in these patients longer than one or two days or even only a few hours. For the most part, however, a simple attack usually lasts six to eight months. On the other hand, the cases are not at all rare, in which an attack continues for two, three or four years, and a double attack double that time. I have seen manias, which

even after seven years, indeed after more than ten years, recovered, and a state of depression, which after fourteen years
recovered.   Albrecht reports a case of melancholia, which
after eighteen years passed over into mania.   The duration
of the first attacks is not usually longer than a few months,
while later on it usually extends more and more, in certain
circumstances by the confluence of several attacks.

Almost always there are free intervals between each two
simple or double attacks.   The duration of these is likewise
subject to extraordinary fluctuation ; it may extend from a
few weeks or months to many years and even to several
decades.   Among 703 intervals, which I have compared,
there were 96, which lasted 10 to 19 years, 34, 20 to 29 years,
8, 30 to 39 years, and 1, 44 years.   Dupouy observed intervals of 25 and 30 years.   Vedrani has collected a series of
cases with long intervals.   He reports a mania, which after
26 years was followed by three more short manic attacks, an
attack of combined depression, stupor, and mania, with a
mania following after 27 years, and a similar case with
depression after 42 years.   He further mentions a case of
mania and depression with a mixed state after 27 years, two
depressions with pauses of 32 and 35 years, two manias with
pauses of 21, 30, 35 and 44 years, lastly, the sequence of
mania-depression or *vice versa* with pauses of 33 and 36 years.
Hübner reports a case of mania, in which after a first pause
of 41 years a regular return of the attacks followed ; in
another case the time between the second and third attacks
was 44 years.

A definite relation between the duration of the attacks
and the intervals does not seem to exist.   Short attacks may
be repeated in rapid succession, but may also be interpolated
one at .a time in fairly long free intervals.   Prolonged and
severe attacks on the one hand probably leave behind an
increased tendency to fresh attacks ; but, on the other hand,
it is also often seen that it is these very attacks which are
followed by a longer pause.   Sometimes the duration of the
intervals is so invariable, that at the usual time the patients
return punctually to the institution ; but for the most part
the disease shows the tendency later on to run its course more
quickly and to shorten the intervals, even to their complete
cessation.   At the same time the duration of the attacks
usually increases gradually.   Thus I saw in one case in the
course of thirteen attacks the duration of these increase from
three or four months up to six or seven, while the intervals

decreased from one year to six or seven months.   But even
in spite of long duration of the disease an attack may once in
a way run its course with unexpected rapidity, especially in
the forms with long intervals.   In the years of involution the
intervals readily decrease and occasionally are again
lengthened later on.

I have tried to form a somewhat more precise idea of
these relations by finding the duration of the individual
intervals in 406 cases with two or more attacks.   By classifying according to their length the median was determined, that
duration which in such a series lies exactly in the middle.   In
this way we get a more correct picture than by reckoning an
arithmetical average, which is influenced unduly by unusually long intervals.   The interval between attacks following each other was according to this reckoning as follows :—

Interval	.	.	I	II	III	IV	V and following
Years .	.	.	4.3	2.8	1.8	1.7	1.5
No. of cases.	.	406	157	64	33	37	

The shortening of the intervals, at first rapid then slower,
with the number of the repetitions is clearly seen in this
summary.   At the same time it has to be remarked that a
series of observations, with very frequent attacks and short
intervals, could not be taken into account because the times
were not certain.   The clinical form of the disorder stands
in clear relation to the length of the intervals, as the following
survey shows, in which the number of the cases made use of
each time is added in brackets :—

Intervals		I	II	III and more
States of Depression Years		6 (167)	2.8 (46)	2 (27)
Manic States	,,	3.3 (53)	4.5 (24)	2 (20)
Combined States	,,	3·4 (185)	2.6 (87)	1.5 (98)

The first return of depression is, therefore, to be expected
after a considerably longer space of time than that of mania
or of a combined attack.   This result is certainly influenced
by the not infrequent cases, in which depression appears in
the age of evolution and then first returns again in the years
of involution, sometimes repeatedly, or in alternation with
manic attacks.   The later relapses also appear to run a somewhat slower course than those of the combined forms.   The
number that falls out of the series for the second interval in
manic cases might be owing to an accidental mistake on
account of the small number of observations at our disposal.

In the remainder the shortening of the intervals with the number of attacks is everywhere distinct.

At times the malady begins with a closed series of very short attacks following very quickly one after the other of manic or manic-stuporous colouring, which is then followed by a longer pause of several years. That is especially the case in a small group of youthful patients, preferably, as it seems, women. The individual states of excitement often last then only a few days, but may be very violent and be accompanied by great confusion. Only a small minority, probably not more than four to five per cent., is made up by the cases, in which the disease steadily and completely fills the whole life from the first attack onwards in regular alternation of colouring. Repeatedly I saw in these cases moodiness set in in autumn and pass over in spring, " when the sap shoots in the trees," to excitement, corresponding in a certain sense to the emotional changes which come over even healthy individuals at the changes of the seasons. As a rule, it might there be a case of forms with a very slight course, hypomania and simple inhibition. Even after a considerably long, uninterrupted course, however, a fairly long remission may after all still occasionally make its appearance.

The different varieties of course taken by manic-depressive insanity, as they are conditioned by the changing behaviour in duration and colouring of the individual attacks, as well as in the length of the intervals, have been analysed into a series of clinical sub-varieties, specially by Falret and Baillarger, who first made us more intimately acquainted with this disease ; these sub-varieties are intermittent mania and melancholia, regular and irregular type, *folie alterne, folie* à *double forme, folie circulaire continue.* I think that I am convinced that that kind of effort at classification must of necessity wreck on the irregularity of the disease. The kind and duration of the attacks and the intervals by no means remain the same in the individual case but may frequently change, so that the case must be reckoned always to new forms.

In order now to give a more exact view of the varieties of course in manic-depressive insanity, I reproduce a number of diagrams, each of which represents the life of a patient ; they were mostly sketched out by Rehm. Blue signifies depression, red manic excitement, both colours being shaded according to the severity of the morbid phenomena. The mixed states were, as far as possible, signified by hatching.

Blue hatching towards the left on a red ground signifies raving mania, towards the right manic stupor, red hatching on a blue ground depression with flight of ideas, cross hatching depressive excitement. The first normal decades were left out in order to save space.

The first case (Fig. 22) represents a periodic depression with almost quite regular intervals, in which curiously in a later attack excitement, appeared at times. With the exception of the first, which has a more rapid course, the attacks

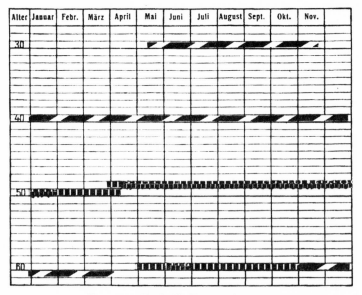

FIG. 22.—Periodic Depression (1).

have almost exactly the same duration. In the second case (Fig. 23) which likewise represents only depression, here also with admixture of excitement in the later attack, we see the disease begin at the age of sixteen. Then follows a pause lasting almost twenty-six years up to the forty-second year, the approach of the climacteric, which brings with it two short attacks, the one following close on the other. The third case (Fig. 24) again runs its whole course in depression, which here

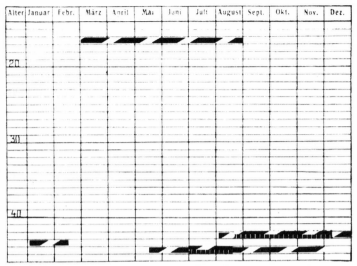

FIG. 23.—Depression in youth and in involution (2).

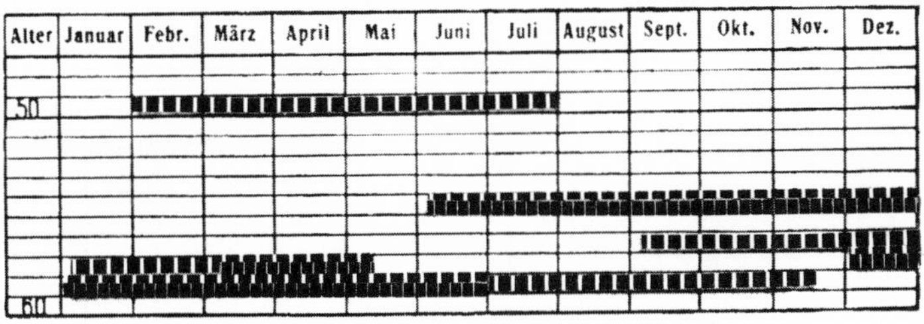

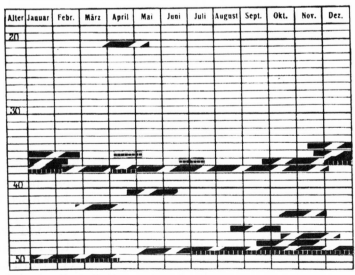

FIG. 24.—Frequent Depression. (3)

FIG. 25.—Periodic Depression after isolated manic attacks (4).

also is accompanied in the later attacks by excitement. It begins first in involution at the age of forty-nine ; then follow with decreasing intervals three similar attacks.

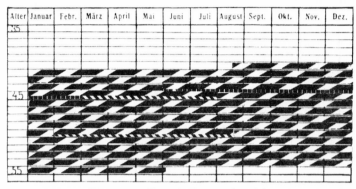

FIG. 26.—Chronic Depression (5).

The fourth case represents another picture. The first short depressive attack in the twenty-first year is followed by a pause of more than fourteen years. Then begins a series of attacks, mostly short but some of them fairly long, with short

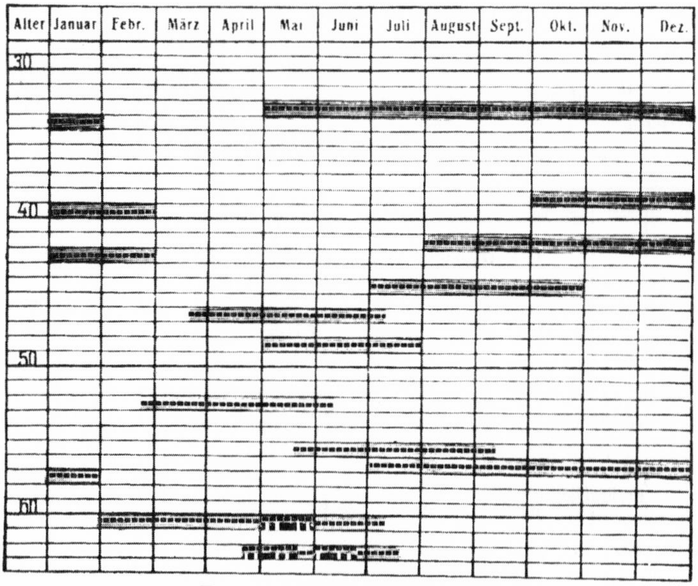

FIG. 27.—Periodic Mania (6).

irregular intervals. The majority of these attacks, ten, are depression, partly, especially the last one, with excitement. But among these, two slight manic periods running a short course are interpolated as first indication of a transition to the circular form. The last of the depressive cases (Fig. 26) shows a single attack of depression lasting almost fifteen years, but still resulting in recovery. It betrays its place in manic-depressive insanity not only by a favourable issue, but

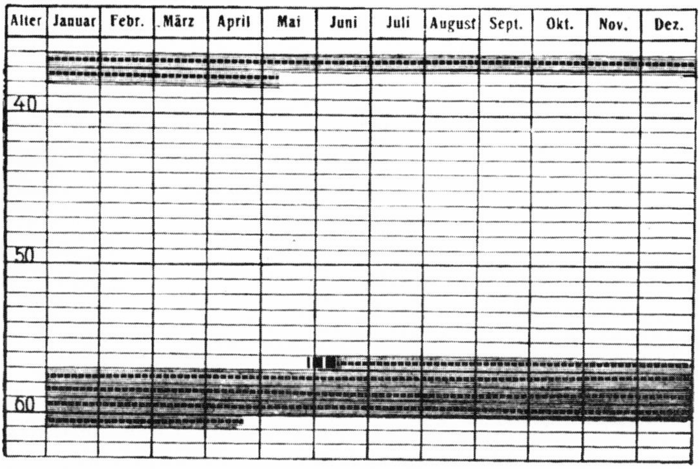

FIG. 28.—Relapsing Mania (7).

also by fairly long periods of excited or grumbling, irritated mood.

The next group embraces manic forms. First we find in Fig. 27 a " periodic mania." The duration of the attacks fluctuates between three and nine months ; the intervals are fairly irregular. The last attacks displayed a more raving

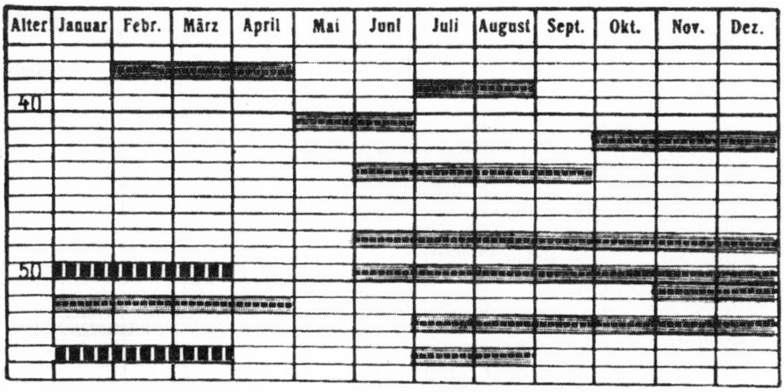

FIG. 29.—Relapsing Mania with isolated periods of Depression (8).

mood. The seventh case (Fig. 28) had two attacks separated by a pause of nineteen years, of which the second lasted almost four years. Its outbreak was peceded by a very short depression, as a first symptom of its place in manic-depressive insanity. These relations become clearer in the eighth case

(Fig. 29) which otherwise presents a picture very similar to the sixth case, only that here a depressive period on two occasions immediately follows the manic attack. The ninth case is very peculiar (Fig. 30). Here we see besides two

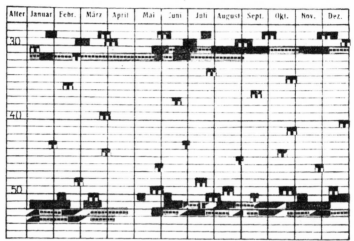

Fig. 30.—Periodic Mania with issue in Circular Insanity (9).

attacks of mania, somewhat longer, but running their course with fluctuations, a large number of very short periods of manic excitement, mostly with raving colouring of mood. After the fiftieth year, as happened before about the thirtieth

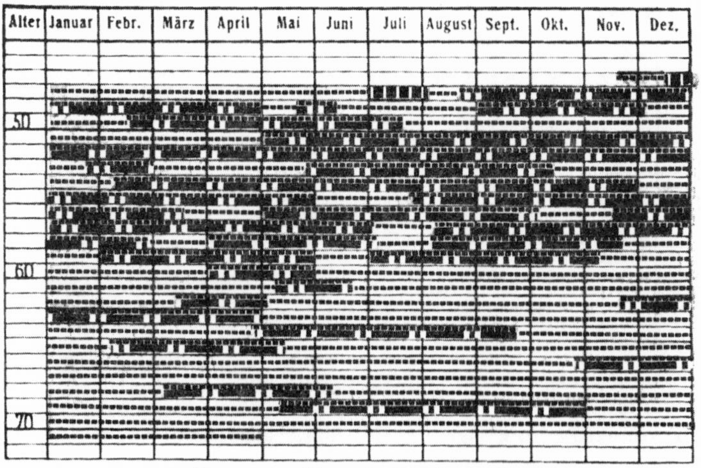

Fig. 31.—Chronic Mania (10).

year, the free intervals become always shorter, and there is at last a regular alternation of manic and depressive periods running a very short course, which lasts for years. The conclusion of this series may be furnished by a case of continuous

manic excitement (Fig. 31), which extends over more than
twenty-three years.   The colouring of mood is often raving ;
at the commencement two short depressive periods were
interpolated.

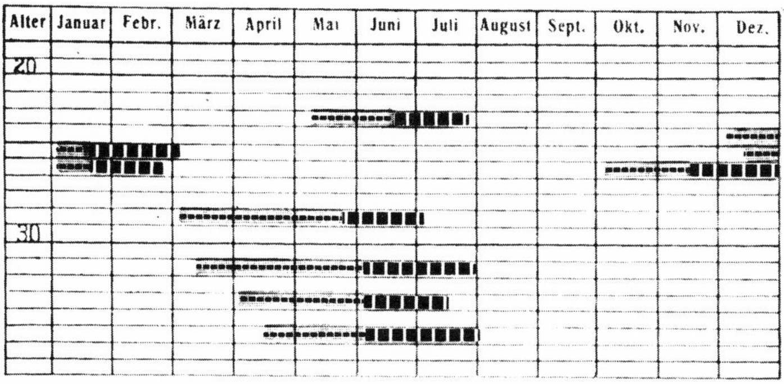

FIG. 32.—Folie à double forme (11).

In the third group we first find a case with fairly regular
return of circular attacks similarly combined ; it would
nearly correspond to the "*folie a double forme*" of the French.

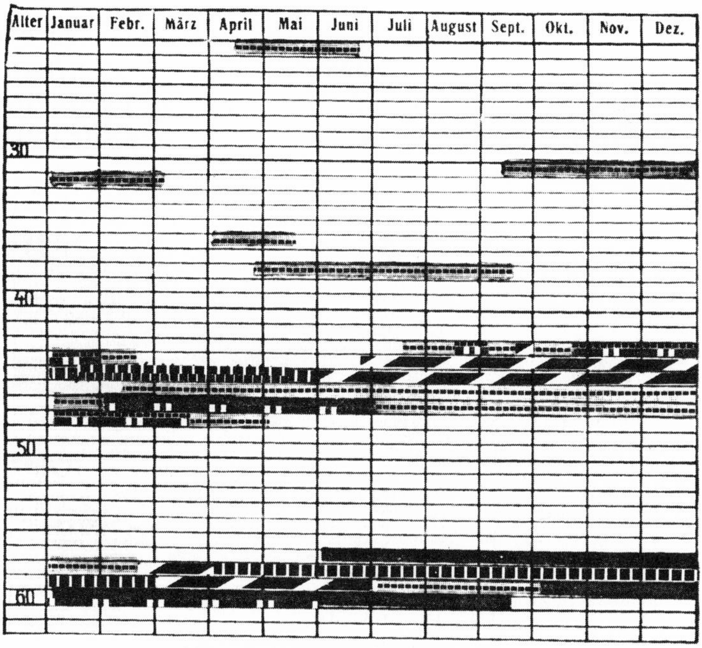

FIG. 33.—Folie circulaire (12).

States like the next case (Fig. 33) are much more frequent.
Here after a few attacks of manic excitement appearing in
irregular pauses, two combined attacks are developed, which

K

show repeated alternation of mania and depression interrupted once by a short free interval. Between these two

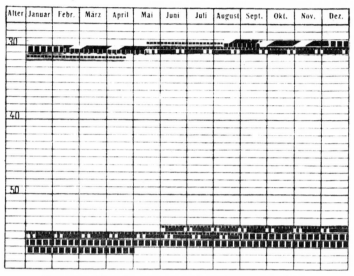

FIG. 34.—Circular attacks with a long pause (13).

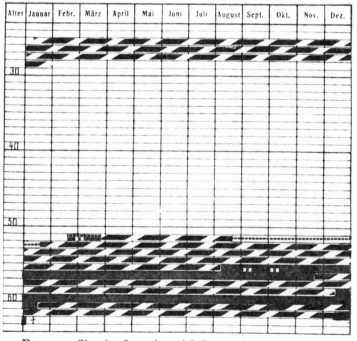

FIG. 35.—Circular Insanity with Depression in youth (14).

series of attacks, each of several years' duration, there is a
pause of nine years. These series themselves, except for

certain irregularities, would correspond to the course of "*folie circulaire.*" We see something similar in the thirteenth case (Fig. 34), but here the attacks are more simply combined ; in contrast there are more mixed states than in the former case. Moreover, here we observe only two groups of attacks

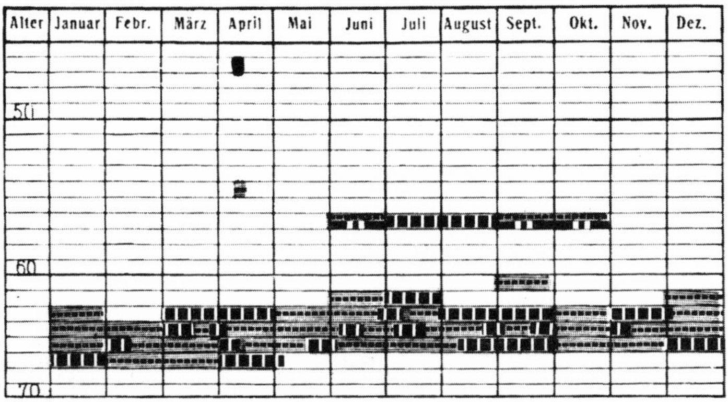

Alter	Januar	Febr.	März	April	Mai	Juni	Juli	August	Sept.	Okt.	Nov.	Dez.

FIG. 36.—Circular Insanity with prodromal delirious attacks (15).

separated by a pause of twenty-three years. Also in the fourteenth case (Fig. 35) we have a free interval of twenty-three years. But the first attack, beginning at the age of twenty-six, is here a simple depression lasting three years. Only at the return of the disease, at the age of fifty-two, does its circular nature become clear. Manic and depressive

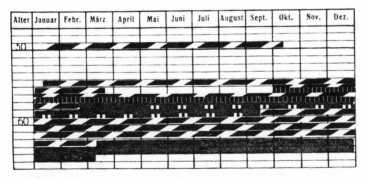

Alter	Januar	Febr.	März	April	Mai	Juni	Juli	August	Sept.	Okt.	Nov.	Dez.

FIG. 37.—Depression with transition to Circular Insanity (16).

periods of very unequal duration now alternate for over six years.

The fifteenth case (Fig. 36). which now follows, began at the age of forty-seven in the form of a delirious state with anxious excitement and hallucinations, which lasted a few days. and which clinically could scarcely be interpreted.

That was followed eight years later by a second attack lasting somewhat longer, then after two years by a third to which was joined a state of simple depression with renewed mixed state.   Only at the age of sixty-one was the first pure mania seen.   From its recurrence, with gradual disappearance of the

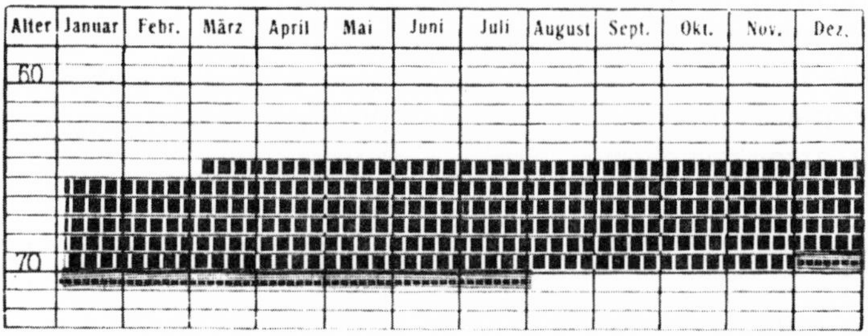

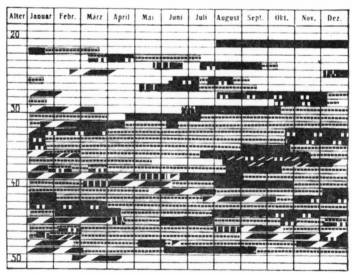

FIG. 38.—Depression of long duration with transition to Mania (17).

free intervals and interpolations of depression, circular insanity was developed, which ran its course in short attacks of changing colour.   The course of the sixteenth case (Fig. 37) presents, along with great deviations, yet in so far a certain agreement, as after depressive attacks similar to begin with,

FIG. 39.—Irregular Circular Insanity filling almost the whole life (18).

a markedly circular form appears in the sixth decade of life, certainly with very long duration of the individual periods. If one should here think first of the development of periodic depression, that is more obvious in the seventeenth case (Fig. 38).   At the age of sixty-five a depression of five and three-quarter years' duration appeared ; only then a state of manic excitement followed. As the last (Fig. 39) I give a case in which almost the whole life is taken up by a chain of manic and depressive attacks. The malady began at the age of twenty-one in manic form, and ran its course also the next ten years essentially as periodic mania with short intervals and occasional depressive interpolations. Then came a period lasting nearly seven years of continuous manic or hypomanic excitement intermixed with all kinds of mixed states and short attacks of depression ; this was followed after a short interval by a fairly irregular, uninterrupted alternation of mania and depression.

. If we give no more examples, that is not because those already given represent adequately the multiplicity of the courses taken by manic-depressive insanity ; it is absolutely inexhaustible. The cases reported only show that there can be no talk of even an approximate regularity in the course, as has formerly been frequently assumed on the ground of certain isolated observations. It is this experience which makes all delimitations and classifications futile, which are grounded on definite varieties of the course.

In the intervals between the attacks the patients appear, at least to begin with, perfectly well. Perhaps after a depressive attack the particularly blooming appearance and enjoyment of life are conspicuous, as after a mania the dejection and the fretfulness, which the patient for a long time cannot overcome. When the disease has lasted for some time and the attacks have been frequently repeated, the psychic changes usually become more distinct during the intervals also. Even though striking morbid symptoms are no longer demonstrable, yet a certain constraint and lack of initiative, depressed, shy behaviour, slight lassitude, great need of sleep and decrease of working capacity are often unmistakable. " In her good times she is still like a person who has some trouble," was said of one patient. Other patients on the contrary display irritability, very much exalted self-consciousness, a quarrelsome disposition, unsteadiness, agitation. A patient spoke of the times when she " had a quite different character, displayed an exaggerated pride in clothes, and had worldly leanings."

The patients often do not acquire clear insight into the extent and the significance of their malady. They perhaps admit that they were excited or depressed, but lay the blame for the most part on chance circumstances, their surroundings, their being brought to the institution. They do not like, therefore, to be reminded of the time when they were ill, evade all discussion about it, and go out of the way of the physician, if they chance to meet him later. A few patients, in whom along with lack of insight, there exists still a certain excitement, complain of the deprivation of freedom from which they suffered during the attack and which they suppose was illegal, or they compose descriptions of their experiences representing them in a half humorous, half enraged way, but always with very personal colouring.

During the intervals very slight, merely indicated attacks are extraordinarily frequent ; the morbid nature of these can only be determined by more exact knowledge of the fully developed phenomena, sudden vivacity, unusual enterprise, the shaking off of daily cares, loquacity, merriment, irritaability, or anxiety without foundation, introspective behaviour, inactivity and indifference continuing for weeks, which then is traced back to overwork, some vexation or something of the kind, but which disappears just as quickly again as it came. One of my patients in a hypomanic attack let himself be defrauded by a fashionable swindler ; the moodiness, which then followed, was explained by the family apparently quite naturally as due to the disappointment undergone. In women fairly short attacks of excitement readily occur in connection with the menses.

The patients themselves feel the approach of a fresh attack sometimes days or even weeks beforehand, without being able to account for it clearly to themselves. One of my female patients frequently made an otherwise quite aimless visit to the institution some time before the outbreak of the attack ; she then showed no trace of morbid symptoms. Others have still time before the excitement begins, to set their house in order and then to go voluntarily for treatment. A patient of that kind once jumped at midnight over the high wall into the institution after a run of several hours.

The transition from one kind of attack to the other takes place sometimes very suddenly and then invariably *during the night*. The depressed patient wakes at the given time contrary to his usual custom very early and is now manic. A patient, who till then had been deeply depressed and thought that he had caused an epidemic, appeared one morn-morning with a red carnation in his button-hole. Another, who was afraid of softening of the brain, appeared to himself " as transformed." A dispirited and dejected patient declared abruptly that happiness had come over her.   The excited patient feels himself one morning tired, done out, inhibited ; he had been " too merry, too frivolous ; now it overtakes him."

More frequently one sees the change of states being pre-pared for a long time beforehand.   The expression of countenance and the bearing of the patient, up till then depressed, becomes gradually freer, his eye more animated ; appetite and nourishment improve.   " I take heart rather than despair," said a female patient.   Another reported an attempt at suicide in the words, " The cord broke, thank God."   And a patient, who had asserted that his lungs were wholly eaten away, declared, " They're growing again." The skin regains its former freshness, the bearing its elasticity.   Gradually the patient becomes more accessible, shows more interest in his surroundings, begins to employ himself more continuously, feels himself easier and in better health, gives utterance to the longing for freedom and his own work, " for spring and the budding trees," looks forward to his discharge, and often for a considerable time makes the impression of a convalescent.   A discharged patient wrote, when she was in this state, that she wished to come in as a nurse, " but only in the quiet wards."

A patient gave us the following information about his state :—

" The weariness also already abates somewhat, and walking is no longer so difficult for me, but a troublesome heaviness is still always in all my limbs and still drags my body like lead down on to the chair or to bed. Yet I think that the Almighty is again strengthening me by his power and is supporting me, and therefore I am now happier again, I praise and adore him, the All-bountiful, who helped me so wonderfully by your hand.   The time of my life " of the soul " dawns for me like midday, and the darkness has become the bright morning for me ; my soul lives, hopes, and rests again in the triune God, our Lord."

The morbid nature of the apparent improvement is often now already indicated.   " I feel myself unnaturally well," a patient declared to me, who later ended in suicide ; she felt herself younger by years, slept a very short time, and was yet always fresh ; " It can't really go on like that."   Isolated actions already perhaps have a manic touch, while in general the symptoms of inhibition still predominate.   I treated a female patient, who, after severe depression in spite of complete sense, was scarcely capable of bringing forth a word, but, at. the same time, was very well physically, often smiled, and, to the astonishment of everyone, suddenly administered a box on the ear as quick as lightning. A lady, who was still troubled by tormenting ideas of persecution, unexpectedly seized hold of a peasant-woman in order to dance round the table with her. Another, as she despairingly went past a draper's shop, had a sudden fancy to buy herself a ball dress, and to the extreme surprise of her relatives appeared in it two days later at a ball, which she had already declined. More and more then the exalted mood gains the upper hand. " To-day is Good Friday, but in me it is already Easter," wrote a patient in her diary.

The dawning of more pleasant pictures is painted very characteristically in the following letter of a patient, from whom I have reproduced above a description by herself of her hypochondriacal sensations. When writing this letter to her mother the patient still suffered from severe depression in spite of considerable improvement ; she died soon afterwards by suicide.

" How I long so terribly for you and for life, and yet I feel that I must die. And I love you and my brothers and sisters more than life—than rich, beautiful, pure life, which I should like so much to share with you, as I should—and instead of this I cause you such grief. O do not curse me, I am indeed ill and not worthy to be with you ; forgive me what I have already said to you.—And to-day I am so comfortable, that I feel that I shall now fall asleep, and everything, everything, that is so wonderfully beautiful in life, appears now so rich and bright before me,—your love and the work—and the garden and the flowers and the forest. And of the linden court, just as it was, when your work and your vigorous hand and your beauty-loving eye decorated it, it appears to me now in such vivid dreams as never before. And do you still remember, how wonderfully beautiful the summer evenings on the verandah were ; where the two tall, slender fir-trees stood in the clear evening sky, and the wild vine stretched as a transparent curtain from the washing-house over to the one fir-tree and from there to the other, and sometimes the wind moved it gently. And the clear, bright moon looked through between the fir-trees. And we sat round you on the verandah and near by the waterfall of the mill-wheel murmured. And when in the evening the rat took a walk on the wire from the granary to the water trough and we watched it and at first did not know what kind of night-reveller it was, that was so mysteriously interesting too, and when Fritz then with a sure aim shot it, that was then vigorous reality. And very specially beautiful it was when the roses and lilies bloomed and the glow worms shone, and then behind the garden the fragrant meadow and at the edge of it our little wood, where we played our games as children, in which Fritz was always the terrible robber-knight ! And when the bees buzzed so in the chestnut-trees decorated with candles—that was too beautiful for sitting underneath and dreaming . . ."

The mixture of hopelessness with sentimental exuberance should be noticed, also the wordy revelling in poetic memory-pictures slightly suggestive of flight of ideas, the constant fresh connection with " and " a sign that ever fresh pictures were crowding in.

In a similar manner the opposite change takes place. The body weight, which had latterly increased in spite of the excitement, begins to fall slowly again.   Now the great over-busyness gradually slackens ; the big plans go into the background ; the patient has " no longer any of that spirit," " would like to rest."   " The capacity for thinking ceases ; before now there was a hurrying of work," declared a patient. *Mood* becomes quieter, more serious, more gloomy.   A young lawyer, who in excitement had composed a prize essay, had not the courage in the following depression to give it in. Fortunately the excitement returned in time, and he won the prize.   Now and then there are isolated remarks about disappointed hopes, attempts that have failed, hard experiences ; movements become slower, more relaxed, feebler ; the expression becomes dull, exhausted, the appearance tired, and now all the remaining phenomena of the former depression reappear one after the other.

For the clearer elucidation of all these extremely remarkable psychic states I reproduce a fragment from the comprehensive description of himself by a tailor, whose father came to his end by suicide, while he himself experienced the first attacks of moodiness in his fourteenth year, which were repeated several times, but never lasted more than a few weeks.   He then got the feeling that he suffered from a " congenital disease."

" My elder brother often said to me, ' You're sitting there as if in a dream.'   He was right too, for my disease is so very like a troubled dream in the waking state.   Already when I was a boy of fourteen, I found life unbearable in this state, and I had at that time already thoughts of suicide. I was so lively before and afterwards, then so sad, that my relatives were struck by it.   I was always asked, ' What's the matter then ? '   ' In head and in heart,' I always said, for how I feel then cannot be described or told. I knew then even at the first appearance of this evil, that it was mental disorder, for I could retain nothing, was clumsy in everything, had no pleasure in anything, not even in money ; finally I was laughed at because I did as if I were going to die immediately.   Each time I feel as if I could not survive these attacks.   I was envious of other people when they were merry.   I always kept away from any amusement, and if I had to go now and then with my companions, I sat there as a dumb person, for I couldn't manage to speak, or only disconnectedly as a stutterer.   In this state I have never yet quarrelled with any one.   I was considered sensible and docile every time, for then I have neither will nor sense, I am a veritable automaton.   As hot-tempered as I am otherwise, just as cold am I in the disease.   Every time a change has taken place in me as if I were a quite different person from other times, and I am convinced that it is so. The past sweeps through my head ; every mistake, which I have made in a normal state, oppresses me.   When ill I could not tell a lie . . .   At the beginning I was making coats, then as the disease gradually became more severe, I had to change to waistcoats . . .   I was again a bungler, no longer a tailor . . .   Then (at the age of twenty-four after many depressive attacks) I felt a peculiar condition come over me, but not depressed and without thought, but the opposite. I was merry, overstrained ; in spite of drinking a great deal of wine at any time, I was still not drunk, for in this excitement no drink whatever could do me any harm ; in contrast to this I can stand little in my normal state. Whether I drank little or much, I remained the same, and when I drank far more than usual, I never had headache or sickness the next day. I did not care at all for money in this excited state, for I considered myself as count, actor, poet, and so on . . . After a few weeks my brother took me to the hospital, for I did stupid things, went into hotels without money, and so on. Work then is certainly child's play to me, but my head was veritably glowing with heat, if I sat for some hours. I was put in a cell for raving mania, a kind of pig-sty, and was there for three weeks ; already I had lost my memory for a fortnight, then I was put in the hospital, where I remained about four weeks. I had smashed everything there, also torn to pieces . . . Shortly before my marriage this mysterious disease stole upon me again. I was described everywhere as a quiet, respectable man ; of course I could not talk much. I had a sad wedding, and I believe that no other man has ever appeared before the altar in such moodiness. Formerly I gave instruction in cutting out, and when I was ill I could scarcely make the simplest suit. The bad memory which I have in the present dull state. I am very bad at remembering names. I may be told a simple name ; next minute I have forgotten it. I often wish that I were a very stupid farm-servant, but only in my present state. It is indeed a singular wish, but anyway a peasant troubles little about where the grass or the grain comes from. When I am ill, these things always occur to me ; I should like to get to the bottom of everything without wishing it. I just have no will ; I cannot take anything in hand, nor can I carry out anything . . . In the excited state I am more than other people ; I can talk nineteen to the dozen. Everything is easy to me ; in short I am easy-going ; then life too is easy to me ; I don't think of to-morrow."

FIG. 40.—Hypomania.

The following verse characterizes, perhaps, still more distinctly the contrast of the states ; it was composed by a patient in the transition period from severe depression to mania, just when the first indications of re-awaking enterprise stirred in him :—

" Krank ist der Sinn, wenn er im schwarzen Jammertal
Ringsum gehäufter Leichen seiner bangen Sorgen,
Ach ! auch das liebend Herz den Seinen selbst verborgen,—
Ein leeres Geisteswrack der depressiven Qual.
Prunkstrahlend andrerseits, nicht fragend wo und wie,
Entfesselt irdschen Seins, erhebt er seine Schwingen,
Lustschwelgend, jubelnd in den Himmel einzudringen :
Ihm spendete ein Gott unsterbliches Genie !——
Nein, ach !—er steigt und fällt im Wahne der Manie ! "

The orthodox course of the gradual transition from one state to the other is often extremely striking. The thoroughgoing contrast of the states usually extends to the smallest details of the conduct of life, clothing, hair-dressing, to all likes and dislikes, so that one might think there were two perfectly different people. This contrast appears very dis-

Fig. 41.—Mania.

tinctly in a comparison of the illustrations, Fig. 17 (p. 80) and Fig. 40, also Fig. 18 (p. 81) and Fig. 41. The first two show the same patient once in stupor with profound clouding of consciousness, then a few weeks later in slight hypomania with a rather affected smile and wearing an enormous bunch of flowers. The other two pictures represent the same patient in mania and in a severe depressive stupor which followed closely, the one time with cheerful appearance ready for enterprise, a flower in his buttonhole, a cane in his hand, and smoking two cigars at the same time, the other time in bed, with rigid features straining anxiously. The specimens of writing 3 and 4 likewise show well the change of states. The first with the careless, disconnected, very much shortened stroke was written in excitement after a dispute with the nurse;

SPECIMEN OF WRITING 3. Manic-depressive Insanity; Excitement after a dispute with a nurse.   (13. ii. 92, 2 p.m.)

SPECIMEN OF WRITING 4. Depression.   (14. ii. 92, 8 a.m.)

whereas the second, which in the small, cramped, very sloping writing indicates the depression that has set in, was written on the morning of the next day. The difference in tone and contents of the notes is also extremely characteristic.

Ascaffenburg made association experiments with the patient portrayed here. In the percentage of clang associations they furnished a clear picture of the gradual disappearance of manic excitement and the transition to the state of depression.   They are reproduced in Fig. 42 ;

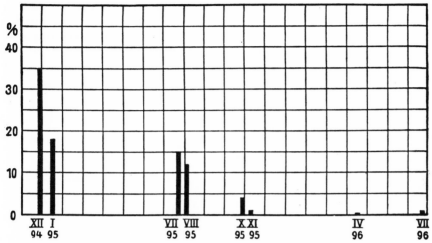

FIG. 42.—Comparison of percentages of clang associations in Mania and Depression.

the segments of the abscissa axis correspond each to a month.   With the disappearance of manic excitement, which at the beginning of the experiment had already lasted more than a year in the most severe form, the number of clang associations falls quite regularly, and completely returns to normal shortly before the discharge of the patient, which took place in December 1895.   About the end of the same month an unusually profound depression with extremely severe inhibition set in, which made association experiments impossible.   The two next experiments in April 1896 furnished not a single clang association, the one in July gave one per cent. We were able to follow the transition from depression to mania, as Fig. 43 shows, by means of perception experiments with the aid of the pendulum tachistoscope.   It is seen here how in the course of about a month the number of correct perceptions, already small at the beginning, decreases steadily while at the same time the number of in-

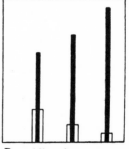

Date of Experiment :

19. VII.	5. VIII.	21. VIII.
to 3. VIII.	19. VIII.	23. VIII.
0.82	0.48	0.22
2.74	2.96	3.75

FIG. 43. — Number of right and wrong perceptions in the transition from Depression to Mania.

☐ Correct perceptions.
■ Mistakes.

correct perceptions increases in far greater measure. At the same time also the patient, who at first was still distinctly depressed, had become definitely manic.

The course of the body-weight in two double attacks of a female patient with slight hypomania and simple inhibition

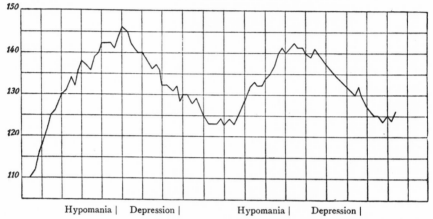

Hypomania | Depression | Hypomania | Depression |

FIG. 44.—Manic-depressive Insanity ; two double attacks.

is shown in the curve Fig. 44. We see how it increases during excitement and again falls accurately with the commencement of depression. Also in the different behaviour of the pulse curve the contrast of the two morbid periods is marked with surprising distinctness.

CHAPTER IX.

PROGNOSIS.

THE prognosis of manic-depressive insanity is favourable for the individual attack. For long the prospect of recovery especially in manic excitement has been considered very good ; with this the circumstance may be connected that mania is preferably a disease of youth. In fact one may, even after very long duration of excitement or depression with reliable diagnosis, still hope with great probability for complete restoration to health. In especial one must not let oneself be deceived by the mental inertia which apparently exists often during mania or after severe raving, and which is usually only the expression of inhibition of thought and later, as a rule, completely disappears, although slowly.

On the other hand in every case which belongs to manic-depressive insanity we must reckon with the possibility that the disease will be repeated several times or even very frequently. How great this probability is, cannot at present be stated with certainty. The following up of a large number of cases throughout life could alone settle the point. As those who have only been ill once, frequently avoid further observation, while those with frequent relapses represent a very conspicuous part of institutional life, it may readily be thought that in general we are inclined to over-estimate the danger of a return of the malady. If we only were able to decide with greater certainty whether the isolated case belonged to manic-depressive insanity or not, it might turn out that in a not altogether inconsiderable number of cases there was only one attack, or, as one may also perhaps express it, having regard to the pauses extending over thirty years or more, that the patients died without a relapse taking place. In any case it must be taken into account that the length of the intervals in almost 20 per cent. of the cases amounts to ten years and over.

As appears from our former comparison, the cases running their course in the two forms show the greatest tendency to frequent repetition. The commencement of the malady with a double attack will, therefore, make the prospects for the future appear more unfavourable. A series of attacks following one another without interruption and changing repeatedly in colouring must be regarded as specially critical. It often signifies the development of permanent circular fluctuations of state, as in our examples 9, 14, 15, 16, 18. But the morbid process may also, as examples 12 and 13 show, again come to a standstill, and there may be pauses of many years. In the years of involution one must be prepared for the return of former attacks; often just at this time there is a considerable series of attacks similarly or variously coloured, as in our cases 2, 3, 9, 14, 16. The time of the return, if a certain regularity has not already appeared, cannot up till now be even approximately foretold. In general frequent return of the attacks with short pauses may be certainly reckoned on in the cases beginning very early and without external cause. If the malady, however, first appears later and in conjunction with far-reaching injuries, perhaps in confinement, relapses do not usually follow so quickly.

How far the clinical peculiarities of an attack to some extent allow reliable conclusions to be made as to the further form of the morbid state, is up to now still quite obscure. Perhaps, however, with very extended observation some prognostic rules may be got, although the incalculable influences of personal predisposition and conduct of life will always be important sources of error. In the meantime one may, perhaps, say that hypomania is most frequently connected with simple inhibition, while severe acute mania is generally followed by strongly marked depression with delusions and a tendency to stuporous states. Clouding of consciousness, hallucinations, and delusions seem, when they appear, readily to accompany both phases of the disease.

Even when manic-depressive insanity lasts a very long time, the psychic state of the patients in the intervals does not usually suffer any considerable injury, if the attacks themselves run a mild course. On the contrary there are many of those patients who in the free intervals do very good, indeed distinguished mental work. Kahlbaum has compared these slighter forms of the disease as " cyclothymia "[1] with

---

[1] Hoche, Über die leichteren Formen des periodischen Irreseins, 1897; Wilmanns, Die leichten Fälle des manisch-depressiven Irreseins und ihre Beziehungen zu Störungen der Verdauungsorgane, 1906; Römheld, Sommers Klinik, ii. 449; Jelliffe, *American Journal of Insanity*, 67, 661.

the more severe forms leading to weakmindedness, which he called " vesania typica circularis." This distinction has, however, only a limited practical value, in so far as the cyclothymics cannot in the ordinary sense be regarded as " suffering from mental disorder," and, therefore, are liable to an essentially different judgment and treatment. But fundamentally it obviously concerns everywhere the same morbid processes. That is made evident not only by the lack of all sharp boundaries between cyclothymia and manic-depressive insanity, but also by the circumstance, that we often enough can observe in the same morbid course along with severe attacks of depression or acute mania numerous slight cyclothymic fluctuations of mood also.

Violent and long-lasting attacks of manic-depressive insanity may likewise end with complete restoration of the former psychic personality, if they only occur once in a lifetime. On the other hand with increase of attacks, in certain circumstances perhaps also with very severe single attacks extending over many years and in advanced age, there exists the greater or less danger of the development of a psychic decline. Perhaps in the other direction we must make the development of lasting changes responsible for the unfavourable course of the disease. The states of weakness, which appear in such cases, invariably let the after-effects of past attacks be recognized. Many patients remain permanently quiet, depressed, uninterested, stand about in corners with dejected or anxious appearance, fold their hands, lament in a low voice, when questioned give hesitating, monosyllabic, but sensible and usually appropriate answers. They are inactive, irresolute, timid, have to be forced to everything, resist energetically when much interfered with. Frequently also the residua of depressive delusions still persist; the patients call themselves the devil, ask for forgiveness, for a mild punishment, are afraid that they will be sent away, that they will have to remain there for ever.

The antithesis of this group, which might be called " chronic melancholia," is made up of those patients, which Schott [1] has brought together under the name of " chronic mania." Here manic features dominate the picture. The patients are in general sensible and reasonable, and perceive fairly well ; memory and retention are also fairly well preserved. On the other hand there exist increased distractibility, wandering and desultoriness of thought, a tendency to

[1] Schott, Monatschr. f. Psychiatrie, 1904, 1.

silly plays on words, poverty of thought.   The patients
have no understanding of their state, consider themselves
perfectly well and capable of work.

Mood is exalted, but no longer exultant, enjoying activity,
but silly and boastful ; occasionally it comes to flaring up
without strength or durability.   The finer emotions are considerably injured.   The patients show little interest in their
relatives, do not shrink from making coarse jokes about them,
do not trouble themselves about their affairs, do not worry at
all about their position and their future, at most once in a
way they beg without energy for discharge.   Only the coarser
enjoyments, eating, drinking, smoking, snuffing, still arouse
in them vivid feelings, further the satisfaction of their
personal wishes and wants ; everything else has become to
them more or less indifferent.   At the same time the patients
develop an activity often very disturbing, without, however,
more serious restlessness.   They like to interfere in everything, act as guardians to the feebler patients, snarl at them,
take from them what they want.   They collect all possible
rubbish in their pockets, make a mess with it all round about,
rub and wipe things, adorn themselves with rags and scraps
of ribbon, talk more than their share, swagger, try to gain for
themselves all possible little advantages.   They can meantime scarcely, or not at all, be employed for profitable work
on account of their unsteadiness and indifference as well as
their inclination to all sorts of mischief.   Schott is of the
opinion that severe hereditary taint specially favours this
issue ; also the residence in an institution continuing often
for decades with its blunting and narrowing influences, as well
as approaching age, might have a certain influence.   In spite
of their smaller share in general in manic-depressive insanity
men are said to suffer somewhat more frequently from this
decline.

At this point we have to mention in a few words another
group of cases, in which the psychic decline reveals itself in
continual, abrupt fluctuation between lachrymose anxiety,
irritability, and childish merriment.   States of this kind
sometimes appear to be developed from a continuous
accumulation of short circular attacks.   The original delimitation of individual attacks becomes more and more
obliterated, so that it finally becomes impossible to
characterize the state at any given moment.   A kindly
word suffices to make the patient sitting in apparent distress
smile pleasantly, clap his hands, sing, dance about, but just

as quickly do tears, self-accusations, or silent brooding again follow, which then perhaps gives place to a jocular outburst of abuse, all without any deep-seated feeling, desultorily changing and easily influenced. Left to themselves the patients appear for the most part indifferent, without desire, poor in thought, they display no specially striking colouring of mood ; they are able to employ themselves diligently.

Finally, the question would still have to be raised, whether in certain circumstances some of the mixed states might not also issue in a peculiarly coloured decline. To myself that appears probable for depressive excitement. But it would be conceivable, that for example manic stupor also or depressive mania might once in a while take such a course. Occasionally, I have come across cases, which seemed to suggest such an interpretation, but further investigation in the field of observation furnished by large institutions are necessary before it will be possible to form a definite opinion about this question.

The prognosis of manic-depressive insanity is to a certain extent made uncertain by its relations to *arteriosclerosis*. I have already directed attention to the fact that the disease by no means rarely develops first in the years of involution and even in still more advanced age, sometimes just after an apoplectic seizure. On the other hand numerous experiences are forthcoming which give evidence for the premature appearance of arteriosclerotic changes in our patients. Albrecht reports that in fifty-four cases he could demonstrate arteriosclerosis eighteen times, and of these more than the half were between fifty and sixty years of age, six were almost fifty. What view should be taken of this connection remains for the present obscure. It might be possible that the frequent and great fluctuations of the blood pressure and of the vascular innervation, which appear in the disease, signify injury to the vessels. If one prefers the assumption of chemical causes, one might think that the same poison, which engenders the alternation of psychic states, affects also the arterial walls, just as one thinks of the relation between syphilitic, that is paralytic, vascular change and the corresponding cortical diseases ; thus the appearance of circular attacks, when arteriosclerosis already exists, is more readily comprehensible. For this view epileptic attacks also might not be without significance ; they occur, indeed, seldom, but now and then they are observed. I saw a patient, fifty-two years of age, who did not suffer either from alcoholism or syphilis, suddenly collapse with apoplexy after repeated, severe epileptic attacks in the fifteenth year of a manic-depressive insanity. Only in the last weeks of his life did the symptoms of arteriosclerosis appear distinctly. His mother also had died of apoplexy.

When in the course of manic-depressive insanity arteriosclerotic changes are added or, what also occasionally happens, fairly severe senile changes, psychic states of weakness may be developed, which obliterate the original morbid picture. I have repeatedly seen patients, who had suffered from a series of attacks without any injury to their psychic capacities worth mentioning, become demented in advanced age and indeed in the well-known form of arteriosclerotic or senile weakmindedness. As we know cases enough of the opposite kind, in which manic-depressive patients suffer no kind of psychic loss at all in spite of advanced age, we must possibly always connect the appearance of a definite dementia of that kind with the addition of a fresh, more or less, independent disease. Pilcz is of the opinion, that the development of dementia is essentially related to the existence of old brain scars. That would probably only happen so far as these are the expression of a morbid process, which is still capable of progression, as syphilis or arteriosclerosis.

Issue in *death* is not very common in manic-depressive insanity. It may be caused by other diseases of various kinds, by simple exhaustion with heart failure (collapse) in long continuing, violent excitement with disturbance of sleep and insufficient nourishment, by injuries with subsequent blood-poisoning, and by fat emboli in the lungs in consequence of extended bruising or suppuration of the subcutaneous connective tissue. Very stout people with insufficient functional capacity of the heart muscle are decidedly endangered in severe manic attacks. Finally outside of institutions suicide also claims a considerable number of victims, especially in the slight cases apparently not yet or no longer in need of institutional treatment. With suitable shelter and supervision this serious danger can be very much restricted, but unfortunately not always excluded with absolute certainty; in particular, premature discharges now and again lead to bitter experiences. In elderly people apoplectic attacks occasionally occur. As yet there is nothing certain to report in the *morbid anatomy*.

CHAPTER X.

CAUSES.

MANIC-DEPRESSIVE insanity in the sense here delimited is a very frequent disease. About 10 to 15 per cent. of the admissions in our hospital belong to it. The causes of the malady we must seek, as it appears, essentially in *morbid predisposition.*

Hereditary Taint[1] I could demonstrate in about 80 per cent. of the cases observed in Heidelberg. Walker found it in 73.4 per cent., Saiz in 84.7, Weygandt in 90, Albrecht in 80.6 per cent., and in the forms with numerous attacks still somewhat more frequently. Taint from the side of the parents he found in 36 per cent. of the cases, in the last-named forms in 45 per cent. The values got in Munich are considerably lower on account of the much less complete knowledge of the previous history. But still *mental disease* or *alcoholism* could be demonstrated in the parents in one-third of the cases, the latter alone in something over 10 per cent, of the cases. Here, as in Heidelberg, I had the experience that cases of manic-depressive insanity in parents or brothers and sisters were disproportionately frequent. Further, I very often found suicide, which points in the same direction. Lastly, the occurrence of psychopathic personalities in the family was also frequently reported, of whom likewise so many have certainly to be reckoned to the domain of the malady discussed here. On the other hand, epilepsy, arteriosclerosis, and, as far as an opinion could be formed, dementia præcox also do not seem to play any part worth mentioning in the hereditary series. Vogt reports that in 22.2 per cent. of his cases mental disease existed in the father or the mother, in 35.2 per cent. in the brothers and sisters, against the corresponding values of 12.2 and 15.3 per cent. in other forms of insanity. Kölpin has communicated a very instructive pedigree, which is reproduced on the following page.

It is seen that of ten children of the same parents, who probably were both manic-depressive by predisposition, no

[1] Fitschen, Monatsschr. f. Psychiatrie, vii. 127.

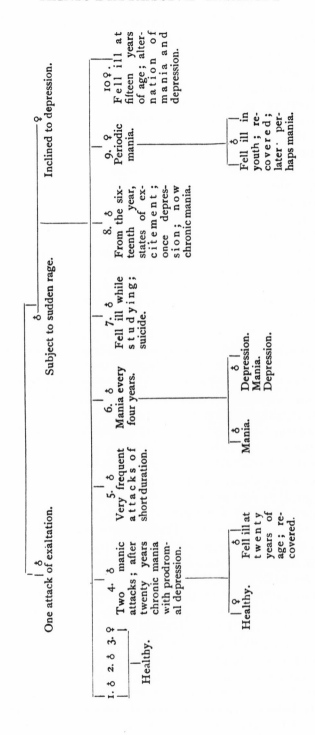

fewer than seven fell ill in the same way ; of the five descendants of the second generation four have already fallen ill. Rehm has instituted investigations about the children of manic-depressive parents. He found among forty-four children from nineteen families signs of psychic degeneration in 52 per cent., particularly in 29 per cent. abnormal emotional predisposition, by preference in the depressive sense. Bergamasco established that among 157 patients from fifty-nine families 109 belonged to manic-depressive insanity ; the remainder were divided among pellagrous insanity, dementia præcox, senile dementia, epilepsy, paralysis, hysteria.

Evidence for the assumption of *inherited syphilis* was present in only a few cases. The *endowment* of our patients was in 62.2 per cent. of the cases, in which information was to hand, said to be good or very good. There were 13 per cent. who had been good scholars, 10.7 per cent. poor. Therefore, although among the patients there were a few who might be considered weakminded, still in general their intelligence seemed to be rather above the average. That *artistic* predisposition is relatively frequent, was repeatedly indicated ; here relations probably exist with the liveliness and mobility of the emotions. Symptoms of *physical degeneration*, especially malformations, distortions, smallness or hydrocephalic bulging of the cranium, infantilism, are often present ; of many patients it was reported that they had suffered from infantile convulsions, and for long from nocturnal enuresis, and had learned late to walk or to speak.

Age.—The distribution of the first attacks of the malady with regard to age are shown in the diagram (Fig. 45). In rare cases the first beginnings can be traced back even to before the tenth year. Friedmann[1] describes in young persons manic or depressive attacks, which run a mild course, and which are often incited by external causes, or series of such ; he calls these " mild forms." Stuporous, delirious, and somnambulistic states are frequent in these ; sometimes complete and lasting cure is said to take place, which indeed could only be established with some certainty after decades. Liebers has described a case of mania lasting six months in a boy under five years of age.

The greatest frequency of first attacks falls, however, in the *period of development* with its increased emotional excitability between the fifteenth and the twentieth year. But

[1] Friedmann, Monatsschr. f. Psychiatrie, xxvi. 36,

in the next decade also the number of attacks is still very great, and only gradually decreases after the thirtieth year. This fall is interrupted between the forty-fifth and fiftieth year by a fresh rise, whose after-effect is seen in the slower descent of the numbers up to the fifty-fifth year. Obviously the influences of the years of involution here play a part. Isolated attacks begin first in very advanced age. Petrén observed a case which began at the age of eighty and at eighty-eight still presented no symptoms of senile dementia.

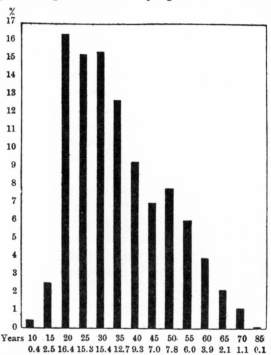

FIG. 45.—Distribution of the first attacks of Manic-depressive Insanity (903 cases) with regard to age.

A further view of the significance of age is afforded by Fig. 46. Here the distribution of the cases beginning at the different ages is given according to their clinical colouring. Purely manic and depressive cases were kept distinct and also those cases in which manic and depressive morbid phenomena were conjoined or were fused to well-marked mixed states. Only states fully developed one way or the other or mixed were taken into account, but not the admixture of isolated transitory morbid symptoms of opposite kind in an otherwise unequivocal clinical picture. From these considerations the noteworthy fact emerges, that the colouring of the clinical pictures is influenced by age *in a very decided manner*. The cases running a purely manic course begin with marked preference in youth, before the twenty-fifth year. If the observations, of which there is certainly only a small number, do not deceive, it seems that with the commencement of the years of involution the tendency to manic attacks once more increases and then rapidly and to a considerable extent decreases. Cases running a purely manic course, which begin after the fifty-fifth year, are quite the exception. The frequency of cases, in the narrow sense manic-depressive, also distinctly decreases with advancing age, although with small fluctuations, an experience which it would not be difficult to bring into accord with the slighter tendency of advanced age to manic attacks. On the other

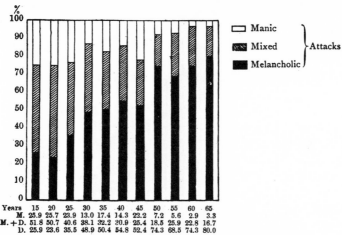

FIG. 46.—Colouring of the attacks at the different ages.

hand, depressive attacks show an *almost continuous increase* from the twentieth to the seventieth year and finally reach the height of 80 per cent. of all cases.

The fact, that states of depression are specially frequent at the more advanced ages, had already before this forced the supposition on me, that the processes of involution in the body are suited to engender mournful or anxious moodiness ; it was one of the reasons which caused me to make a special clinical place for a portion of these forms under the name of melancholia. After the purely clinical foundations of this view were shaken by the investigations of Dreyfus, our representation also now lets the causal significance of age appear in a light somewhat different from my former view. It is certainly incontrovertible that after the forty-fifth year, thus with the beginning of the climacteric in the female sex, which principally controls the numbers, a great increase of depression begins.   On the other hand, consideration of the whole diagram makes it probable that it here only concerns the increase of a change in the clinical behaviour of the morbid attacks which had been coming on long before. The increase of depression is already so pronounced in the third and fourth decade and relatively progresses with such regularity, that a separation of the years of involution from the previous periods of life cannot be carried out from this point of view.

We are, therefore, forced to the conclusion that the increase of depression is not caused by the special circumstances of the years of involution, although it seems to be favoured by them, but that it in general stands in a certain relation to the *development of the psychic personality*.   We have here to remember the fact, that the suicidal tendency of mankind also experiences a progessive increase in the course of life, and that children possess the ability to make good again the influence of emotional injuries in far higher degree than older people.   The tendency to elaborate the incitements of life and probably also morbid disorders in the sense of depressive states, appears accordingly to increase with the maturing and the final torpidity of the psychic personality, it may be that with the gradual loss of pliant adaptability to the circumstances of life, the internal and external struggles become harder, or it may be that in the more richly developed consciousness the reverberation of mournful moods is less easily obliterated, or lastly it may be that with the greater demands of the struggle for existence the wounds which it causes become deeper.

At this point the experience which I had of the form of manic-depressive insanity among the natives of Java, is perhaps not without significance.   There was a whole series of cases there which I thought I should include in this form ; these were relatively not fewer than among the European patients examined at the same time.   On the other hand the clinical pictures diverged in so far from our observations, that almost exclusively states of excitement, and often confusion, were concerned.   Well-marked states of depression lasting for some time, such as fill the observation wards at home, I could not find at all ; they are thus in any case rare. To this corresponds the absence of ideas of sin and of suicidal tendency.   These observations confirm the view, that for the form of the clinical picture, which our morbid process produces, the idiosyncrasy of the psychic personality in question is of great importance. A comparison might be made between the behaviour of the Javanese patients and that of our youthful patients, a *psychically undeveloped* population with the *immature* European youth. We might bring forward similar considerations with regard to the states in dementia præcox, and we shall later have to come back to them again in the discussion of hysterical disorders. The circumstance is also noteworthy, that the frequency of manic-depressive insanity appears to be different in different races. Reiss specially emphasizes the occurrence of numerous states of depression among the Suabians.

The distribution of a considerable number of single cases of manic-depressive insanity in regard to age will also give us information about the part which age plays in the form of the malady. I give here the percentage distribution of 1704 attacks in periods of five years. Unfortunately many cases with very numerous attacks could not here be taken into account, because the time of their appearance could not be accurately ascertained :—

Years . .	—10	—15	—20	—25	—30	—35
Per cent. .	0.2	1.4	11.2	12.3	15.2	12.5

Years . .	—40	—45	—50	—55	—60	—65
Per cent. .	11.6	8.0	9.1	7.3	5.0	3.8

Years . .	—70	—75	—80	—85
Per cent. .	1.8	0.3	0.1	0.2

Here it is seen that the greatest frequency of the attacks naturally falls later than that of the first attacks, about a decade. It can further be seen that between the forty-fifth and the fiftieth year also an increase of cases takes place. As it is relatively greater than the increase recorded above of the first attacks, we may conclude that the return of the attacks in the time mentioned is also facilitated ; otherwise the difference on account of the considerably increased number of observations would rather have been obliterated.

The following summary gives particulars about the distribution of single attacks according to their colouring in the different decades :—

Years . . .	—20	—30	—40	—50	—60	over 60
Manic . . .	38.4	32.3	33.2	30.6	18.2	15.9
Manic-depressive	20.1	19.8	14.4	13.1	17.2	15.9
Depressive . .	41.1	47.9	52.4	56.3	64.6	68.2

The contrast in the behaviour of manic and depressive attacks is very distinct. The greatest decrease of manic attacks and the greatest increase of depressive attacks takes place between the fifieth and the sixtieth year, somewhat later than in the first attacks ; the depressions, which appear in great number between the forty-fifth and fiftieth year, have thus the tendency to be repeated in the same form. In general, attacks composed of a sequence or a mixture of manic and depressive phenomena decrease likewise with age, yet they appear after the fiftieth year partly to take the place of the manic attacks, which decrease in disproportionately great measure. Unfortunately combined and mixed attacks were not kept separate from each other ; I suppose that the former

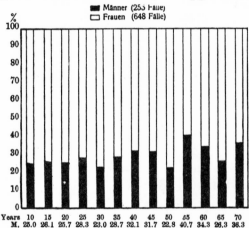

FIG. 47.—Share of the sexes in manic-depressive insanity (first attacks)
at the various ages.

predominate in youth, the latter in age. In any case it can be said with certainty that in manic-depressive insanity depressive attacks are progressively substituted for manic attacks which at first are almost equally frequent.

The form of the clinical states *in detail* appears also to be influenced by age, a question about which more minute investigations are necessary. While of the depressed cases, with simple delusion of sin and indefinite ideas of persecution, 37.6 per cent. had not yet passed the thirtieth year at the commencement of the disease, only 35.3 per cent. of those with well-marked, and often extraordinary delusions remained under that age. Delusion seems thus to be somewhat more active in the later years of life, as we saw in dementia præcox. In the forms running a circular course also, very elaborate delusions certainly come under observation even in youth. The cases with states of profound anxiety belong with great preference to the later years ; only 12.7 per cent. of any cases were under the thirtieth year. This circumstance also formerly strengthened me in the opinion, that a special place must be made for " climacteric melancholia."

Of the manic forms the slighter appear to begin at an earlier age ; 66 per cent. of that kind of case began before

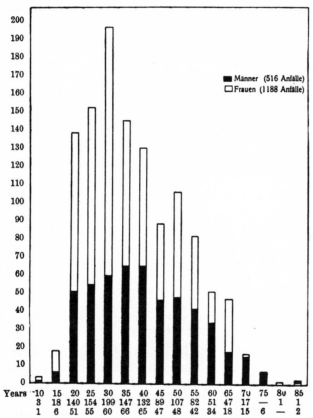

Years	ˉ10	15	20	25	30	35	40	45	50	55	60	65	7ɷ	75	8ɷ	85
	3	18	140	154	199	147	132	89	107	82	51	47	17	—	1	1
	1	6	51	55	60	66	65	47	48	42	34	18	15	6	—	2

FIG. 48.—Distribution of 1704 attacks of manic-depressive insanity at the various ages.

the thirtieth year, against 58.4 of the states of severe excitement. Further we find in youth specially the cases with more severe clouding of consciousness, confusion, and states of stupor ; 67.6 per cent. of these began before the thirtieth year. It would not be inconceivable, that here the tendency of youth to hysterical disorders, in especial to dazed states, influences the clinical picture. The cases with compulsive ideas had all begun before the thirtieth year ; a specially severe and peculiar morbid predisposition might be the foundation of these.

Sex.—The share of the two sexes in manic-depressive in sanity is very varied. Among ourselves about 70 per cent. of the patients belong to the female sex with its greater emotional excitability. Peixoto reports what is worthy of note, that in Brazil there are among the men 6.2 per cent. manic-depressive patients, among the women 6.8 per cent. In general the women fall ill somewhat earlier ; of them 49.7 per cent. were at the commencement of the malady under thirty years of age. of the men only 45.5 per cent. The share of the two sexes in the cases at the various ages is shown in Fig. 47. The share of the women is greatest in youth up to the years of development, and in the time between the twenty-fifth and thirtieth year and lastly in the climacteric. The processes connected with sexual life, the beginning of the menses, which not infrequently starts the first attack, parturition and puerperium, and also involution, without doubt here play a part. In more advanced age the share of the male sex is greater ; injuries caused by life, among which arteriosclerosis appears to have a certain significance, may be causal factors. But the decrease in frequency of cases among women in more advanced age is probably more important for the displacement of the ratio.

In order to have a clearer view I have illustrated in Fig. 48 the distribution of 516 attacks among men and 1188 attacks among women in periods of five years according to the original figures. The greatest frequency of the attacks among women is seen between the twenty-fifth and thirtieth years ; among men, where the fluctuations are much less, it falls somewhat later. Very noteworthy is the decrease of attacks among women before, and the increase after the forty-fifth year ; the explanation might be found in the cessation of the work of reproduction on the one hand, in the commencement of the involutionary processes on the other. A considerable part of the general fall in frequency of attack is, of course, due to the death-rate. The fact appears all the more striking that also in the male sex after the forty-fifth year not only a retarded decrease, but even a slight increase of the cases becomes perceptible, a sign that here also a certain unfavourable influence of the involutionary age is present. The later diminution of the attacks takes place relatively more slowly than among the women, although their longevity should give them a preponderance.

The share of the sexes in the principal clinical forms is shown in the following summary :—

Years	—20	—30	—40	—50	—60	—70
A.—States of Depression.						
First attack, Men	46.7	53.5	58.3	69.4	73.6	77.8
Attacks in general, Men	39.7	48.7	43.5	56.8	55.3	51.2
First attack, Women	20.0	39.7	54.7	62.9	72.7	81.0
Attacks in general, Women	41.6	47.6	56.6	57.6	69.9	78.8
B.—Combined and Mixed States.						
First attack, Men	26.6	12.7	16.7	8.4	20.5	21.1
Attacks in general, Men	24.1	14.8	16.0	7.4	18.4	14.7
First attack, Women	51.5	42.2	33.6	23.7	23.7	19.0
Attacks in general, Women	18.6	21.5	13.7	14.3	16.6	16.6
C.—Manic States.						
First attack, Men	26.7	33.8	25.0	22.2	5.9	1.1
Attacks in general, Men	36.2	36.5	40.5	35.8	26.3	34.1
First attack, Women	28.5	18.0	12.7	13.4	3.6	—
Attacks in general, Women	39.8	30.9	29.7	28.1	13.5	4.6

If we now consider only the first attacks, we see that among women states of depression in youth are relatively considerably rarer than among men ; in their place combined forms appear more than any other, which, apart from the most advanced ages, remain permanently far more frequent than among men. The difference in the frequency of first attacks of depression certainly disappears more and more, especially after the fiftieth year ; the same is true for the combined forms. Manic first attacks are, except in early youth, much rarer among women. In the male sex the frequency of states of depression increases continuously with age, to a considerable extent before the fiftieth year, with simultaneous decrease of the combined forms. Manic first attacks after an increase at the beginning, become progressively rarer and in more advanced age disappear almost entirely ; they are associated more and more with phenomena of depression.

The total number of attacks shows a frequently divergent picture. The increase of depressive states with age is here substantially less and more irregular, a sign that these have less tendency to frequent repetition than the manic and combined forms. On the other hand the decrease of the frequently returning manic attacks is much less, especially among the men. They come more into the foreground here because of their great tendency to relapse, among women chiefly at the expense of the combined forms, among men of the depressive forms. In consequence of this the difference between the sexes in the frequency of the depressive, as well as of the combined attacks is almost completely obliterated ; the share of the manic attacks among the women remains, however, permanently smaller after the twentieth year. The circumstance is noteworthy, that the share of states of depression in all the attacks taken together among men is permanently smaller, among women on the other hand at first greater than in the first attacks. That signifies that these states exhibit among men a slight tendency, but among women, at least in the first decades, a great tendency to similar recurrences. In the combined form, especially among women this tendency is obviously slight ; in their stead manic attacks appear later by preference. As the general result of these considerations it can, therefore, be stated that men comparatively often have attacks of depression with slight tendency to repetition, but then also have manic attacks which often recur. Women on the other hand begin most frequently with combined attacks or mania ; moreover, periodic depression often occurs among them, which only in later years gradually gives place to simple attacks.

With regard to the frequency of the individual clinical forms, the investigation gives the result that among men states of simple depression appear to be more frequent, among women on the contrary those with extraordinary delusions or with anxiety. In the male sex further purely manic attacks are more frequent, while among women we often find combined attacks, and stuporous and confused states.

The length of the intervals between individual attacks appears to be not essentially influenced by the sex of the patient. According to my classification it amounted for both sexes after the first attack to 4.6 relatively 4.3 years,

after the second attack to 2.8 relatively 2.0 years, after the
third and subsequent attacks to 1.2 relatively 1.4 years.
If any value is placed on these differences, at most it might
be said that women at first usually have a recurrence sooner
than men.

Personal Idiosyncrasy is, as Reiss also demonstrated
lately, without doubt a coefficient for the clinical form of the
disease, unless from the other point of view it must be regarded as already the expression of the existing malady.
While on the average the proportion of manic, depressive,
and combined forms in the patients with recognizable morbid
temperament, quite corresponded to the general frequency
otherwise of those forms, the behaviour was seen in detail
to be according to the following summary of percentages :—

	Depressive.	Manic.	Combined forms.
Depressive Temperament . .	64.2	8.3	27.5
Manic Temperament . . .	35.6	23.3	41.1
Irritable Temperament . .	45.5	24.4	30.1
Cyclothymic Temperament .	35.3	11.7	53.0

It is seen that from the depressive temperament preferably
states of depression arise, while purely manic attacks are rare.
As the latter meanwhile with the combined forms still make
up a third of the cases, the moodiness arising on a depressive
foundation will scarely be able to claim a separate clinical
position. From the other side we see, namely, that with the
manic temperament the depressive cases only amount to a
little over a third of the total. The preponderance of manic
forms alone is certainly by a long way not so considerable as
that of the depressive forms in the first group, but there we
probably have only the expression of the general predominance of states of depression among ourselves in contrast to the behaviour of the Javanese patients mentioned
above. The irritable temperament yields morbid forms
almost in the average distribution, but rather more manic
and rather fewer combined forms. It might accordingly be
the most general as well as the most frequent, and exercise
the least influence on the special form of the clinical picture.
Finally, the cyclothymic temperament appears, so far as the
small numbers permit of a judgment, to favour the development of combined forms, which in any case is obvious.

External Influences.—Compared to innate predisposition
external influences only play a very subordinate part in the
causation of manic-depressive insanity.

Alcoholism occurs among male patients in about a quarter of the cases, but is to be regarded as the consequence of debaucheries committed in excitement, not as a cause. Now and then an alcoholic colouring of the attacks is observed, which may reveal itself in very vivid auditory hallucinations, hearing long dialogues of not very flattering character, seeing illusions with reflectors, visions of animals, night terrors with heavy perspiration and trembling. Sometimes I have seen a manic attack begin with well-marked delirium tremens.

I found *syphilis* in about 8 per cent. of my male patients ; it is, however, to be judged from the same point of view. Ziehen has certainly described cases of periodic or circular psychoses, which he traces back to acquired or inherited syphilis. According to my view it can only be a case there of the fairly frequent association of manic-depressive morbid phenomena with syphilis or of syphilitic psychoses with circular forms, but not with a circular insanity engendered by lues. It is noteworthy that manic-depressive patients very rarely fall ill of paralysis, while symptoms of cerebro-spinal syphilis are not altogether rare among them.

Recently it has been emphasized by Pilcz and others that manic-depressive insanity is often connected with *coarse brain disease*. Pilcz reports seven cases of apoplexy, which the malady is said sometimes to follow closely, further ten cases with tangible brain conditions. Hoppe, who twice found cysts of the pia, thinks that brain scars act to a certain degree as irritating foreign bodies and so bring the psychic disorder to development. Saiz and Taubert have described cases with brain scars. Neisser saw a circular psychosis appear after an attack of apoplexy with paralysis. I myself observed a patient in whom, after periodically returning states of depression, which immediately followed an attack of apoplexy with paralysis, a circular form developed. In spite of all isolated experiences of that kind, it must still be doubted, having regard to the enormous mass of cases developing without tangible cause, whether it here concerns more than chance coincidence. At most one might in a similar way, as holds good for a great number of other influences, regard the irritation of brain scars as the exciting cause of isolated attacks. Or one must assume that there is a special " periodic focal brain psychosis," corresponding, perhaps, to traumatic epilepsy. For this view there are, however, up till now scarcely sufficient grounds forthcoming.

The number of other causes, which are made responsible for the appearance of attacks, as well as for the origin of the whole malady, is extraordinarily large, a sure sign that no single one of them possesses really decisive significance. First, *head injuries* might be named, which, indeed, might produce brain scars in the sense just indicated. Mönke-möller, in the previous history of fifty-six cases of periodic insanity, found thirteen cases of cranial traumata. Among my own observations also there was a series of similar cases. But the head injuries had almost always occurred many years and even decades before the outbreak of the disease, and they were almost entirely absent in the female sex with its special tendency to manic-depressive insanity. As real causes of this malady they can, therefore, not be taken into consideration.

The same holds true for the *bodily illnesses* which, not rarely, precede the development of manic-depressive insanity. Typhoid, erysipelas, pneumonia, disease of the stomach and ear operations, pleurisy, cholera nostras, influenza, blood-poisoning, hæmoptysis, were specified to us as causes. Among twenty-eight cases of that kind, however, in seventeen either there had been attacks of a similar kind previously or they followed later without external occasion.

Far more frequently an attack of manic-depressive insanity follows a *confinement* closely, or it begins during *pregnancy*. Among thirty-eight cases of the former kind similar attacks appeared twenty-five times, among ten cases of the latter kind five times, also before or afterwards spontaneously. A patient suffered from mania after two confinements, but besides that frequently from manic or depressive attacks. Another woman fell ill first after confinements ; this happened three times and afterwards several times spontaneously. A third became manic after a confinement and likewise after the death of a child, and depressive after giving up her business, but also had otherwise several manic and depressive attacks.

Psychic Influences.—A still greater rôle is usually ascribed to psychic influences. In especial the attacks begin not infrequently after the illness or death of near relatives. Among forty-nine observations of that kind, attacks were also observed twenty-four times without cause. A woman fell ill three times of depression after the death first of her husband, next of her dog, and then of her dove. Another patient was depressed after the death of her husband, manic after a confinement and after a dental operation. Again, another became depressed during pregnancy, and manic after the death of her husband, but on other occasions she had attacks of various colouring. The case of another patient was similar, who became depressed after a fright and after the death of her uncle, and manic after her mother's death. Still another fell ill of mania after a confinement and after the death of a child, and of depression when she gave up her business.

That here incalculable accidents have their share is shown by the case of a patient who frequently suffered from manic and depressive attacks; she became depressed after an operation and after the suicide of her fiancé, but stood the death of her mother without falling ill. Another fell ill first after an abortion brought about by herself, and again after a confinement, but in the interval gave birth to a child without suffering from any disorder.

Among other circumstances there are occasionally mentioned quarrels with neighbours or relatives, impending or threatened law suits, fear of a misfortune, disputes with lovers, unrequited love, excitement about infidelity, financial difficulties, losses, purchases, sales, removals, fatiguing sick-nursing; engagements also and the first sexual intercourse are sometimes the occasion of an attack. Among forty-five patients, whose attacks were traced back to such causes, there were twenty-seven, who also otherwise had similar attacks. A man fell ill after an advantageous purchase of depression, but had suffered from it already previously. In another case the sale of a property, which was regarded as the cause of a depression, was successfully made null and void, but without any influence on the disease; later on there were further manic and depressive attacks.

The certain conclusion, which can be drawn from these and similar extremely frequent experiences, leads us to this, that we must regard all alleged injuries as possibly sparks for the discharge of individual attacks, but that the real cause of the malady must be sought in *permanent internal changes,* which at least very often, perhaps always, are innate. At the same time the individual case may strongly suggest the assumption of close causal relations between external occasion and attack. Thus a man fell ill of depression first after the death of his mistress, then after that of his wife. A woman twice became melancholy, each time after the death of a brother. If such attacks remain the only ones in life, nothing appears more natural than to see in such melancholias the increase of well-founded grief going on to morbidity. That this interpretation is not appropriate, the cases prove, in which the morbid state differs completely from that of the discharging emotional shock, by the development of extraordinary delusions or by manic colouring. Further, the observations are instructive in which, in spite of the removal of the discharging cause, the attack follows its independent development. But, finally, the appearance of wholly similar attacks on wholly dissimilar occasions or quite without external occasion shows that even there where there has been external influence, it must not be regarded as a necessary presupposition for the appearance of the attack.

Certainly it happens that further independent attacks are often absent, or they are difficult to prove. Of two women, who both had depressive attacks on the death of their husbands, the one had already had an attack thirty-seven years previously; the other fell ill twenty-one years later in the same way without occasion. If, however, a survey is made of a larger series of observations, it can be easily seen that exactly the same clinical states attain to development, the one time in close association with injuries of the kind mentioned above, the other time quite independently of them, and that between these two limiting cases all imaginable transition states are demonstrable, not only in different patients, but also in one and the same case. Unfortunately the powerlessness of our efforts to cure must only too often convince us that the attacks of manic-depressive insanity may be to an astonishing degree *independent of external influences*.

Nature of the Disease.—About the nature of manic-depressive insanity we are still in complete uncertainty. Both the frequent return of the attacks and the peculiar alternation of excitement and inhibition are complete enigmas. We may first of all refer to the fact that in our nerve tissue the tendency to a periodic course of inhibitory and excitatory processes occurs in the most different domains. Meynert has searched for the explanation of the alternation of opposed states in *periodic disturbances of vasomotor innervation*. In consequence of increased irritability of the vasomotor centre, a state of reinforced tension is said to be developed in the whole arterial field with simultaneous cerebral anæmia as cause of the depressive moodiness. And exactly the deficient nourishment of the vasomotor center caused in this way is then said further to bring about a paralysis of the centre itself, dilatation of the vessels, and hyperæmia of the brain, and the development of manic-excitement is regarded as the expression of this. It is indubitable that changes in the behaviour of the pulse correspond to the two periods of an attack ; for the rest, however, the view given reckons with wholly unknown quantities. It would also be difficult to reconcile with the fact of single attacks lasting for years and even for decades, and moreover fails completely at the fact of the mixed states.

The very considerable *fluctuations of body-weight* might here also suggest more general changes in the *metabolic processes*, but our knowledge is not sufficient to provide useful points of view. Lange [1] has assumed as the foundation of periodic depressive states with psychic inhibition, which indubitably belong to the domain of the malady here described, a *gouty* mode of development, a view which, however, till now cannot be regarded as proved or even as probable. Stegmann found in " periodic neurasthenia," which certainly belongs to manic-depressive insanity, diminution of uric acid excretion at the time of the moodiness. Pardo, who has carried out comprehensive investigations into the " coprology " of the disease, is inclined to regard as its essential foundation the *intoxication* of the body by the metabolic products of *intestinal bacteria*. He observed during the attacks a change and enrichment of the intestinal flora, especially the appearance of a definite cocco-bacillus. He also thinks that the attacks are frequently started by dietetic errors and ended by diarrhœa, the two explanations would scarcely be applicable to any extent worth mentioning. The constipation beginning during the attack is said to be a protective measure of the body which by digestion destroys the injurious bacteria.

Parhon and Marbe suggest an *insufficiency of thyroid gland activity*, Muratow a special significance of the *suprarenals* for the development of the disease. Obviously in all these unproved and unprovable views there is only the reflection of the influence of current opinion. Stransky also searches for an explanation of manic-depressive insanity from the point of view of metabolic disorders. On the one hand he directs attention to the indubitable near relationship of this malady with other forms of insanity of degen-

---

[1] Lange, Periodische Depressionszustände und ihre Pathogenesis auf dem Boden der harnsauren Diathese, deutsch von Kurella, 1896.

eration, and emphasizes the ancestral relations between emotional life and periodicity. Further, he supports his views on the relations between Basedow's disease and manic depressive morbid phenomena and conjectures *auto-intoxica-tion by glandular products*, which specially influence the vascular system, perhaps disorders in the metabolism of iodides. Our patients are said to be by their peculiar pre-disposition hypersensitive to those poisons or to be incapable of counteracting them sufficiently.

The remarkable changes of state often beginning so suddenly in the patients and the form of the clinical pictures recalling many intoxications (alcohol, products of fatigue), lastly, the appearance of very similar states in paralysis do, indeed, suggest the thought of *internal poisons*, but on the other side again great difficulties stand in the way of this view. The regularity, with which in many cases the alterna-tion of states continues throughout a great part of a lifetime, the almost unlimitedly long duration of the morbid states without lasting injury to the psychic personality, the often distinct exciting influence of emotions, lastly also, what is emphasized by Stransky himself, the clinical and hereditary near relationship of the malady with other forms of insanity of degeneration would better fit an explanation of the morbid processes, which laid the chief responsibility on an *abnormal behaviour of the nerve tissue itself*. The circumstance is, perhaps, also worth mentioning that in manic-depressive insanity the special form of the picture appears to be in greater measure dependent on the psychic personality than we are accustomed to see it in pure effects of intoxication.

In connection with Morel and Doutrebente, Anglade and Jaquin have chosen the *relations between manic-depressive insanity and epilepsy* for the starting point of their con-sideration. They lay stress on the fact, that the neuroglia in both diseases presents an infantile appearance ; from this we may conclude that there are hereditary abnormal peculiarities in it, and that it may perhaps represent a patho-logical anatomy of the predisposition. It concerns in both diseases *an interference with the state of equilibrium between neuroglia and nerve tissue*, of the kind that even slight causes may call forth considerable disorders, it may be in the sense of epilepsy, or in the sense of " folie." The taking together of the two diseases, which in the most different directions diverge far from each other, seems to me to be just as little a forward step, as their being traced back to a struggle between the two tissues which are opposed to each other, as is said, " like two hostile sisters."

The opinion, which Thalbitzer has formed of the nature of manic-depressive insanity, is likewise connected with pathological anatomy. As the foundation of the malady he regards *diseased vasomotor paths* for the nourishment of the brain, the course of which he relegates to the triangular tract described by Helweg in the cervical spinal cord. A peculiar fineness of the fibres, which causes the tract to stand out more distinctly, is said, as developmental inhibition, to prepare the soil for the appearance of vasomotor disorders and with these of manic-depressive insanity.

CHAPTER XI.

DELIMITATION.

THE morbid form of manic-depressive insanity, as it has here been delimited and described, is composed of a great number of clinical component parts, which otherwise frequently receive a different interpretation. The starting point of the conception of the disease is formed by the doctrine of the *periodic*, or, as Magnan named them, *intermittent* psychic disorders. This doctrine was elaborated principally by the French alienists. The attention of these investigators was then directed to one of the most strking characteristics of our morbid groups, to its tendency to multiple repetition in life. At the same time it could not escape their notice that the return of the attacks takes place sometimes in the same, sometimes in changing form. This experience led next to the separation of periodic mania and melancholia ; then, as already mentioned, the compound forms were again divided according to their changing course into a series of varieties till they were collected later under the name of circular insanity, which originally was valid only for the continuous alternation of mania and depression.

Further experience, as it could not permit of the individual kinds of circular insanity being regarded as separate diseases, has also taught that the separation of the simple periodic forms from the compound cannot be carried through. As before discussed in detail, the purely manic attacks without any association with depressive symptoms, as introduction, conclusion, interpolation, or admixture, belongs to begin with to the rarities, and when we meet with one or other attack of that kind, we yet see, as in our cases 7, 8, 9, and 10, at least at another time depressive periods attain to development. But the clinical pictures of the manic attack itself resemble each other completely, whether they belong to a so-called periodic mania or to a circular form. There is no alienist, and, according to my conviction there can be none, who would be capable of recognising from the picture of the state alone, whether a given manic attack belonged to the one or to the other group of forms. Although the manic attacks may diverge from each other ever so much, yet these differences tell us absolutely nothing about whether we have to do with a periodic mania or with a circular insanity.

The question in regard to periodic melancholy is considerably more difficult. If we are convinced that in periodic mania we have to a certain extent to do with a form of circular insanity, in which all the attacks are changed into the manic form, the idea is naturally suggested, that cases here also occur, in which the depressive attacks alone hold the field. This view gains fresh support from the fact that in association with the states of depression not only can slighter indications of manic symptoms be demonstrated with extreme frequency, as temporary exalted mood, ideas of exaltation, laughing, singing, dancing, feeling of happiness in the time of recovery, but also between the pure periodic depressions and the circular forms all conceivable transitions may be seen. Finally, attention must still be called to the mixed states for whose peculiarity and multiplicity we only gain an approximate understanding, when we regard all the opposed manic and depressive symptoms as equivalents, which can mutually replace each other and actually do appear for each other with extraordinary frequency.

In spite of all these weighty reasons, the extraordinary frequency of the cases, which run their course in several or many periods of purely depressive form without a trace of manic features, stands in the way of the temptation to unite without hesitation the whole domain of periodic melancholy with circular insanity. It is in any case incomparably much greater than that of pure periodic mania. Especially in more advanced age we see numerous patients of that kind with a few depressive attacks repeated in similar form, somewhat like our third case. But there is also the fact, that the clinical form of depression in general is far less characteristic of a definite disease than the manic type. While here in the essential point only the delimitation from paralytic (syphilitic) or catatonic states of excitement, perhaps also once in a way from expansive paraphrenia, comes into question, which for the most part is capable of rapid accomplishment, a state of depression may besides that be also of *psychogenic* or *arteriosclerotic origin*, and it may further represent the introduction to one of the *anxious* or *paranoid psychoses* of the involutionary years so little understood by us as yet. Although we have grounds for the assumption, that the composition of the clinical picture in all these cases will show certain differences, it is yet up till now often scarcely possible from the psychic state alone to come to a reliable decision.

Certainly there is added in our case as an auxiliary character-istic the return of the attacks. From the outset, however, the possibility must not be disregarded, whether other forms do not also possess this peculiarity. On the one hand the cases appearing as a simple increase of a morbid, depressive predisposition might have the same tendency without on that account being related to circular insanity, on the other hand the depressive attacks of the involutionary years which do not recur often, even perhaps appearing only once. In the former case further investigation has shown that from the depressive predisposition states of depression, indeed, develop most frequently, but that along with them periodic manias also and combined attacks occur. There is thus no sufficient reason forthcoming for separating off those first forms. But for the comprehension of the last forms, observations, like our cases 16 and 17, are instructive, in which it is seen that here also in certain circumstances, after depression frequently re-peated or lasting many years, manic periods may still be developed. But further, as was formerly explained, it has turned out that the predominantly depressive colouring of states in the involutionary years only signifies the last part of a general change of the morbid picture with advancing age, which has begun already long before, and does not at all permit of a fundamental separation of the depressive forms of the involutionary years. We are, therefore, forced to the conclusion by all these considerations, that periodic melancholy also is not an independent disease, but a form of manic-depressive insanity. Its peculiarity consists only in this, that it develops, certainly with a somewhat different clinical signification, with special preference on the soil of the depressive predisposition and further in more advanced age.

As *periodicity* was regarded as a very important char-acteristic of disease, the periodic psychoses were from the outset placed in opposition to those which appear only once in a lifetime. The beginning was made with those cases, in which throughout a considerable time an approximately regular return of similar attacks actually took place. And just that kind of example led to the making of sub-divisions, which were characterized solely by the different relations between the attacks and the free intervals. But the minute examination of a comprehensive series of cases very soon teaches, as already the small selection of our examples shows, that a regularity, even only approximate, of the course forms a comparatively rare exception among the recurrent cases. In an overwhelming majority of the cases we have to do rather with a wholly incalculable sequence of attacks sometimes more frequent, sometimes more rare, sometimes more uniform, sometimes alternating or combined, between which pauses are interpolated of extraordinarily fluctuating duration. The greater number of these cases must of course be excluded from the domain of the genuine periodic psychoses. It was assumed that here it concerned " relapsing " attacks of mania or melancholia or isolated attacks quite independent of one another. That, of course, held good especially for the cases with very few attacks in a lifetime or even with only a single one. Experience has certainly everywhere shown that the number of such cases on more accurate examination shrinks to a remarkable degree, and simple mania at least becomes an always rarer disease [1]; but without doubt there are cases enough in which only a single attack of mania can be demonstrated thoughout life.

It must meanwhile be emphasized that this fact, for the establishment of which a series of investigators have exerted themselves, is of very little significance for deciding the question of the relations between simple and periodic forms of mania and melancholia. What it depends on, is obviously the ascertaining whether the return of the attacks in those clinical forms represents an essential or a more secondary symptom. In the former case we shall have to place the " periodic " forms separate from the " simple " forms as a special group, in the latter case not so.

About this question it must first be remarked that no border line at all can be drawn between the strictly periodic forms and those which run an irregular course. Of special significance for this question is the fact, that a periodicity, in some degree satisfying, exists in numerous cases only for a certain part of the course, that it develops first in the course of the malady or even again disappears. This proves that here it concerns not a fundamental and inviolable peculiarity of the morbid process but a fluctuating characteristic ; the

---

[1] von Erp Taalman Kip, Allgem. Zeitschr. f. Psychiatrie, liv. 119 ; Hinrichsen, ebenda, 86 ; Mayser, Archiv f. Psychiatrie, xxxi. 500 ; Parant Annales médico-psychol., 1910, 68, 395.

cases with a very regular course are not fundamentally distinct from the others. Moreover, we see a similar, more or less incomplete periodicity develop also in a series of other diseases, particularly in epilepsy, also in hysteria, and in certain forms of dementia præcox especially in their terminal states. We conclude from this also that the periodic recurrence of morbid attacks cannot be the standard characteristic of a definite morbid process.

That which decides whether a case of illness belongs to a certain disease or not, is rather the incontrovertible placing of the clinical details within the limits of the known forms. But no one will wish to deny that between the individual attacks of the strictly periodic forms and of the forms which only " relapse," whether manic or melancholic, the most perfect agreement exists. All attempts to find here any useful distinguishing characteristics have completely failed. We shall be able, therefore, to give up the boundary between strictly periodic and irregularly recurring forms and bring them all together to a unity.

But quite similar considerations hold good for the number of attacks in the individual patient. We know cases, in which many dozens of attacks in unending series have to be recorded. Then there are patients with six, eight, ten attacks in life which follow one another with fairly long pauses intervening. If it is admitted that these cases belong to periodic insanity, so neither can it be denied of the cases, where perhaps every fifteen or twenty years from the period of development an attack breaks out, thus altogether three or four during life. But who will assert that here the limit of " periodic " insanity is finally reached ? There are, as we have seen, cases in which twenty, thirty, indeed, more than forty years pass between the attacks ; naturally here the number of possible attacks in general is restricted at most to two or three, especially when the malady begins first in more advanced years.

As can be seen, it might be admitted that even the cases with only one attack belong to a strictly " periodic insanity " by the assumption of very long pauses. Since, however, in the form here discussed we are not at all concerned with an actual periodicity. but only with a tendency, sometimes stronger, sometimes weaker, to the recurrence of the same disorders, we are not at all in need of such subtleties. What rather solely and alone concerns us is, as ever again must be emphasized, the *fundamental and complete agreement of the general clinical morbid picture.* We are wholly incapable of judging by one manic or melancholic attack, whether it will remain the only one in life, or will recur several times, or even very frequently ; only the further following up of the case, which assuredly under certain circumstances would have to be continued for thirty years and more, can clear up the matter for us. At most subsidiary circumstances, the existence of a depressive or manic predisposition, an attack in early childhood, the occurrence of frequent attacks in the parents or brothers and sisters, the general probability of recurrence, give special help ; also the combination of manic and depressive periods could be made use of in this direction. But beyond that all evidence is lacking. Neither does the subsequent examination of attacks appearing only once or repeatedly disclose characteristics of any kind which permit of a separation. These are the reasons, which have caused me to gather into the unity of manic-depressive insanity, besides the circular attacks, not only the periodic and relapsing forms, but also the simple forms of mania and melancholia.

A difficulty stood in the way of this conception, namely, the peculiar clinical form of the depressive states of more *advanced age.* Without regard to the fact already discussed, that here in general a very conspicuous tendency to depressive attacks appeared, which must arouse the suspicion of morbid processes of a peculiar kind, very frequently also in these forms volitional inhibition which otherwise is so characteristic of depression was absent, and often also inhibition of thought. In their place anxious excitement appeared, mostly with abundant delusions. Moreover, the course was very chronic, so that frequently after a fairly long series of years still nò recovery had taken place, but rather the issue in a state of mental weakness seemed to have begun. A number of patients were also indubitably demented.

Under these circumstances I had at first thought that I should separate that kind of depressive attack of the involutionary years as a special clinical form, as " melancholia " [1] in the narrower sense, from manic-depressive insanity, since here with regard to the composition of the state, of the course and issue, in a certain sense with regard also to the history of origin, essential divergencies appeared to exist. At the same time I did not conceal from myself,

[1] Hoche, Die Melancholiefrage, 1910 ; Volpi-Ghirardini, Rivista di freniatria sperim, xxxvi. 161.

that in a whole series of depressive states of the involutionary years the fact that they belong to manic-depressive insanity could not be doubted both on account of their clinical form and also an account of their earlier or later association with manic phenomena. I therefore strove to find some useful distinguishing characteristics, certainly without any satisfactory result.

Further experience then taught, as in the discussion of the presenile psychoses has already been explained, that the arguments in favour of the separation of melancholia, were not sound. The dementias could be explained by the appearance of senile or arteriosclerotic disease ; other cases after very long duration of the disease, some of them displaying manic symptoms, had yet still recovered, The frequency of depressive attacks in advanced age we have come to recognise as an expression of a general law which governs the change of colouring of the attack in the course of life. Lastly, the substitution of anxious excitement for volitional inhibition has proved to be behaviour, which we meet with in advancing age in those cases also which decades previously had fallen ill in the usual form, as our first and second examples demonstrate. Hübner has likewise had the experience, that melancholic attacks may run their course sometimes with, sometimes without inhibition. There is, therefore, no longer sufficient cause to separate from manic-depressive insanity the depressive states of more advanced age, which till now have been called melancholia.

A further, not inconsiderable addition to this morbid form was furnished by the mixed states, which so far had been classified each according to its colouring under the most different terms, as stupor of exhaustion, as acute dementia, amentia [1] and so on. Here at the first glance the principle laid down above appears to fail, that the form of the whole clinical morbid picture must be authoritative in order that it may be assigned to a disease, since the mixed states frequently fall outside the limits of the ordinary states in a very conspicuous way. The changes in the composition of the clinical phenomena observed in the transition periods between mania and melancholia served here as guide. They taught us that our customary grouping into manic and melancholic attacks does not fit the facts, but requires substantial enlargement, if it is to reproduce nature. At the same time it turned out that this enlargement ran out in

[1] Confusional or delirious insanity.

the direction not of the fitting in of fresh morbid symptoms, but only of the different combination of morbid symptoms known for long. Further, it was seen that the mixed states, even when they appeared not as interpolations but as independent attacks, behaved with regard to their course and issue quite similarly to the usual forms, and lastly, that they might in the same morbid course simply take the place of the other attacks especially after a somewhat long duration of the malady. With all these established facts the proof that the mixed states belong to manic-depressive insanity appears secure.

From still other directions morbid forms have been drawn into the territory of manic-depressive insanity. Specht and Nitsche have rightly pointed out that a number of querulants who used to be reckoned to paranoia, are in reality nothing but persons with manic predisposition. Specht has even made the attempt which certainly goes too far, to let the whole of paranoia be included in "chronic mania," delimited by himself, which in essentials is covered by the manic predisposition here described.

On the other hand, Hecker and Wilmanns have emphasized that a considerable number of the patients described as psychopaths, neurasthenics, hysterics, suffer from cyclothymic fluctuations of mood, and, therefore, likewise belong to the domain of manic-depressive insanity. That naturally holds good very specially for "periodic neurasthenia," Dreyfus then, following Wilmanns, ascribed in particular nervous dyspepsia essentially to cyclothymic moodiness. Kahn spoke of "circularisme viscéral," which is said to be characterized by alternation of diarrhœa and constipation. Finally, in agreement with Bleuler I think that I may without hesitation include in manic-depressive insanity "periodic paranoia" which runs its course in isolated attacks with favourable issue, since it is invariably accompanied by distinct fluctuations of mood, frequently also by transitory states of excitement, confusion, or stupor, and cannot be in any essential point delimited from states, which otherwise also we now and then meet in the course of indubitably manic-depressive psychoses.

It cannot be denied that by all these new acquisitions the range of manic-depressive insanity has increased to a very considerable extent. That in itself is, of course, no reason for doubting its unity, as little as perhaps the frequency and multiformity of tuberculosis or of syphilis can arouse in us hesitation about the clinical states. For the present also I see no possibility of undertaking to make fundamental divisions anywhere in this wide domain. On the other hand the attempt may well be made to characterize still somewhat more precisely individual sub-groups as to their clinical peculiarities. In this direction Reiss has made an experiment with the forms which grow on the soil of well-marked manic-depressive predisposition, while Hecker, Hoche, Wilmanns, Römheld have described minutely the important morbid state of cyclothymia to which also probably in essentials "neurasthenic melancholia" described by Friedmann[1] must be reckoned. Dreyfus has given us a glimpse, though certainly still incomplete, into the specific character of the forms developing in more advanced age. Specht and Nitsche have set forth in detail the behaviour of the permanent manic states. Although the same morbid process lies at the foundation of all these forms, they are yet so different in clinical behaviour, in course, and in prognosis, that one might perhaps speak of a morbid group springing from a common root with gradual transitions between the individual forms, rather than of a uniform disease in the customary sense of the word.

Mugdan[2] has recently made the attempt to separate from the circular attacks the "alternating" cases as a special clinical unity. In these, which do not quite amount to a third of the cases of "manic-depressive insanity," we find only purely manic or depressive states, in the circular cases a conjunction of both. The former are said to be further distinguished from the latter by the greater frequency of hallucinations and delusions, by more infrequent attacks, and by more favourable prospects of cure. From my own experience I can confirm the fact, that cases with close association, and especially mixture, of manic and depressive phenomena are in general to be regarded as more severe ; but I do not consider it possible in view of the numerous transition forms to draw any boundary at all here.

The extraordinary enlargement of our conception of the disease is subjected on the other hand also to noteworthy *limitations*. It must first be remembered that only a part of the cases formerly called "mania" and "melancholia" have been included in manic-depressive insanity. A considerable number of cases, which formerly were taken

---

[1] Friedmann, Monatsschr. f. Psychiatrie, xv. 301.
[2] Mugdan, Zeitschr. f. d. ges. Neurol. u. Psychiatrie, i. 242.

together under those names, have been included in dementia præcox, many also in toxic insanity and other smaller morbid groups. But also from the periodic cases certain forms have been split off. Without regard to circular paralysis, which we can delimit to-day with certainty, dipsomania must be remembered, which formerly was often reckoned to periodic melancholia, but which to-day has a place given to it in several groups. Further we are convinced that dementia præcox also presents cases with a periodic course, which according to their other behaviour must be removed from manic-depressive insanity.

The so-called *delusional* forms still make up a disputed domain. As far as I can judge at present, I do not think that the morbid conception of delusional insanity is a unity. I would without hesitation reckon it with manic-depressive insanity. There certainly occur, as I have already indicated above, states which are externally very similar, in certain diseases of the involutionary age ; these run a very unfavourable course, and obviously are the expression of widespread destructive processes in the cerebral cortex. The clinical pictures, however, remind one more of catatonic morbid forms. " Manic delusion," which is defended by Thalbitzer, might likewise include component parts of different kinds, at one time perhaps chronic manic cases with well-marked delusions, but at another, cases of expansive paraphrenia, with unfavourable issue, which has already been described elsewhere.[1] Certainty about these questions can only be obtained by further investigation of this domain, especially from the anatomical side.

[1] Kraepelin, *Dementia Præcox and Paraphrenia*. Translation Edinburgh, p. 302. (Oct. 1919).

CHAPTER XII.

DIAGNOSIS.[1]

THE diagnosis of manic-depressive insanity is easy in those cases, in which a series of alternating or similar attacks has already preceded. In the meantime it must be noted that also in paralysis and in dementia præcox a similar alternation between excitement and mournful moodiness or stupor may occur just as here. In such cases the distinction must take account of the peculiar clinical symptoms of the attacks themselves, which we have already discussed in detail.

The slighter and slightest forms of manic-depressive insanity pass over quite imperceptibly into the forms of the morbid predisposition which we described before. In the cyclothymic forms the periods of groundless moodiness or unrestrained merriment may for long be considered as simple capriciousness, and brought into connection with all sorts of chance occurrences. Such patients, who perhaps never come into the hands of the alienist, are, as Hecker very properly has emphasized, frequently judged by the physicians, who are consulted, solely according to moody states, and they are considered to be hypochondriacs or neurasthenics, as in the corresponding manic periods they pass as healthy. Very frequently, however, in the period of depression which drives them to the physician, they have themselves a distinct feeling of the morbidity of the excitement, of which they are sometimes very much afraid. It is, therefore, in most cases easy to find out the alternation of states and the recurrence of the individual attacks and thus the nature of the malady in question.

Simple irresolution appearing suddenly without cause is so specific that it often without anything more furnishes the right key for the interpretation of the state. Such cases are extremely frequent, and are found everywhere in sanatoria, where they go through the most varied cures. If the cure coincides exactly with the transformation of mood,

[1] Bornstein, Zeitschr. f. d. ges. Neurol. u. Psych. v. 145 ; Thomsén, Allgem. Zeitschr. f. Psych. 1907, 631.

it attains a brilliant result, which now is ascribed to it, but unfortunately the same result does not appear, when the patient the next time in the beginning of the attack hopes for healing from it. Moreover, here also the people in the surroundings may at any time be surprised by a severe attack, although mostly the whole lifetime usually passes in an alternation between all sorts of wild actions and the presumed repentance for them, between feverish delight in enterprise and the apparent reaction after overwork.

It is often essentially more difficult to judge of the permanent manic or depressive states. Patients of the former kind, who frequently fall into conflict with their surroundings and with the public authorities, are mostly considered to be *swindlers*, or *rascals*, often even to be suffering from *moral insanity*. Without having regard to the fluctuations of the state, with which also once in a while a short transformation to depressive mood may be associated, the clinical picture is also helpful in leading to a more correct view, the permanently confident, self-righteous, often jovial mood, the lively emotional excitability, the aimlessness, unsteadiness, and the great busyness, the inaccessibility to admonition, regulations, and unpleasant experiences, the jocular derailments, the absence of criminal intentions. Just these states, but also hypomanic attacks, which run a very chronic course, present not infrequently the picture of *querulants*. Whether the querulant delusion, as Specht thought, is in general to be conceived as a form of manic-depressive insanity, will be discussed later. Here I would only remark that manic volitional excitement, otherwise than in the delusional querulant, is invariably conspicuous in the whole conduct of life, not only in common legal relations. Moreover, the manic querulant displays as a rule a more amused, exultant mood with an inclination to humorous tricks, in contrast to the measureless exasperation and animosity of querulant delusion. Finally in him, the manic patient, fluctuations of the state are frequently conspicuous, which under certain circumstances may cause a sudden, repentant renunciation of the struggle till then carried on passionately.

The permanent state of depression is perhaps to be regarded as less unequivocal as an expression of the manic-depressive predisposition. Where, however, distinct fluctuations in the severity of the states, exacerbations of the nature of a seizure, or even an occasional transformation to unfounded merriment are observed, the relation cannot be doubted. Peculiar caution in judging is required with regard to compulsive ideas and obsessional fears, which only exceptionally make their appearance in well-marked attacks in manic-depressive insanity. Besides that there remains to be noticed the permanent disposition, which in depressive moodiness is gloomy and hopeless, in compulsion neuroses on the contrary stands in the closest connection with the appearance of the compulsion phenomena. The patients may in the latter, when they are diverted, especially also in conversation with the physician, be quite calm and even cheerful, while the psychic oppression, which accompanies the depressive predisposition, is usually much less, or not at all accessible to momentary external influence.

To decide whether an isolated state belongs to manic-depressive insanity or not without a survey of the whole course, is not always easy. The principal difficulties arise in general with *paralysis* and *dementia præcox*. If in the former disease cytological and serological investigation has now made certainty very great, the distinction between the states of manic-depressive insanity and of dementia præcox, simple as it is in the great majority of cases, may under certain circumstances be very difficult. The points of view, which here come into consideration, have been already explained in detail.[1] Here it will merely be added that to decide between the two diseases, the consideration of their history of origin may be of value. As manic-depressive insanity in general begins somewhat earlier, the probability in this direction will be somewhat greater in an attack before the twentieth year. Moreover, attacks in advanced age will much rather rouse the suspicion of manic-depressive insanity. A well-marked manic or cyclothymic predisposition scarcely leads to dementia præcox; also the occurrence of mania or melancholia in parents or brothers and sisters will point in this direction, though certainly by no means absolutely. The question is more difficult to decide in individuals with depressive or irritable predisposition. It appears that here we must keep separate several, externally similar forms. Softness, sensitiveness, dejection, lack of self-confidence are found to a greater extent in the previous history of manic-depressive insanity, shy, whimsical, repellent conduct in that of dementia præcox. Further, to the former correspond the easily inflammable,

---

[1] *Dementia Præcox and Paraphrenia*, p. 260.

sentimental, passionate natures, to the latter the incalculable, stubborn, rough, and violent natures.

The least occasion for mistaken diagnoses is given in general by manic states. Leaving aside paralytic and catatonic states of excitement, only the confusion with *cerebral syphilis* really comes under consideration, in which, although not exactly often, states are observed, which display very great similarity with manic states. The difficulties may be increased up to the impossibility of a certain decision, when not only the chance combination of mania with lues exists, but also one or other of the morbid symptoms as well, which point to the nerve tissue having a share in the syphilitic disease, loss of pupillary reflexes, difference in the reflexes, tabetic phenomena. Such cases are not altogether rare. If there are disorders of speech and writing, seizures with unconsciousness or even convulsions, one will be obliged to think of a syphilitic foundation for the whole state, and likewise when with relatively slight excitement and preserved sense, gross disorders of memory, weakness of judgment, and emotional dulness are conspicuous. If, however, it should turn out that the first-mentioned bodily symptoms have existed already for years unchanged, and, if the patient with increased distractibility is clever, quick at repartee, witty, his mood exultant, his conversation and actions in fine style and clever, the probability of mania with lues becomes greater. It becomes an almost absolute certainty, if already previously similar or depressive attacks have been present. In certain circumstances also the exhibition of anti-syphilitic treatment may clear up the situation ; a rapid and obvious result would speak for cerebral syphilis, its non-appearance certainly not against that.

The diagnosis of states of depression may, apart from the distinctions already discussed, offer difficulties specially when the possibility of *arteriosclerosis* has to be taken into consideration. It may at a time be an accompanying phenomenon of manic-depressive insanity, but at another time may even itself engender states of depression. Especially the physical symptoms of arteriosclerosis, increase of blood-pressure, tortuosity and rigidity of accessible vessels, vertigo, paralytic phenomena, aphasic disorders, will direct attention to this possibility. If already states of depression or mania have preceded, the causal significance of the vascular disease will be rejected for the psychic disorder ; in the other case, however, the decision will be very difficult. One is thrown back solely on the valuation of psychic morbid phenomena. Great disorder of memory and of retention without distinct inhibition of thought, further, scantiness and uniformity of the delusions, poverty of thought, emotional barrenness with convulsive weeping or laughing, weakness of volition and susceptibility to influence will speak for an arteriosclerotic foundation of the depression.

The attacks of manic-depressive insanity accompanied by greater clouding of consciousness and vivid hallucinations are frequently regarded as *amentia*.[1] The points of view, which appear to me to be of significance for the delimitation, have been taken into account in the discussion of amentia. Schmid[2] has followed the fortunes of a considerable number of patients who had presented the picture of acute confusion, when dementia præcox was thought of, but they had completely and permanently recovered. He comes to the conclusion which is certainly right, that just those states of confusion, even when they present all kinds of " catatonic " symptoms, represent forms of manic-depressive insanity far more often than is usually assumed. Many patients of that kind, especially when the attack runs a rapid course, call to mind *hysterical* half-conscious states ; indeed, I have the impression, that now and then in reality great hysterical admixture comes into consideration. But, however, flight of ideas, the merry exultant colouring of the mood, the great distractibility, and the fearless joy in enterprise are absent in the purely hysterical states of excitement. This excitement is connected by preference with definite occasions, and appears in the form of unlimited outbursts of feeling ; it discharges itself more in single actions with conscious aim, in contrast with the permanent, general manic pressure of activity. Moreover, hysterical excitement after short duration disappears for the time being rapidly and completely, while even the slightest forms of manic attack last far longer and only gradually return to the position of equilibrium.

Under certain circumstances it may become very difficult to distinguish an attack of manic-depressive insanity from a *psychogenic* state of depression. Several times patients have been brought to me, whose deep dejection, poverty of expression, and anxious tension tempt to the assumption

---

[1] Confusional or delirious insanity.
[2] Schmid, Zeitschr. f. d. ges. Neurol. u. Psych. vi. 125,

of a circular depression, while it came out afterwards, that they were cases of moodiness, which had for their cause serious delinquencies and threatened legal proceedings. As the slighter depressions of manic-depressive insanity, as far as we are able to make a survey, may wholly resemble the well-founded moodiness of health, with the essential difference that they arise without occasion, it will sometimes not be possible straightway to arrive at a correct interpretation without knowledge of the previous history in cases of the kind mentioned. At most it may be evident that the individuals in question are considerably more constrained and confused at the visits of the physician than in the interval.

But even when the occasion is known, caution in judgment is necessary, as, indeed, genuine circular states of depression also may be occasioned by emotional excitement. Here the circumstance is important that in the latter case the course of the attack is independent of the exciting cause. The patients are comparatively little affected by the further development of affairs, in especial not relieved even by a favourable turn of events; they bring forward delusions, which no longer stand in any relation whatever to the starting-point of their illness. In psychogenic depression on the contrary it is seen that every discussion of the sore point, every piece of news about the business, calls forth lively emotional storms, further, that every decision in the uncertainty, and let it be even unfavourable, generally exercises a reassuring effect. The judgment may be supported by the appearance of other psychogenic phenomena, tremors, disorders of gait, fainting attacks, convulsive laughing and weeping, which certainly may also occur in manic-depressive insanity, but which do not present such close relations to the exciting circle of ideas.

Not altogether infrequently manic patients, occasionally also inhibited patients, are considered *weakminded*, even when otherwise their malady has been correctly diagnosed. That is specially true of mania with poverty of thought, which is easily thought to be " imbecility with excitement ". As already mentioned a judgment of that kind is extremely deceptive, as long as any distinct symptoms of mania or depression are still present. I knew a patient who for months only laughed quietly to herself in an idiotic way, at most now and then struck her neighbour, and who was regarded by myself as weakminded ; after her recovery, however, she appeared unusually clever, cultured, and refined. Another patient for more than a year made the impression of a wholly demented individual in consequence of his lack of understanding and complete incapacity to bring forth a word ; he gradually came to himself and proved to be cheerful and lively, though certainly only moderately endowed. Still another patient was for many months almost completely mute, and lay in bed apparently without interest in his surroundings and with a rigid expression of countenance ; but he obeyed orders, turned somersaults with a pleased look when desired, and exercised on command ; later he recovered completely. As soon as the symptoms of a manic attack are clearly seen, such as indications of flight of ideas or susceptibility to influence, a merry mood or occasional jocular actions, the probability of a curable inhibition of thought will have to be kept in view. Further the absence of catatonic symptoms will, of course, have great weight.

CHAPTER XIII.

TREATMENT.

A TREATMENT according to cause of manic-depressive insanity with its roots deep down in the personality does not exist. Binswanger in one case in which the approach of an attack appeared to him to be announced by retention of nitrogen certainly succeeded in aborting it by lessening the supply of nitrogen, but this experience has hitherto remained isolated. That a very even tenor of life in *protected circumstances,* especially also with *avoidance of alcohol,* may have a certain prophylactic effect with individuals who are liable to attacks, may be regarded as probable considering the frequently indubitable influence of external injuries. Also in the quiet life of institutions attacks are often seen to run a comparatively mild course.

How far it is possible to suppress in its origin the individual attack which threatens, we do not yet know. Kohn has tried such experiments especially for the forms with short attacks quickly following the one after the other in which the appearance of a fresh exacerbation can be more accurately foreseen. He ordered very large doses of *bromides. Twelve to fifteen grams* are given daily, if possible beginning some days before the expected outbreak of the attack, whose first symptoms should be very accurately noted. It occasionally in fact succeeds in preventing the appearance of excitement. After the specially dangerous days are past, the dose of the remedy is very gradually decreased, and on the approach of the next expected attack it is again increased to the large quantity mentioned. Hitzig judging by a few cases has recommended the use of atropine injections ; the results, however, appear to be meanwhile rather uncertain.

The appearance of attacks in pregnancy or the puerperium has now and then led to the attempt by the induction of *artificial abortion* to shorten the attack or to prevent its outbreak. The observations, which I was able to make with regard to this, were not encouraging. The disease comes and runs its course as otherwise. Just as little does a normal confinement as a rule influence the morbid state favourably; on the contrary an exacerbation is sometimes seen. At most, therefore, measures for the prevention of pregnancy might be considered in the case of women liable to attacks, but these in themselves are also not altogether harmless from a psychiatric point of view. On the other hand we often enough see that quite irregularly in the same woman in the course of the work of reproduction, at one time an attack of manic-depressive insanity appears, at another time not. We, therefore, by no means possess any evidence at all of the greatness of the danger on a given occasion.

The treatment of manic excitement will be above everything to prevent external stimuli as far as possible. This indication is met by the placing of the patient in an *institution*, which may be dispensed with in very slight forms, as soon as the limitation of freedom is badly borne and the malady does not lead to serious injuries and inconveniences. As we know further that the excitement is always more increased by activity, we shall limit the pressure of occupation as far as possible and keep all restless patients *in bed*, which especially in physical weakness and bloodlessness is urgently to be recommended.

In very great excitement the *continuous bath* is to be advised instead of bed-treatment. The continuous bath may here be frankly called the specific means of treatment. Its beneficent and sedative effect is extremely surprising. All the other disagreeables so much feared, isolation, dirt, destruction, violence, can be wholly or at least almost wholly avoided by this measure. All other hypnotic and sedative remedies become almost superfluous, if the baths can be continued during the night also; otherwise recourse must now and then be had to paraldehyde, trional, veronal, luminal, or such things. In cardiac weakness small doses of caffeine or digitalis are in certain circumstances indicated. After the excitement has abated, the bath treatment can be very well combined with temporary stay in the open air. All injuries and furuncles must from the outset be treated with the greatest care, as they, especially in corpulent and very restless patients with weak hearts, may give occasion for severe infections and thus quickly bring about very serious danger.

The *nourishment* of the patients requires special attention; it frequently suffers by their restlessness. Abundant, easily digested food should be given often, and according to the circumstances administered with great patience. In more severe cases *daily weighing* is to be recommended in order to judge accurately the condition of the body-weight and in case of necessity to begin tube-feeding in time.

The *psychic treatment* of acute mania has, of course, to take into account the irritability of the patient. Quiet friendliness, at a suitable moment more a humorous entering into his cheerful mood, cautious, patient tacking, do a great deal to facilitate intercourse, and often make the patient, who in unskilled hands is dangerous and stubborn, docile and good-natured. When quietness sets in, special consideration must be given to the avoidance of external incitements and temptations.

Not inconsiderable difficulties may arise in fixing the time for *discharge*, as the patients are often very impatient and urge to get out in every possible way. But even patients, who have become quite quiet, may in freedom, especially under the influence of alcohol, immediately become excited again and carry out extremely dangerous actions. The most certain indication for judging the condition is here also given by the *body-weight*.

In states of depression *bromides* are usually employed with occasional hypnotics, further, evening baths with cold douching. In greater anxiety *opium* is given with or without bromide. The dose is quickly increased from *ten up to thirty or forty drops of the tincture thrice daily*. I have not seen any more benefit from larger doses; in certain circumstances they appear to have an exciting effect. After quietness has set in, the dose is slowly reduced, and, if need be, again rapidly increased. Besides that there must be remembered strengthening nourishment, regulation of digestion, further, *rest in bed* with regular stay in the *open air*.

As the patients are in general mostly excited by those persons and things which concern them most nearly, by their relatives, their home, their vocational activity, it will be desirable, as a rule, to remove them from their accustomed surroundings. Patients, in whom there is any danger of *suicide*, must not in any circumstances be treated in the family or in a hospital run on the open-door system, but should be placed unconditionally in a closed hospital under constant observation by day and by night. An attendant sleeping in the same room, or worse still in a side-room, is not sufficient under any circumstances in cases at all serious.

Feeding often causes great difficulty because the patients resist vigorously on account of lack of appetite or in consequence of delusions ; they do not consider themselves worthy to eat, they think that they cannot pay, they suspect poison or nauseating things in the food. *Kindly persuasion*, patient waiting for the right moment, careful choice of food, however, in most cases lead to the goal ; in certain circumstances sensible patients abandon their resistance when they are convinced that otherwise tube-feeding is imminent.

Psychic treatment will have to be essentially limited to the keeping of emotional stimuli far off. Long conversations, letters, business arrangements, are, as far as possible, to be avoided. In cases connected with betrothals personal as well as written communication with the other partner must be stopped to begin with, but the final decision for the future is to be postponed to the time of recovery, if at all possible.

Visits of relatives also may have a very exciting effect, but I am convinced that their unfavourable influence is mostly overrated, in as far as it concerns intelligent people and only short interviews. Long seclusion of the patients from their own relatives, as formerly was often considered necessary, has frequently a very unfavourable effect. Specific comforting encouragement at the height of the moodiness is for the most part fairly ineffectual ; later when the mood is clearing up, the benefit without doubt often appears greater than it is in reality. But still the consciousness of being able to confide in the physician, and especially to leave all the little daily decisions in his hands, is for many patients very reassuring ; also the constantly repeated assurance that all self-tormenting is morbid and that there will be complete recovery, is often felt as a comfort in the thronging of doubts and fears. In slight cases hypnotic influence may be so far useful in combating unpleasant sensations, sleeplessness and dejection.

Great caution must be advised in the case of depressed patients with regard to discharge from the protection of the institution, as just in convalescence the danger of suicide is often especially great. Frequently considerable difficulties arise here by the impulsive home-sickness, which develops in the patients, and causes the relatives to carry through the discharge against all the warnings of the physician. Sudden, very considerable exacerbations, indeed suicidal attempts, are often enough the consequence. " I immediately regretted everything," declared one of these patients.

Many patients also wish to leave the institution only on that account, in order to be able to accomplish their suicidal intentions outside. In such cases they often manage to conceal their real mood with great skill from the physician and from their relatives. Only when the impatient urging disappears, and perfect insight with a calm quiet mood exists, when nourishment has returned to the former standard and sleep is undisturbed, may recovery be regarded as complete, and the time ripe for discharge. Exceptions are advisable only under specially favourable conditions.

PARANOIA

CHAPTER I.

INTRODUCTION

THE history of the conception of paranoia [1] is very closely connected with the whole development of our clincial views of psychiatry. The term, paranoia, which was used first by Kahlbaum in 1863 in a special sense, then by von Krafft-Ebing and Mendel, took the place of the older name *Verrücktheit*, which was given to a form of insanity essentially affecting *intellectual activity*. According to the older teaching of Griesinger, which in the main point assumed a single kind of psychic malady running a regular course in various stages, *Verrücktheit* was always the issue of a previous disorder of the emotional life. Each psychosis was said to begin with a melancholic stage, which might be followed by a period of manic excitement, then of *Verrücktheit*, of confusion and, lastly, of dementia when recovery did not take place at any point. At that time, therefore, one spoke exclusively of a "secondary" *Verrücktheit* as the unfortunate issue of a psychic disorder which had not attained to cure. As, moreover, confusion was also called "general *Verrücktheit*," which was conceived as an extension over the whole psychic life of the disorder

---

[1] Snell, Allgem. Zeitschr. f. Psychiatrie, xxii. 368 ; Griesinger, Archiv f. Psychiatrie, i. 148 ; Sander, ebenda, 387 ; Westphal, Allgem. Zeitschr. f. Psychiatrie, xxxiv. 252 ; Mercklin, Studien über primäre Verrücktheit, 1879 ; Neurolog. Zentralbl., 1909, 846 ; Amadei e Tonnini, Archivio italiano per le malattie nervose, 1884, I, 2 ; Werner, Die Paranoia, 1891 ; Schüle, Allgem. Zeitschr. f. Psychiatrie, l. 1 u. 2 ; Cramer. ebenda, li. 2 ; Sandberg, ebenda, lii. 619 ; Smith, Journal of Mental Science, 1904, Okt. ; Pastore, Giornale di psichiatria clinica e tecnica manicomiale, xxxv. 3 ; Sérieux et Capgras, Les folies raisonnantes, 1909 ; L'année psychologique, xvii. 251 ; Binet et Simon, ebenda xvi, 215 ; Sommer, Leydens Deutsche Klinik, 297, 1906 ; Alberti, Note e riviste psichiatria, 1908 ; Wilmanns, Zentralbl. f. Nervenheilk, 1910, 204.

originally more limited, the systematized delusion restricted to a few parts of the psychic life was contrasted with that as " partial *Verrücktheit*."

It was first the investigations of Snell, Westphal, and Sander, which in the 'sixties of last century led to a " primary " manner of development of *Verrücktheit* being generally recognized. The effect of this undeniable progress was that the newly recognized form of disease was as a primary disease of the intellect placed over against mania and melancholia, in which were seen the standard disorders of the emotional life. The emotional reactions occasionally observed in the former malady were said to arise as " secondary " phenomena by means of delusions and hallucinations, just as it was thought that the emergence of intellectual disorders in the " emotional diseases " could be derived as a result from the primary cheerful or mournful temper. It was, therefore, of the greatest significance for the diagnosis to know in the individual case, whether the disorders of emotion or those of intellect had been the first morbid phenomena.

The conception of *acute* paranoia, first briefly indicated by Westphal, became of special importance for the further development of the question of paranoia, with which later " periodic " paranoia was brought into connection.[1] By the displacement of the original conception which only took into account chronic, incurable states, the delimitation of the morbid state according to external phenomena became much facilitated. If the course and issue of the disease were no longer authoritative, the intellectual disorder, the appearance of delusions or hallucinations, remained as the only tangible characteristic of *Verrücktheit*. Thus it came about that a series of morbid pictures were now incorporated with it, which, regarded clinically, possessed nothing whatsoever in common with the original *Verrücktheit*, as, for instance, amentia,[2] alcoholic insanity, and numerous states which, without doubt, belong to dementia præcox or to manic-depressive insanity.

We learn from paralysis, from dementia præcox, and in a certain sense also, from manic-depressive insanity that a disease in itself may present acute and chronic forms. Here,

---

[1] Köppen, Neurolog. Zentralbl, xviii. 434 ; Thomsen, Archiv f. Psychiatrie, xlv. 803 ; lv. 3 ; Böge, ebenda, xliii. 299 ; Kleist, Zeitsch. f. d. ges. Neurol. u. Psychiatrie, v. 366.

[2] Confusional or delirious insanity.

however, the acute attacks are everywhere only parts of a course fundamentally chronic ; on this account the prognosis with regard to the final state remains in principle the same for each morbid process. But just this characteristic fails in application to cases of so-called acute paranoia. The sifting of the morbid cases corresponding to this picture after a sufficiently long period of observation, shows undeniably that from year to year an always larger number of these belong to wholly different well-known diseases. In any case the greater number of cases of so-called acute paranoia display neither a peculiar cause, nor a special course and issue, nor any other clinical characteristics, which would permit of their being separated from other states. Personally I even doubt if with more detailed exanimation any remnant clinically of value remains over of the cases. But yet if one wishes to retain it, it is in any case more expedient not to give the name of paranoia to the morbid state, because by so doing essential characteristics of the forms of this disease generally recognized are obliterated, the insidious course, the unfavourable prospects of recovery, the permanent continuance of the delusions which appear.

There was a time when the number of the paranoiacs in our mental hospitals had grown to from 70 to 80 per cent. of all cases. The demonstration of a few delusions or hallucinations sufficed for clinical characterization. The starting-point was the conception that each paranoiac had essentially a delusion mentally worked up, " a system ", which also was regarded as the foundation of his states of depression and excitement and also of his morbid actions. Certainly observation itself showed that in very many cases nothing really could be demonstrated of a delusional system, but that only a few meagre, disconnected or confused delusions were given utterance to. In order to explain the contradiction between hypothesis and findings, it was usual to seize upon the assumption, either that the patient did possess a delusional system but for some reason or other did not speak about it, or that a system had formerly existed in his mind, but that, however, it was already " disintegrated." In this case it concerned an " old paranoiac ", who certainly might still be very young in years. Further experience has taught that both assumptions, although they might be appropriate once in a while in a single case, could not explain the absence of a systematized delusion in an enormous number of presumed paranoiacs. Rather it became clear that here it concerned morbid states which according to their essential character, were accompanied, as a rule, not by systematized delusions, but by incoherent, contradictory, changing, meagre delusions. According to the principal point it concerned those forms which we now gather together under the name of dementia præcox. With these, perhaps, a few cases also of senile, epileptic, or syphilitic disease came into consideration.

But when now for the diagnosis of paranoia one came back to the demand for a delusion to some extent fixed and mentally worked up, it was seen that the group of such cases, still very large, did not at all appear to be clinically uniform. Above everything the fact stood out that the development of the disease was usually accompanied by more or less vivid and extended hallucinations, while in a smaller number of cases the development of the delusion permanently, or at least for many years, took place solely by means of morbid interpretation of actual events or by pseudo-memories. The attempt was made to rectify this difference by making a classification into hallucinatory paranoia and systematized or simple paranoia. Further, it was seen that many cases, and, indeed, by preference the forms with vivid hallucinations, displayed the tendency to relatively rapid transition to states of mental weakness, which made itself known in the extraordinariness of the delusions, lack of judgment, incoherence, and emotional dulness. In contrast to that, other patients were seen, especially those with purely systematized delusions, who remained unchanged sometimes for decades without essential loss of psychic ability.

These experiences of necessity suggested the assumption, that there would be a difference in the character of the morbid process corresponding to the difference in the course and issue. For this reason I decided first to separate off from the others the forms which develop very insidiously, and which do not lead to states of pronounced psychic weakness, as paranoia in the narrower sense. The remainder, which was far more comprehensive, represented the " paranoid " disease, a group in itself, still by no means uniform, but put together of very different component parts. As the greater number of these consisted of cases, which in many clinical features, as in course and issue, displayed unmistakable points of agreement with dementia præcox, I thought that I should first, till these questions were further cleared up, incorporate them with that disease as paranoid forms. But further experience has caused me, as was formerly explained in detail,[1] to separate off a few smaller groups again from the paranoid forms of dementia præcox under the name of the paraphrenias, because of the divergent form of their terminal states.

Consideration of the causes and of the history of the development of paranoiac and paranoid diseases teaches us that in this direction there is very great multiplicity. Formerly, when morbid states were the principal guide for the delimitation of diseases, no special weight used to be laid on this circumstance. It seems to me, however, that with progressive knowledge of the true causes of insanity, the dependence of the clinical state on the conditions of its development becomes more distinct, although our insight into these circumstances as yet is still lamentably inadequate. If the attempt is made to classify according to this point of view, it appears that both among the paranoid and also among the paranoiac diseases in the sense delimited above, a certain number of cases is found which certainly, or at least with the greatest probability, must be traced back to definite external causes. Here there are on the one hand many alcoholic and syphilitic psychoses, but also and especially a series of psychogenic forms of insanity. It is, therefore, to be recommended, as has been done in our discussion, to separate out at the beginning cases of that kind and to combine them in special groups. We then have remaining for " true " paranoia, which alone occupies us at present, only those cases which are *developed from purely internal causes*.

Peculiar difficulties arise, as already indicated, in connection with the placing of *querulant delusion*. It was held for long to be the most characteristic form of paranoia. In it, for example, the following features are distinct, the systematization of the delusion, its uniformity and stability, further, the limitation of the morbid process to certain circles of ideas, the permanent preservation of the psychic personality, the non-appearance of phenomena of dementia. These peculiarities of querulant delusion have also served me as type for the delimitation of the conception of paranoia. It is, however, unmistakable that in one aspect a striking difference exists between querulant delusion and forms of

[1] Kraepelin, *Dementia Præcox and Paraphrenia*. Translation Edinburgh, Introduction (Oct. 1919).

paranoia otherwise similar in all the directions mentioned. In the former the delusion is connected *with a definite external occasion*, with a real or supposed legal wrong which stirs the emotions greatly. In this respect it rather resembles other psychogenic diseases, especially many forms of prison psychoses and traumatic neuroses. The question will, therefore, have to be examined whether the relationship of querulant delusion to the clinical forms named is closer than to the paranoiac diseases. On the ground of the experiences before me, I thought that I must answer this question in the affirmative, and on that account I have placed querulant delusion, which formerly was regarded as a sub-form of paranoia, in the group of the psychogenic psychoses, in the neighbourhood of those other morbid forms which likewise take on querulant features.

It must, however, be emphasized that this displacement has only a comparatively subordinate significance. In a certain sense a psychogenic mode of development may be ascribed also to paranoia; in it definite actual experiences may acquire a decisive influence on the formation of the delusional system. The difference lies only in this, that here the real driving powers for the morbid working up of events are solely in the patient himself, while in the various querulants the external occasion furnishes the deciding factor for the beginning of the illness. It certainly must be pointed out that in the latter case also a peculiar predisposition must form the general foundation for the development of querulant phenomena, as even with the same external conditions only a fraction of the cases take this direction. The differences in the history of origin of querulant delusion and paranoia, therefore, run out only in the direction of a certain displacement of the relations between external, psychogenic influences and internal morbid causes. But besides that there is still further the special idiosyncrasy of the querulant tuned to strife with legal authority, the development of which by external occasion is driven into a very definite direction diverging in manifold ways from the conduct of the paranoiac.

If with the help of these explanations the attempt is made to define the conception of paranoia, as it forms the foundation of the following exposition, stress would be laid on this feature of it, the *insidious development of a permanent and unshakable delusional system resulting from internal causes*, which is accompanied by *perfect preservation of clear and orderly thinking, willing, and acting.* At the same time that deep-reaching transformation of the whole view of life that " *Verrückung* " of the standpoint in regard to the world around, is usually accomplished, which was characterized by the name " *Verrücktheit* ".

The development of the morbid conception here discussed has been essentially different in French psychiatry. While in Germany it concerned principally questions of separating and grouping mental disorders, the French investigators made far more effort to describe isolated clinical forms in the most vivid way possible. The manifold content of the delusions, of the " délire ", was taken into account, its origin from hallucinations or delusional interpretations, " interprétations délirantes," its elaboration (délire systématisé), the general psychic state of the patients (" folie lucide, raisonnante "). The works of Falret and Lasègue were of special significance for the question discussed here. The former described the progressive development of the delusional formation, from the preliminary period to that of systematic building up, and lastly the monotonous fixation of the delusion, and so characterized a peculiarity of the course which we often find in true paranoia, but also in dementia paranoides and in paraphrenic disease. Lasègue described the morbid picture of the persecuted persecutors, of the " persécuteurs persécutés," which includes, namely, the querulants, but also other forms of the delusion of persecution in which the patients finally proceed to dangerous attacks on their supposed enemies.

From an essentially different standpoint Magnan came nearer to the solution of the question of paranoia. His clinical views are dominated by the endeavour to separate the mental disorders of the degenerate from the forms arising on a healthy foundation. The characteristic paranoid disease of the last group is " délire chronique à évolution systématique," already discussed by us, while to the first belong the persecuted persecutors and the querulants, and also those delusional morbid forms which are more or less remote from the type of " délire chronique " by reason of their " atypical " formation, by suddenness of development, combination of delusions of different kinds, and divergencies in the course. If the ground of classification which was authoritative for Magnan can scarcely any longer at present be regarded as justified, yet his classification, which to a certain degree separated the querulants and true paranoiacs from other paranoid diseases, signified a decided step in advance.

The latest development of French psychiatry has brought conceptions of the doctrine of paranoia, which, notwithstanding many differences in detail, yet move pretty much in the same paths as the discussion attempted here. Régis has postulated a "psychose systematisée progressive" which with its chronic development of a delusional system without hallucinations might correspond in the main to "true" paranoia. Sérieux, who has written a great deal about these questions, separates sharply from each other the "délire d'interprétation" and the "délire de révendication"; the former corresponds accurately to our paranoia, the latter to querulant delusion. That I consider this separation well-founded, and why I do so has been already explained. Finally, various investigators, especially Dupré, have described a "délire d'imagination," in which pure imaginations, relatively pseudo-memories, without connection with real perceptions, are said to be the driving power of the delusion formation. Neisser also has spoken of a "confabulating paranoia." If I disregard confabulating paraphrenia[1] already described, it seems to me that no genuine paranoiac state can be separated off from the point of view mentioned. Certainly fantastic inventions and pseudo-memories frequently play a considerable part in the history of origin of the delusion, but yet always only along with other delusional occurrences. When the former exclusively dominate the condition, it might rather concern morbid liars and swindlers, "mythomanics" according to Duprés.

---

[1] *Dementia Præcox and Paraphrenia*, p. 309.

CHAPTER II.

GENERAL MORBID SYMPTOMS.

THE morbid picture of paranoia is comparatively poor in detail, as the more striking disorders only extend over limited domains of the psychic life, and leave others wholly untouched or nearly so. Observation and perception in general proceed without hindrance, although the impressions are often morbidly interpreted. The patients remain permanently sensible, clear, and reasonable. Genuine hallucinations do not occur, as according to more recent experience and in agreement with Sérieux I must assume. In one of my cases, in which after the disease had lasted for many years numerous hallucinations of hearing were developed, it turned out later that syphilitic brain disease probably existed.

Visions.—On the other hand the patients not infrequently tell of isolated or fairly frequent *visionary experiences*, which are mostly referred to the night-time, but occasionally also are said to have appeared during the day on any special occasion. They see stars, shining figures, divine apparitions. It is possible that here it frequently concerns states of dreamy ecstasy. In other cases natural occurrences are misinterpreted ; in the full moon God the Father becomes visible ; a cloud takes on the form of an apocalyptic animal. But sometimes the descriptions given by the patients, which are mostly connected with events which took place long ago, arouse the suspicion of pseudo-memories ; thus a female patient alleged that at the age of four she saw heaven opened. Sometimes on these occasions the patients also receive orders or assurances from God ; the blessing of Esau was given to a patient on the left shoulder, the blessing of Jacob on the right. Others are threatened by the devil, strangled, endure conflicts. Such experiences are always regarded by the patients as supernatural events which do not belong to ordinary experience. A few patients also perhaps assert that they are in constant communication with God, that they receive inspiration from him, but there it never is a case of real hallucinations of hearing, but always only of the emergence of exhorting, warning, assuring thoughts, which in the manner of the " voice of conscience " are traced back to supersensual influences.

Memory and Retention show no disorder in domains lying outside of the delusion. *Pseudo-memories* are, however, extremely frequent ; they usually stand in the closest relation to the morbid circle of ideas. Sometimes it is only a wrong valuation and a transformation of experiences subsequent to their occurrence, sometimes it is the emergence of wholly invented utterances or events in the form of memory pictures. The patient reports communications, which have been made to him in a mysterious way, meetings, which he has had with prominent people, strange attacks, to which he was exposed. The blind implicit confidence is always very remarkable in these cases, which is given to the alleged utterances of any individuals whatsoever about the most important secrets. Often very complicated experiences are narrated with all details. The jealous man saw and heard his wife misdemean herself in the most shameless way with his rival ; a shot fell on the patient which tore off his hat and stretched him on the ground ; at the same time someone appeared with a knife in order to mangle his face past recognition.

Sometimes one can trace directly how such memories emerge in the patient and become fixed. Some patients allege that they already knew beforehand of the occurrence of this or that event, thus of their being brought to the asylum ; it has all of a sudden occurred to them again. One patient said that everything that he had thought to himself had come true already before this ; others assert that they can prophesy. The extraordinariness and undisguised improbability of the proffered narratives often makes it easy to recognize them as pseudo-memories. Here belong the statements of those, who are expecting thrones, about the information which was given to them already in their youth about their birth and about their claims.

In other cases when the patients with absolute conviction report observations which are within the limits of the possible or even of the probable, it may become extraordinarily difficult to discover the morbid history of origin of the pseudo-memories. Thus in delusions of jealousy one is often in doubt how far real occurrences or delusional inventions are the foundation of what the patients say about the alleged suspicious observations, indeed about the apparent admissions of the husband. Apart from general grounds of probability, the latter assumption will be justified if the patients adorn their narrative with very exact details always increasing on repetition, when they only produce their alleged observations a long time after the event, and also when their conduct at the time of the events and after has not in the least corresponded with what would have been expected in reality.

In my opinion, the part played in paranoia by pseudo-memories has often been underestimated. The statement is not infrequently found that the delusions in such cases may go back to early childhood, a circumstance which has been regarded as a strong argument in favour of the origin of the malady being a morbid disposition. Although the correctness of this view may be acknowledged without reserve, I yet consider that its substantiation by the statements of the patients about delusional experiences in childhood is not sound. Obviously these are the expression of pseudo-memories just as the corresponding narrations are in dementia præcox and paraphrenia.

Delusions of Reference.—In a still far higher degree than the picture of the past, the psychic appreciation of present experiences is influenced by the delusional processes. The disorder here dominating the morbid state can, perhaps, best be characterized by the expression delusions of reference. Numerous impressions and occurrences are not accepted in their sober every-day character, but they enter into some or other relation to the patient's own fortunes and misfortunes. Above everything the doings of his fellow human beings suffer this prejudiced interpretation.

The demeanour and the glances of the passers-by, a movement of the hand, a shrug of the shoulders, have a mysterious meaning for the patients ; it is sometimes painful and tormenting, sometimes elevating and beneficent. People wish in that way to insult him, blame him, make him contemptible, warn him, encourage him, impart to him some or other important information. A phrase accidentally caught up, a remark at the neighbouring table contains a hidden allusion ; it is " the customary picture-language " ; " They thought that I did not understand it," said a patient. The conversation of the party at table points dimly to a secret understanding ; the patient " notices that there is something there, but doesn't know what it is."

The same phrases are done to death with obvious intention on quite definite occasions. Certain songs are whistled in a remarkable manner in order to point out trivial occurrences in the patient's past, to give him hints for his work. In plays, in the most recent novel, in the newspapers there are references to his doings ; the clergy-man in the pulpit, a stump orator makes allusions to his person which cannot be misunderstood. It suddenly comes about that he continually meets the same people, who apparently watch him, and follow him as though by chance ; people stare at him, clear their throats, cough on his account, spit in front of him or avoid him. In public restaurants people edge away from him or stand up as soon as he appears, look at him with stolen glances and criticise him. Cabmen, railway guards, workmen talk about him. Everywhere attention is directed towards him ; his clothes in spite of their strangeness are copied by numerous unknown people. Isolated remarks which he has let fall immediately become public catchwords. One of my patients had called yellow the colour of the intellect ; the next day everyone was wearing yellow roses, as the rose is the symbol of silence in order to indicate to him that he was clever and should be silent. " Who will reckon up everything that speaks to me here ! "

All these experiences are in themselves of wholly indifferent content ; they appear " quite natural to every one who is not initiated," as chance accidents, but the patient perceives only too distinctly that everything is " arranged " with consummate cunning, that it is a case of " the artificial production of chances," behind which a base conspiracy, an important state affair is concealed. Certainly the whole game is extremely cleverly managed in order to deceive him or in order not to disclose great plans for the future prematurely. As often as he asks anyone to explain frankly, giving him to understand that he sees through everything, the person assumes an innocent air and invents all kinds of subterfuges ; people do not steer straight to the goal but by round-about ways, while the real aims are only alluded to in veiled indications. People cone to meet him with a friendly manner in order to deceive his vigilance, entangle him in peculiar conversations, misrepresent the facts to him with mental reservation ; the true meaning of this he certainly understands at once.

The following passage from the diary of a patient, who

believed that he was aimed at by a secret league for the
furtherance of pederasty, gives perhaps an idea of the very
peculiar displacement which is accomplished in the relation
of the patient to the external world :—

" That a confederacy with aims, such as are evident from these lines,
makes every effort that these aims should not become public and therefore
tries to make propaganda in hidden or symbolic form, is enlightening. As
it now cannot be certain what attitude the individual influenced by it will
assume with regard to the matter, it tries by all kinds of ingenious devices
running parallel, as it were, with the main effort but in themselves innocent,
to confuse him, relatively to protect itself from unpleasant disclosures.
Thus, *e.g.* I had at that time got into the habit, as is indeed the case with
almost everyone, of using a few stereotyped phrases, among others,
" Certainly ! " and " Scarcely to be believed," and lo and behold !
I found these two sentences and many others as well in rapid sequence as
heading to an advertisement in large letters in the *Generalanzeiger*. From
that I could of course only conclude that chance and my life are thus *day by
day* composed of nothing but chances, so that it would finally have become
the purest fantastic double life.—That, however, is scarcely to be
believed !—"

Internal connections between two events following each
other by chance are very frequently assumed. A patient
laid before the prime minister of Baden a map, on which
the regions of the world not yet occupied were marked ;
immediately afterwards the German colonial policy began.

Sometimes also natural occurrences acquire a special
significance for the patient. The peculiar twinkling of the
stars, the changes of weather, the flight of birds, the sound
of bells, symbolize in some or other way events in the life
of the patient or his future. They terrify him or encourage
him ; they contain threats or promises. Usually it concerns
isolated occurrences which find the patient in a peculiarly
susceptible mood. Here there are points of contact with
ordinary superstition, which likewise ascribes to chance
occurrences in the external world profound relations to the
individual's own fate ; one need only think of the motives
which may cause any one to try his luck in the lottery with
just this or that number.

Delusional interpretations lead occasionally to peculiar
mistakes about people in which external resemblances play
no part at all. An officer riding past is the sovereign or at
least his adjutant who thus wishes to give the patient a
sign ; a lady in a carriage is a princess who is trying to come
into relations with him. His persecutors, who emerge
everywhere, are at once infallibly recognized again by the
patient in spite of their disguises and external changes ; the
mysterious loved one may also in certain circumstances
assume the most manifold forms.

As the common source of pseudo-memories and of delusional interpretations we may well regard the tendency to *morbid imaginings*, as it has been described by Dupré and Logre[1] as " délire d'imagination." Series of presentations appear before the mental vision of the patients, sometimes a net of secret machinations, in whose meshes they are hopelessly entangled, sometimes delightful hopes for the future, to the fulfilment of which they look forward with confidence.

Uneasy forebodings may thrust themselves also on a healthy individual with or without external occasion ; he may build castles in the air, occupy himself with the picturing of alluring possibilities of good fortune, and accept with satisfaction tokens of coming bliss. But while he always remains conscious of the unreality of his play of imagination and rectifies it by deliberation, it appears to the patient as the trustworthy expression of reality. It acquires an authoritative influence on the whole of his thought and activity and instead of being driven away by reflection and experience, it convincingly transforms treasures of memory, the mental working up of events of life, and the view of the universe.

The mental disorder which dominates the morbid picture of paranoia can, therefore, be characterized in two directions. In the first place the whole system of thought bears a morbidly personal stamp. The patient is the centre of a surrounding area which in the most multifarious way occupies itself only with him and his fortunes ; what happens in his neighbourhood is not indifferent or casual, but has a profound relation to himself. But further, he lacks the capability to measure the products of his powers of imagination with the scale of sober experience. For him they have that immediate certainty of belief which leaves no room at all for doubt.

Delusion Formation.—The results of these disorders is the delusion formation peculiar to paranoia which may develop in the two fundamental directions of *ideas of injury* and *of exaltation.* The delusion here usually matures very slowly, taking many years. At first it remains within the limits of suspicious conjectures, arrogant and overweening self-conceit, secret hopes ; but these draw ever fresh nourishment from the prejudiced evaluation of the experiences of life, and they become more and more fixed. Occasionally under the influence of particular conditions or internal

[1] Dupré et Logre, L'Encéphale, 1911, 209.

states, it appears that the delusion progresses more by exacerbations, unless the descriptions of the patients about such occurrences are coloured by pseudo-memories. On some or other occasion scales seem to fall from their eyes, secret connections become clear to them like lightning; the present and the future are disclosed to them by inspiration. At other times the delusion formation may apparently stand still for many years; the same ideas, at most decorated by a few pseudo-memories, are produced unchanged without being enriched by fresh delusional experiences.

The delusion of the paranoiac is invariably "systematized," mentally worked up, and uniformly connected, without gross internal contradictions. The patients exert themselves to gain a picture, certainly distorted in an extremely ego-centric fashion, of their place in the mechanism of life, a kind of view of the universe. They bring their experiences into relation with each other, they search for cause and effect, for motives and connections. Obscure points and contradictions are as far as possible set aside and smoothed over by laborious thought, so that a delusional structure arises, which, however, with all the improbability and uncertainty of its foundations, does not usually contain any apparent absolute impossibilities. The patients will even listen to objections up to a certain point. They can at once refute them, it is true, by pointing out their special internal and external experiences, but yet, at least, they acknowledge the necessity of substantiating their assertions and of defending them against doubts.

It is exactly this internal working up of the delusion which leads to its *becoming a component part of the psychic personality*, to its passing into the flesh and blood of the patients. With this is connected its irrefutability. Although the patients themselves, perhaps, admit that they seldom or never can produce a really convincing proof of the correctness of their view, yet every attempt to convict them of the delusional character of their ideas rebounds as from a wall. At most they allow that the recognition of the inner connection of all the apparent chance circumstances can only be acquired from the standpoint of that personal conviction, "which just irrefutably has existed and will exist," as a patient said. "I live in the imagination that that is no imagination." The patient, therefore, feels occasionally that an uninitiated cannot follow his trains

of thought everywhere, and so fears that his persecutors
might make use of this state of affairs in order to assert that
he is afflicted with the delusion of persecution.   Of morbid
insight there is never any question.   A patient, indeed, said
that he now knew himself that he was mentally ill, for

> "so long as a human being knows that he is still separated from the
> holy and living God, his creator and preserver, still through sin and guilt or
> his own inner evil spirit, which lives by devouring and drinking, thus knows
> that he is not yet one with God, in spirit and in his conscience, therefore
> does not yet feel justified by the Holy Ghost, it is self-evident that he must
> feel himself mentally ill."

That is, of course, no morbid insight, but a paranoid
interpretation of a concept, behind which the assumption
of a peculiarly strict and orthodox apprehension of the
relation to God is distinctly recognizable.   The patient
then added further, " To the holy triune God all men are
mentally ill."

The *fundamental unchangeableness* of the delusions is
considered with a certain amount of right to be a chief
characteristic of paranoia.   Only very recently doubts have
arisen whether a too literal acceptance of this pronounce-
ment corresponds with experience.   On the one hand " mild
forms of paranoia " have been described by Friedmann[1];
in these after a few years the delusion gradually recedes
again.   On the other hand Gaupp has called attention to
cases of " abortive paranoia," in which, under the influence
of unpleasant conditions of life, less rigid delusional systems
are developed, which without actual rectification may gradually be obliterated.   We shall later have to examine how
far it appears feasible to place these cases within the morbid
conception of paranoia.   It must, however, also be taken
into account that the absence of susceptibility to influence
of the paranoiac delusion can scarcely be present at the
beginning.   Rather must we assume that in the many years
of preparation the delusion grows only very gradually, that
the patients offer resistance to the suppositions which are
thrust upon them, rejecting them at first, and then after
many inward struggles they are finally overpowered.   The
possibility can, therefore, scarcely be contested on principle
that the development of the malady does not progress
through such a period of preparation with fluctuating
delusions.

Mood corresponds throughout to the content of the
delusions brought forward.   Many patients are shy,

---

[1] Friedmann, Monatsschr. f. Psychiatrie u Neurol., xvii. 467.

suspicious, dejected, irritated, others self-conscious and confident. Frequently, there is in general no conspicuous colouring of mood at all recognizable, but it perhaps appears more distinctly when the delusional ideas are discussed. Great fluctuations of emotional equilibrium do not belong to the morbid picture, as I should like to emphasize in opposition to the statements of Specht. Nevertheless one may assume with Bleuler [1] and Specht that in the history of origin of paranoiac delusion emotional tension plays a considerable part, although I consider that Bleuler's tendency to regard definite " complexes emphasized by affect " as the starting-point of paranoid delusion formation, goes too far. The two opposed directions of the delusions which are often associated with each other appear, however, to point to a close relation with emotions; we have to do with, as Maier [2] has expressed it, " katathymic " delusion formations. Their content shows, although in a morbidly developed form, such a remarkable agreement with those fears, wishes, and hopes, which even in normal individuals proceed from the feeling of uncertainty and the endeavour after happiness, that one is tempted to believe in a similar foundation here. On the one side we find the fear to be despised and mocked, threatened by a systematic persecution; deceived in wedlock, on the other side the delightful conviction of being of aristocratic descent, the favourite of a highly-placed personage, inventor and benefactor of the people, the chosen of God.

Activity and **Conduct** often remain without any very definite disorder. The patients are mostly able even to earn their living permanently without being specially conspicuous in their surroundings. Certainly all kinds of peculiarities frequently appear in the conduct of their lives. A patient expressed himself as far as possible only in writing, because he had need of quiet and of communion with God; he often fasted for several days and he gave the following explanation of this :—

" Fasting and prayer do not weaken men at all, but just the opposite; they strengthen the spirit, purify the heart, and make a man free from his sinful nature."

Many patients withdraw themselves, bury themselves in books, compose comprehensive documents; others wander

[1] Bleuler, Affektivität, Suggestibilität, Paranoia, 1906; Specht, Über den pathologischen Affekt in der chronischen Paranoia, 1901; Zentralbl. f. Nervenheilk. u. Psychiatrie, 1908, 817.

[2] Maier, Zeitschr. f. d. ges. Neurol. u. Psychiatrie, xiii. 555.

about restlessly, change their situations frequently, make
their appearance sometimes at one place, sometimes at
another. There is little inclination for regular and continuous employment. A merchant, who had gained a small
competence in America and had returned home ill, spent
his money little by little till he fell into the hands of the
Guardians, as he was too proud to undertake work not suited
to his high valuation of himself. Now for the first time it
came out that for almost twenty years he had suffered from
pronounced ideas of persecution and exaltation. Often the
patients, in spite of good abilities, do not accomplish anything
rightly, but are always unsuccessful; they spend far more
than their circumstances allow, busy themselves with the
most difficult problems, without sufficient understanding and
without knowledge. Nevertheless they not infrequently are
capable of exercising an important influence on their
surroundings, of procuring for themselves a certain amount
of consideration, of convincing some people of the correctness
of their delusions, and possibly also of turning them into
enthusiastic adherents, as we have described more in detail in
the section about induced insanity.

The patients invariably come into contact with the
alienist only late, if at all, and even then for the most part
only temporarily, if they have made themselves conspicuous
or given·offence by any action in line with their delusion.
They usually possess so much self-mastery that they
habitually avoid all conflict with law and authority. Besides
that they are never so tormented that they would be driven
to regardless deeds of violence by overpowering inward
tension. It, therefore, for the most part does not go further
than comparatively harmless actions, abusive language,
threats, advertisements in the newspapers, complaints to
the police, attempts to force an entrance to highly-placed
persons, unreasonable religious practices, the exploiting of
people on the ground of delusional claims. Now and then,
perhaps, a suicidal.attempt may occur.

Bodily Symptoms.—In the bodily domain no tangible
divergence from normal exists; appetite and sleep are as
a rule not disordered. Many patients bring forward all
kinds of hypochondriacal complaints, they complain of
nervousness, oppression in their head, digestive weakness,
for which the medical treatment is readily held responsible.
They then, perhaps, take refuge in all kinds of singular
cures, some of them self-invented.

CHAPTER III.

CLINICAL FORMS.

THE clinical classification of paranoiac states offers peculiar difficulties because, as it has been well expressed, there are as many forms as there are individual patients. In fact here *personal peculiarity*, which is relatively little affected by the malady, exercises a far-reaching influence on the configuration of the morbid phenomena. The multiplicity of individual features will, therefore, be much greater than, say, in the grossly destructive morbid processes of paralysis or even of dementia præcox. Nevertheless, at least, certain general trends of delusion formation are repeated so invariably, that they may well serve as starting-point for a division of the material observed into some smaller sub-groups. Here we shall perhaps best begin with separating the morbid states with predominating delusions of injury and those with ideas of exaltation ; in both directions some other special kinds will then be distinguished.

Delusions of Persecution.—This is the most frequent form of paranoia. The patient, who already for a long time has perhaps felt himself neglected, unjustly treated, oppressed, not sufficiently valued, makes the observation, that on some or other occasion people no longer greet him in such a friendly way as formerly, that people are now more reserved towards him, and avoid him, and, in spite of many, as he says, hypocritical proofs of friendship, will have nothing more to do with him. In consequence of this his irritability and his distrust increase ; he begins to notice the behaviour of the people round him, and gradually finds numerous indications that people are systematically planning to injure him in every way, to undermine his position, to make him impossible. " I read everyone's thoughts from his face and I have good hearing," declared a patient. He is watched and spied on, detectives are sent after him, whose duty it is to keep their eye on him and collect material against him. On the street he has a feeling as if he must run the gauntlet. People look at him contemptuously, whistle and laugh behind his back, challenge him, try to irritate him. Harmless remarks are full of concealed malice; certainly people do not speak out, they say nothing definite. In the "*Fliegende Blätter*" there is offensive abuse; everywhere there is hounding and backbiting, jeering and chicanery. "It is all lies and deceit, hypocrisy; I don't trust anyone any longer; no one wishes me well," said a patient. He is treated in the most insulting way, people ape his voice, call him by nicknames, whistle to him as to a dog, throw snowballs and stones at him. It is a concerted game; all blow the same horn; "Manus manum lavat," said a patient. Now and then the delusion is also supported by pseudo-memories; the doctors had allowed she was quite right in her ideas, declared a female patient.

The kind and the range of the continual chicanery are very multifarious. The lodgers give false names, do not pay, put beer-bottles before the door, throw them on to the street in order that people may think that the patient is a drinker. Letters directed to him are opened and read, purloined; a female patient received at the instigation of her opponent a forged denial from the district court. Consignments for customers are spoiled and rendered dirty, so that complaints constantly come in. The chimney of the stove is stopped up, boots are damaged, suits and under-clothing are ruined. In lawsuits hostile machinations are instigated, so that they will be lost; the lawyers are bribed; financial intrigues, swindling and fraud are going on; the tenant is being incited to pay no rent any more. Calumnies are scattered abroad about the patient as if he had brought on himself a nervous disease by debauchery, as if he were syphilitic, or addicted to pederasty. His photograph has been sent to brothels in order to represent him as an habitué there. Forged bills were made public as if he daily took a senseless amount of alcohol. By such means he is driven from his situations, he is ruined, he loses his inheritance, and, finally, people plan to seduce him to sexual outrages, to onanism, to make him go mad, or even to make away with him altogether. The physicians are bribed, give doubtful medicines; there is poison in the beer; the taste of the food is extremely suspicious and causes colic, dizziness and noises in the ears. "I know very well what that is," declared a patient. His neighbour at table fell ill, after he had by accident drunk from the glass destined for the patient.

Thus the circle of persecutors is gradually extended further and further. If the patient changes his place of residence, he has peace at first perhaps for some time, but he very soon notices that people meet him as a personage who has already been announced, and they have complete information about him and the whole of his previous life. In all sorts of indications secret threads are spun from his former to his present surroundings. People spy after him everywhere ; some individuals whom, in spite of supposed disguise, false beards, dyed hair, he recognizes everywhere again, follow his every step, so that his position is often " worse than that of a man pursued by a warrant of arrest " ; it is a " boycott and a vehmgericht."

In connection with observations of this kind the patient usually has extremely remarkable ideas about the originators and the extent of the persecutions directed against him. A definite person is sometimes regarded as the real driving force, a faithless lover, a former fiancée, a sister-in-law, a colleague, the mayor. Or the freemasons, the social democrats, some or other secret society is behind it all. Of course, they have at their disposal enormous means and resources, everywhere they have aiders and abettors ; not only all possible private persons, but also officials, courts, police, clergymen, physicians, journalists, authors, have a share in the general conspiracy.

The following extracts from a letter written by a female patient afford a glimpse into this circle of ideas :—

" During the fourteen years that I have lived here, I have led the life of a martyr which mocks at all comparison. It concerns the embezzlement of inherited money, and on account of this all imaginable evil and cunning was exercised, that I might be passed off as insane and so on, or that I should be made so, and that the necessary means of living, credit and honour should be taken from me. This inexcusable behaviour by day and by night is carried on by the secret police and their aiders and abettors, female and male, young or old, poor or rich—all must assist ; since it is for the police ! The hounding was ordered in all houses and districts of the town and no regard was had for an old widow full of years. Since I came to Munich, all my letters have been kept back, opened, and delivered without a stamp. Letters about inheritance were simply suppressed, so that I never could be present at the distribution like the other heirs. Every effort is made that I may not be seen and that I should not come into contact with anyone ; indeed it is horrible and incredible that such abominable occurrences can happen, carried out by certain lawyers, who have embezzled my money ; of course they have also a certain police jurisdiction at hand, which facilitates for them their infernal ongoings in order that 'it should not come to light ; besides they are rich, with which one can close the mouth of many a crime . . . When I arrived in Munich I found my house in the greatest disorder, although, before I left home, I left everything punctiliously in order. The furniture was covered with a layer of

.dirt and dust, the bed-clothes were thrown about anyhow, every drawer and cupboard was opened, although I had carefully locked up everything, closed the box of keys and taken it with me ; in the kitchen the pretty mirror was in fragments. It went so far that I was forced to hesitate about eating anything, for after these rascally tricks people are capable of anything, whatever can be conceived horrible and mean . . .''

Along with the delusions of persecution other delusions of all kinds, which come less into the foreground, invariably appear. We frequently find *hypochondriacal* fears. The patient notices that his memory is giving way, he is afraid of softening of the brain ; he complains of pains in his head and back, oppression in his chest, cramp in his stomach, spitting of blood ; his health is seriously injured, his whole body is done for. Now and then *ideas of jealousy* are present. But on the other hand an *exalted self-consciousness* frequently exists. The patient is very religious, cleverer than all other people, understands everything better, gets through " literally the double " amount of work, wanted to be something really great, to be respected, honoured, to take a higher position. A female patient had the conviction that " money must be hanging somewhere." Others assert that they must demand large sums as compensation, as inheritance, from the father of their illegitimate child.

Mood is for the most part excited, irritated, and embittered. " For me the sun has not shone and will never shine," declared a patient, " life is abominable ; for me it remains empty of love. Men are wicked ; already in the child there is malice and guile, scorn and derision ! Why do people continually speak about me and spit in front of me ? People cannot look at me and will not look at me— that is how it is."

The patient, of course, tries in every way to withdraw himself from the persecutions, changes his place of residence and situation, brings actions for damages, provides himself with weapons and dogs for his protection. He addresses querulant petitions to the authorities, the ministers, to Grand Duke and Kaiser, in which he generally makes use of very violent language, speaks of " beastly government and a brigand state," demands the removal and punishment of his opponents and makes claims for compensation. Further, he tries to stigmatize the infamous game of his enemies publicly by means of the newspapers or by broadsheets and to defend himself against the concealed charges. He also, perhaps, sets about doing something conspicuous in order to direct general attention to his endangered position, causes a street riot, throws a petition among the assembled representatives in parliament, or tries to force his way to the reigning Prince. Some patients make suicidal attempts; others publicly ask their supposed antagonists to explain, abuse them, threaten them with violence, so that the interference of the police becomes necessary. In certain circumstances, as the morbid foundation of his procedure is not always easily recognizable, measures follow next, which still further embitter the patient. "At first a fellow like that plagues a diligent and capable man for years, and if this latter, reduced to extremity and without prospect of help, takes to self-defence, then—punishment, severe punishment!" wrote a patient.

As the patients, apart from the activities mentioned proceeding from their delusions, always behave in an orderly way and do not usually commit really serious acts of violence, they do not, as a rule, lose their freedom more than temporarily. In their behaviour they are sometimes passionate, vivacious, talkative, clever, sometimes reserved, morose, repellent. They hold firmly and resolutely to their delusions, although at times they do not speak about them at all. "He wished to remain the evil conscience of his opponent," declared a patient. Only after the morbid phenomena have lasted for decades, does the internal tension perhaps yield and with it the vividness of the delusions, without, however, a rectification of the paranoiac view of life taking place.

Delusions of Jealousy[1].—This is in many respects related to the form just described. The patient is very gradually seized by the suspicion that his wife is deceiving him and he now notices all kinds of things which strengthen him always more in the idea. His wife appears to him colder; she rejects advances, she quarrels and scolds; she goes out whenever she likes to the restaurant and to the theatre, visits a relative or a neighbour extremely often even at an unusual hour and remains an excessively long time. When she returns home, she is embarrassed, makes all sorts of evasive excuses. People make allusions, speak in a mysterious way, so that his suspicions cannot but be aroused; there are "spiritual proofs." "There are many things which taken together make a complete chain of proof," declared a patient. Another, who thought that his brother was his rival in love, got pains on cohabitation,

---

[1] Jaspers, Zeitschr. f. d. ges. Neurol. u. Psychiatrie, i., 567.

when his brother was infected; "I can explain the whole train of thought to myself," he said.

A considerable rôle is often played here by *pseudo-memories*. The patient reports serious charges made by his wife and confessions which she has made to him. He remembers that all sorts of suspicious men came to the house, who under various pretexts asked for his wife and had nothing to say when they only found him. Occasionally afterwards it becomes clear to him that these were the very people whom he was now suspecting, that they, therefore, had obviously had relations with his wife for a long time already. A patient narrated with all detail how his wife had repeatedly shut herself up with her lover in the water-closet. He then wanted to search out the latter quickly and he threatened to force open the locked door; on this the lover then slipped out quickly making no noise, an occurrence which happened again in exactly the same way a few weeks later. Once also he saw through the sitting-room door how his brother-in-law used his wife from behind. Another patient, described by Jaspers and observed also by myself, noticed how at night a cloth was laid over his face and his wife in bed beside him accomplished cohabitation with his rival, how both whispered together and how the lover then left the house. The too exact description of what went on, in the first case the similar repetition also, lastly, the alleged purely expectant behaviour of the patients in such circumstances make the existence of pseudo-memories indubitable.

In connection with his delusional experiences the patient brings forward the most serious accusations against his wife. She has always led him by the nose, she keeps a whole lot of lovers for herself, she has intercourse indiscriminately with hawkers and lodgers. A patient asserted that his brother continually carried on incest with his mother and adultery with his wife. Another accused his wife of having intercourse with her sons; a female patient stated that her husband had let himself go with their little daughter since her earliest childhood. The patient does not acknowledge his children any longer because they are not his, they do not resemble him; he notices in them unmistakable features of his rivals. They are bastards for whom he refuses all responsibility.

Often he brings forward still other reproaches against his wife. She is rude, extravagant, wants to get rid of him, to put him into jail or the madhouse, to kill him ; her lover is helping her. A patient declared that his wife was " mentally below par, depraved in morals, and of common, base, bold, and stupid origin " ; she was good for nothing either on land or water. Many patients give utterance to all kinds of ideas of persecution. They are pursued by the parish authorities, watched by secret police agents ; everything is found out by spies, letters are opened, details of their life are told everywhere ; the doctor is in the conspiracy with the wife. The patient mentioned above, described by Jaspers, constantly asserted after a medical examination that he had been officially declared insane, and in spite of being told over and over again and in the kindliest way that there was no foundation for his idea, he carried on for many years an embittered struggle to obtain the annulment of this supposed " declaration of insanity ".

At the same time a greatly *exalted self-consciousness* frequently exists. The patient boasts of his " sense of duty and unwearied diligence," he is a respectable citizen, he only wants what is right, he helps everyone if he can, and if it is right. " I always endeavoured to raise my standpoint," declared a patient. The patient of Jaspers, who was a very skilful watchmaker and had constructed a large and very elaborate clock, spoke of the ingratitude with which the Fatherland rewards its great sons. Others again make the impression of good-natured, weak-willed personages. Understanding for the morbidity of the ideas of jealousy is entirely absent, though a patient did say to me that he had always had a feeling of terror lest his delusion might really be true. According to this it seemed that a period of doubt had preceded in the patient who was wholly without insight ; he even bored holes in the door in order to obtain certainty by watching his wife.

Invariably great *irritation* at the husband or wife supposed to be guilty develops in connection with the delusions. It comes to violent reproaches and disputes. The patient abuses his wife, tries to wring a confession from her, threatens and ill-uses her. A patient carried about a revolver with him and put it under his pillow at night, because he had to shoot his wife or stab her. Another spoke of ripping up his wife's belly. He did say afterwards that that was " only a mouth expression." " That is a thing that one does not do ; one says it only that the jaw may have work." Nevertheless he became later very violent towards his wife. Even the children are abused and beaten. A female patient threatened girls in whose company she had seen her husband. Another brought a complaint against her husband of alleged incest. A male patient brought an action against his supposed rival. Another prosecuted three of his colleagues simultaneously for adultery with his wife. Generally it comes to divorce or at least to separation, and then the patients usually quiet down by degrees without, however, the delusion being rectified.

Hypochondriacal Delusions.—A hypochondriacal form is frequently described as another kind of paranoiac delusion with depressive colouring. It is certain that hypochondriacal delusions are frequently expressed by paranoiacs. Nevertheless I have not found it possible in careful sifting of my experiences to find an indubitable case of paranoia characterized only, or at least predominantly, by this kind of delusion. I think, therefore, that I should meantime abstain from the delimitation of a hypochondriacal paranoia.

Delusions of Grandeur, Inventors.—In the various clinical forms of paranoiac delusion of grandeur the principal trends of human endeavour come to expression. The delusional inventors form a first group. The patients do not feel satisfied with their ordinary vocational activity, and occupy themselves along with that with all kinds of far-reaching, high-flying plans which gradually become the real substance of their lives. The idea at one blow to become world-famous and to acquire measureless riches by inventions which cause sensations, hovers before them. Without rudimentary knowledge, with wholly inadequate resources, they set about realizing the ideas which occur to them. They sketch out drawings, build models, search for people who will give money, and they exert themselves about patents. Sometimes it concerns plans for definite practical machines or useful objects, for railway points, a boot sole with a joint, an electrical regulator of beer-pressure, a condenser for a refrigerator, a valve for hot air apparatus, a motor plough, an aluminium coffin. In certain circumstances it may even happen that a usable idea is the foundation ôf such inventions, but the patients wholly lack the capacity to bring it into a useful form, as they are not at all familiar either with the technical, or with the business preliminary conditions. In their unprofessional ignorance of the real circumstances they even frequently occupy themselves with problems, which long ago have been satisfactorily solved by others.

It is just this naive ignorance which causes them very commonly to turn straightway to the most difficult, indeed to wholly insoluble tasks. Specially liked are the following, aeronautics, the utilization of the sun's heat and of natural electricity, but especially perpetual motion, a "cheap machine for the utilization of power without any supply of power." With untiring ardour in spite of all dissuasions and derision, drawings ever more extraordinary are made, with which the patient expects to come nearer to his goal. For years he works at an impracticable model, fitting in or replacing here a cog-wheel, there a weight or a stay, so that the most remarkable monsters of wood, wire, lumps of lead, gas-pipes, old bits of brass, arise, to the completion of which the patient sacrifices every free hour and every penny which he has saved.

The peculiarity common to all these inventors is the unshakable faith in their star, in their great and unique endowment, and their brilliant future. He arrived at his inventions, of which he was still planning many, by his innate talents, declared a patient. As one cannot sing without a voice, neither can one invent anything, if one has no organ for it. Another, a very poorly endowed patient, compared himself with a well-known inventor, who had the same name as his mother; he visited in devout mood the great man's grave, and developed the firm conviction that he had left him an inheritance. The importance and especially also the economical value of their own inventions are immeasurably overestimated; in the opinion of the patients it invariably mounts up to at least millions. They, therefore, are for the most part very secretive and fear that their ideas, their intellectual treasure, may be stolen from them. They consider that their task is completely accomplished when they have brought forward some idea or other and perhaps made a few clumsy drawings to illustrate it; there is no question of any real working-out of their plans with accurate entering into detail. They are always extremely satisfied with their models, innocently overlook all difficulties and mistakes, and in spite of the most obvious failures, ever again confidently declare that only a quite unimportant improvement is still necessary in order to reach the desired goal in a short time.

In other domains also this *over-estimation of self* is often

seen. The patients make great plans for marriage, worry
with their proposals ladies who are unknown to them or
who absolutely refuse them, and are extremely astonished
that they are not accepted with open arms. A patient
said, " A Rockefeller would perhaps have said to me, ' Well,
my friend, all honour to you ! Here you have my daughter ;
I am your helper.' " They raise unfounded claims to
money, demand support from the state for their efforts,
expect confidently to be employed in prominent posts, as
they feel themselves equal to the highest demands. Pseudo-
memories may also be coloured by their exalted ideas ; a
patient related that the minister had assured him that
money was lying ready for the working out of his inventions.
In their conduct the patients often display a certain dignified
reserve ; one patient let his hair grow long like an artist.

Naturally the actual results do not at all correspond to
the high-strung hopes. First of all the efforts to make a
practical use of the inventions supposed to be so brilliant,
to sell them, to obtain patents, fail. Perhaps the patient
has luck once and succeeds with some trifle, but the hoped-
for millions do not come in. The blame for this, in his
opinion, lies not only with his lack of means, which does
not allow him to take the realization of his plans into his
own hands, but also with the lack of sense of people who
do not know how to value his importance.

But often hostile machinations are what rob him of the
well-deserved fruits of his labour. He is hoaxed ; price-
lists of wine are sent to him in mockery of his poverty ;
people work against him everywhere, hinder him from
getting on, steal his inventions and make use of them. A
patient, to whom the idea, in his opinion quite new, had
suddenly come to construct a motor plough, and who shortly
afterwards found one advertised in the newspapers, at once
clearly saw that his childish drawings had been stolen from
him and with all haste made use of ; he always, therefore,
called himself the " plundered inventor." He said that by
his desperate poverty he was now a " laughing-stock,"
plundered, deceived, perhaps in the eyes of the whole world
ridiculous and despised as well. As aider and abettor in
the theft he suspected a young girl who had rejected his
proposals of marriage. Another patient wrote threatening
letters to a government official whom he considered
responsible for his not receiving a considerable sum of money
from public funds which he had asked for.

As a rule, the patients lead a quiet, depressed existence but lighted up by the unconquerable hope of ultimate success. They are not permanently discouraged by any failure and they continue to work unswervingly at their plans. Since for the most part they still earn their living in some other way, they give no occasion for difficulties, unless once in a while they are driven to unusual steps by the struggle against their opponents or the attempt to procure more means for themselves.

Delusions of Grandeur, High Descent.—A further form of paranoia is dominated by the delusion of high descent, which proceeds from the wish for power and riches. The French speak of " genealogen," " interprétateurs filiaux." [1] After perhaps long years of racking their brains and dreaming, the certain conviction arises in the patient that he is not the real child of his parents, but is of much higher and more glorious descent. An affair of no importance often provides the external occasion for the origin of this delusional idea, which for him immediately attains to indubitable certainty. In a dispute his father makes use of a violent expression which he would never employ towards his own child. The patient notices that his parents whisper in the adjoining room, turn pale on his entrance, greet him with peculiar seriousness ; in his presence the name of a highly-placed personage is mentioned " significantly ". On the street, in the theatre, some or other aristocratic lady looks at him in an unusually friendly way. While he is contemplating the picture of a count or a prince or the bust of Napoleon, a surprising resemblance with himself suddenly occurs to him, or finally a letter falls into his hands, between the lines of which he easily reads the significant information. A patient spoke of mysterious revelations which he dared not communicate to anyone.

With peculiar satisfaction the patient recognizes that also by the people in his more immediate and more distant surroundings the superiority of his person and of his position is more or less openly acknowledged. Wherever he goes, he is treated with unmistakable respect ; strangers take off their hats to him with profound politeness ; the royal family try to meet him as often as possible ; the band on the parade or in the theatre begins to play as soon as he appears. In the newspapers which are laid before him by the waiter, in the books which the bookseller sends

[1] Sérieux et Capgras, L'encéphale, i. 113, 1910.

to him, he finds more or less figurative allusions to his fortunes ; the passers-by on the street accompany him with approving remarks full of meaning.

This delusion also is frequently accompanied by *pseudo-memories*. In especial a number of alleged experiences of childhood betray this origin. The patient remembers how as a small child he was taken out of a beautiful castle from his real parents, dragged about in the world, and finally given a home with his alleged parents. He is still able perhaps to describe the magnificent furniture and decoration of the rooms, the beautiful park, in which he spent his childhood. Many utterances and actions of his foster-parents, the cut and colour of his clothes, the treatment which he received at school, prophetic dreams, all events great and small of his life have from his earliest youth up pointed to his descent, to his future high calling. From different sides straightforward communications were made to him about his origin and his descent ; agents were commissioned to offer him considerable sums of money to come to terms, but he did not accept these.

In the further course the patient then gradually attempts to make his supposed rights known. He confides in an intimate friend, applies to the authorities, writes letters to his highly-placed parents. For the most part he has the feeling that he will scarcely find full recognition, and so he endeavours to get at least the greatest possible sum that can be agreed on. He considers himself justified in making special claims for his position, sets a value on his appearance, and at the same time has usually little inclination to lower himself by regular work. Thus he finds himself obliged to procure money on the strength of the recognition of his important claims of which there is a certain prospect. As he acts with great confidence, exerts himself to suit his behaviour to his aristocratic descent and really takes steps to further the matter, he often succeeds in finding credulous people who help him in expectation of great profit later.

He certainly meets with great opposition. Aristocratic relatives try in their own interest to prevent the recognition of his claims ; his life is attempted ; people try in every way to render him harmless. Even the removal to a mental hospital, which then follows when the patient has become inconvenient by his always more urgent steps to make good his claims or by the exploitation of his followers, is considered by him as a specially cunning trick of his opponents, who have already for long indicated to him that he must end in insanity. At first he submits, as he is sure that his mental soundness will soon be recognized. In all his utterances he is very reserved, evades searching questions, and conceals his delusional ideas under blameless behaviour, till a special occasion, an emotional excitement, draws them out.

Gradually it becomes clear to him that the physicians are hired for the purpose of rendering him harmless and, if possible, mentally ill, as he could not be got at in any other way. Small unpleasantnesses and annoyances, changes in arrangements, occasional remarks, show him that the opposition and intimidation are set in motion by the people in the new surroundings also. His fellow-patients are not ill at all but bribed malingerers or police spies who by their conduct and nonsensical ongoings are to " prove " him.

Or the patient recognizes that the stay in the institution only represents a necessary link in the chain of the tests which he has to go through in order ultimately to reach his high aim. Indeed, on more careful reflection it becomes clear to him that already in his past life many indications of this purgatory in the madhouse were present. Far removed, therefore, from dejection and despair he draws fresh hope of the attainment even of his last and highest aims from the exact fulfilment of all that fate had previously destined for him. This view of his not infrequently finds special confirmation in the observation which he forthwith makes that also in the institution the mysterious indications of his brilliant future do not fail. He is treated with special attention ; attar of roses is poured into his bathwater ; he is flattered in figurative language ; newspapers and books find their way into his hands, whose contents concern him. It cannot, therefore, escape him that the physicians detain him " on higher command," and do not at all think of considering him really ill. Among his fellow-patients he discovers very highly - placed personages who have been placed in the institution under false names as companions for him.

Sometimes the patients carry on prolonged and extra-ordinary struggles for their liberation and recognition. Others resign themselves to their fate with dignity in the certain expectation that their time will come some day. Sérieux and Capgras have brought forward a whole series of historical claimants to thrones, of whom many have, perhaps, been patients of the kind here described.

Delusions of Grandeur, Prophets and Saints.— The delusion of another group of paranoiacs, the prophets and saints, of the " mystics," as they are, indeed, usually called, goes out in the direction of the relations to the transcendental world. A patient described the first beginning of the malady as follows :—

" When I was abroad from 1866 to 1873, I gradually gave up all religious ideas. I was led to this by my travels in connection with my work as carpenter or draughtsman in countries and among peoples of different religions. So in this connection I thought at last that my conscience told me what a man has to do and to leave undone, and if I act accordingly, I do not need to be afraid even of death. But unfortunately in spite of that, I felt an indescribable unrest in myself day and night which always got worse. From this God by his grace at last set me free by means of a letter from my mother to Vienna in the spring of '73, so that afterwards I had rest and peace in myself, and on this account in gratitude for this I at the same time also vowed to God the Lord to live and die for his holy word. For this reason I returned to Saxony, and I caused a disturbance in Leipzig in August '73 by some placards which I was going to post up during the night, but I was hindered by the police, so that I was put in prison for some days . . . On these placards I had given expression to my faith, that I believe that God, who speaks to us in the Bible is our only Lord, which I am obliged to believe unconditionally by reason of holy baptism and the triune God, and at the same time I expressed myself in a contemptuous and insulting manner about Kaiser Wilhelm . . . Till Whitsunday '75 I worked at my calling again practically and theoretically. But my relations to my parents became at last so strained that I completely disowned them on the ground of my belief in God's word, and I even gave up the filial relation to them and spoke to them as Mr and Mrs F. . . ."

The patients frequently occupy themselves with subtle religious speculations of all kinds, theosophy, spiritism, sectarianism. Visionary or ecstatic experiences then usually acquire a decisive significance. The patient sees in the night divine manifestations, and experiences at the same time an indescribable blissfulness ; he hears the voice of God, receives orders from him ; he sees the devil as well. Christ appears ; at the same time a voice rings out, " Feed my sheep ! " Gods calls out to him, " You are the only one ! " A female patient perceived St Magdalene who announced to her, " You were not born a beggar ; you are chosen for something higher." " With this dream the spiritual experiences began," she declared.

Now and then similar experiences take place during the day. A patient beheld God at the moment when he prayed, " Deliver us from evil " ; it went through and through him like a higher, invisible power, as if air were breathed into him, as if fire passed through his flesh and bones, as if the soul were leaving the body. Another suddenly heard a voice from above, " You must go forth ! " and after that he felt himself guided by a higher power ; on another occasion when the clock struck three he felt the Trinity in his breast which announced to him, " You are the salt of the earth." He also once saw the sun rising like an egg, and noticed that a gloriole surrounded him. A female patient felt how she hovered above the ground in church. It is certainly necessary in all stories of that kind to reckon with the possibility of *pseudo-memories*. Invariably such experiences, which are usually very exactly described and referred to a definite day, remain isolated, although now and then they are repeated in a similar manner.

Generally an extremely *personal, self-confident* working-up of the experiences of life develops. The patient always sees better into the truth, " sees all connections in his head," does not require to read any newspapers in order to know what is going on in the world. When he has visitors he feels immediately whether they have the right faith ; he receives signs if people are pleased with him. He makes " continuous observations," notices that his views are carried further, his conversations are made use of. If he has said anything beautiful, a beautiful man with a lilac-coloured tie meets him, otherwise an ugly man with an unpleasant colour. A patient attributed secret significance to the appearance of the dogs which he met on the street, " Black dog with a red ribbon round its neck—reactionary who decorates himself with progressive feathers ; white dog with blue bow—mawkish way of acting which points to narrow-mindedness ; white dog with red ribbon—sickly sweet behaviour with radical utterances."

The conviction apparently sometimes flashing out like lightning, that he is a chosen one of God, becomes now more and more fixed in the patient. He feels that he is a prophet, " Elias redivivus," Redeemer, the Son of God, the heavenly giver of the marriage feast who is to fulfil the parable of the repeated invitation to the marriage feast, to fight the great fight with Anti-Christ and to bring in the millenium. He is the only one who has known God, " knowing all, he alone only knowing," the highest judicial authority in ecclesiastical and secular things, sent out from the Father, called to redeem all mankind ; he must warn the law-givers, he waits for what God purposes for him. A patient declared that the heavenly Father sent a man every two hundred years who should make known to the Jewish people (1) their fall, (2) the true faith. Another perceived that his brothers had got up a comprehensive organisation " with authoritative head, central personage, compensating middle point," and he added, " I suffer from the megalomania that I should be this centre ; that is my disease." He described the origin of this delusion in the following terms :—

" That my brothers got up the organisation, I can only with difficulty decide, for I believe that is more a matter of feeling in me. But I will try to explain how I arrive at this view. Although I cannot prove it I have in myself the firm belief, that it is actually so. A very trifling incident was the occasion. On the performance of some duty in the shop a workman let fall the expression. That is one of the A. W.'s (initials of all the three brothers). This saying of the workman confirmed in me what I had long supposed."

It becomes clear to the patient that mankind is in terrible confusion. Men do not look up to God ; what astronomers and law-givers say, is untrue. The pope is antichrist ; the resurrection of the dead and the last judgment are at hand. Jesus was the serpent in the wilderness, a magician, a lazy fellow, a thief, a murderer, a liar and deceiver ; Paul, Peter, and James were false prophets. The Kaiser is Saturn or Satan, whose son is the serpent that tempted Eve. The reigning sovereign is well-disposed towards Satan.

Occasionally " genealogical delusions " also emerge. A patient said that his true spiritual father was Kaiser Franz Joseph ; his alleged father had appeared to him before in a dream, and slid about before him on bloody knees, and had asked him for pardon, because he had not known what his son really was. Other patients have made important inventions. Now and then ideas of persecution appear ; the clergy wish to oppress the patient, the Kaiser causes him the greatest torments ; in the bread there might be something wrong.

Pseudo-memories frequently appear to acquire great significance here again. The patient tells how everyone was astonished at his beauty when he was born ; a neighbour said, " That will yet be a Redeemer." Later some one said, " A Messiah must come." A patient at the age of four saw heaven opened. A female patient at the age of five had a dream which was fulfilled, which then occurred to her later. When her stepmother was going to punish her, she dreamed it each time beforehand, and the same thing happened when her sweetheart embezzled 15,000 marks.

Many patients ascribe to themselves the gift of prophecy.

A patient asserted that he had foretold an earthquake ; another prophesied, as it was said, conflagrations, the recent wars, the cholera, the death of her sister, her removal to the hospital. She saw a woman in Italy, who was believed to be ill, standing before her house quite well and combing her hair. In consequence of this she had a great number of believers, and she asserted that there would be a religious war, after which King Otto would become Head of the Holy Roman Empire. Other confabulations are also brought forward. A patient had met the apostle Paul in the inn at his home, as an inward voice disclosed to him. Another was cheated of threepence at a card game by Judas ; a third stated that this was not the first time he had been in the world.

A few patients apparently possess the power to put themselves into *ecstatic states*. A patient said that the theosophic discipline could develop in human beings organs of sense and states of higher consciousness, of which the ordinary average European knew nothing ; in this way he perceived facts and phenomena in nature, which he had not noticed before. A female patient made journeys at night which she distinguished from her dreams. According to her description she was then in her astral body ; she did not need to drag her ordinary body with her ; she was accompanied by an angel and a female saint. On her return " her spirit oozed into her body like oil in blotting-paper " ; at the same time a hollow voice announced to her the goal of her next journey (the underworld). As the patient once slept for six months on end with short daily intervals, it was probably a case of hysterical phenomena.

After a considerable period of preparation the patients set about fulfilling their supposed *mission*. They try to recruit followers by conferences, circular letters, sermons. Generally they succeed in this. Their confident behaviour, their firm convictions and knowledge of the Bible do not usually fail of effect. Besides there is also the fact, as a patient said, " In matters of faith no one can refute another " ; " In matters of faith and conscience God himself can be the only judge," declared another. The neighbours next assemble out of curiosity in the patient's house, and are astonished at his alleged power of prophesying, his addresses richly garnished with verses from the Bible ; they give him presents, hold prayer meetings with him and hope for special grace from him.

The " heavenly giver of the marriage feast," already mentioned above, a master shoemaker, had a small congregation of seventeen people gathered round him, who for the most part received his prophecies of the approach of the millenium after the great and decisive battle with Antichrist very literally. Statutes of nobility were found in his house and divisions into ranks and classes, as also regulations for the most varied court servants (huntsman, chamber-lackey, keeper of the wardrobe, master of ceremonies, officer in immediate attendance for private affairs) " of his Allholy Royal Majesty of the King of the eternal Jerusalem of the kingdom of God on earth, of the King over all peoples of the earth ruled by the sceptre of his Father the Creator of the world, originated by the sign servant King David." This was worked out with extreme neatness and in great detail by one of his followers. The following short extracts may give an idea of those remarkable documents :—

" The officials of the immediate surroundings of the King are :—1. the General of the throne ; 2. the General Lord Chamberlain ; 3. the General Comptroller of the Household ; 4. the Officers in immediate attendance on the King ; 5. the General Adjutant,. Aide-de-Camp, and the other Adjutants ; 6. the General Master of Ceremonies with the other Masters of Ceremonies ; 7. the Quartermaster-sergeant of the King ; 8. the Head Body Servant of the King ; 9. the Huntsmen of the King, also the General Officials of the Allholy Royal Lord Chancellor . . . That the Office of an Allholy Royal Lackey 1st Class be established according to the ordinance of the King of the Allholy Royal 2nd Class of Court rank of the Officials of Magnificence of the date of 11th May 1898 at Würzburg for the official with a definitely fixed yearly salary of 16,000 florins (ten and six thousand Gulden), which is to be paid in monthly instalments of 1333 florins. Likewise an allowance for clothes of 960 florins will be allotted to the Chamber-Lackey 1st Class, which also like the yearly income is to be paid in monthly instalments at 80 florins per month . . . The change of dress of the King takes place after each high service and that is in the morning at 4 o'clock, and 6 o'clock and at midday at a quarter past 1 o'clock in the afternoon till half past 3 o'clock, and if an excursion is fixed for the day in question the change of dress takes place 20 minutes before the hour of departure . . . The King's beer goes to the account of the restaurant of the officials of magnificence, for which purpose the beer account book lies in the Chancellor's Office of the Head Body Servant . . . In all the apartments of the Allholy Royalty wax lights will be maintained during the night to the end of the world, which will be the wax lights of the large chandelier and the wall brackets of the halls and rooms . . . If a chamber-lackey has to accompany the King during the promenade, he must walk on the left side of the King, but the chamber-lackey must observe silence, unless the King enters into conversation with him. For as always so also in such walks the King must give the actual audience to his spirit, for which the King must be undisturbed . . . The Huntsman must appear in strictly prescribed service uniform which consists of coat, breeches, service shoes, huntsman's hat, gloves, sword, spurs, and the usual service underwear. For service the high official must have his hair dressed by his hairdresser and must also be shaved every day, if there is a strong growth of hair. A beard may be allowed . . . At 6 o'clock sharp in the morning the General Adjutant and the General Master of Ceremonies with two Masters of Ceremonies receive the King in the cabinet, after which the remaining cortège in active service then must take part. The remaining cortège joins the immediate cortège from the hall of mirrors for attendance on, and further service of the King at the table. Both the Huntsmen when they come to the table must place the chair at the table for the King and place the menu card lying there in front of him, after which then the girding of the King and the serviette service must take place ; in the same way also the huntsmen must serve the King with the newspapers lying on the table, that is the huntsman must ask the King if he wishes a newspaper and which newspaper . . . During the time of service in the table-hall all unsuitable approaches to ladies, which might reveal a kind of love-affair or paving the way to it, are most strictly prohibited, as it would be a gross breach of the etiquette of the Court."

Further on the subject is the " Order of the two heavenly brides," by which a knight of the realm is raised to the highest rank of the nobility with elaborate ceremonial, the four-in-hand with silver trappings which the knight must keep, the ancestral hall, which he must furnish for himself, the service dress which may not be spoiled by rough wear or perspiration, the necessity for the court officials '' to take a bath often," and by means of beard-brushes to clean the moustache from soiling by tobacco. The investiture of all the officials of magnificence takes place " on the day of the elevation of the king over all the peoples of the earth " ; the kingdoms of Judea, Samaria, Galilee, Idumea, and Perea will be incorporated in his seat of government. As garments of the King there are mentioned, " vestments of the service of the absolving power," highpriestly service vestments, official teachers' garments, ornaments of the government, ornaments of church festivals, ornaments of secular festivals, house-garments, which are all accurately described. The number of the court officials runs up to 157, from the first throne-bishop primate, general throne master, throne general, general treasurer, general keeper of the archives, a crowd of directors general (and others of the cabinet upholstery school, hat-making school, cuirass-tailoring school, of the private journals) to the general court marshal, general equerry, general master of ceremonies, physician to the King, barber, hairdresser, chef, general master of fisheries, throne notary, stamp officials, and so on. The naive view of future magnificence which appears in those documents, returns frequently in the formation of sects and in religious foundations. It can easily be understood that paranoiac patients of the kind here described have not infrequently become the founders of large communities.

Further steps which the patient may take, consist in

directing letters to the spiritual and secular authorities and explaining his mission to them or declaring feud. An example of this is given in the following extract :—

> "The hour namely has now come when you catholic clerical brood have played out the game with your mockery of Me and My sacred writings ! Now follows namely the reckoning for your misdeeds ! *i.e.* I now challenge you yourselves along with your antichristian scoundrels on the sacred chair in Rome to come, and meet me again and my scriptures with your well-known mockery and your other base calumnies and therefore this, that according to the Revelation of St John the preparation for the settling of accounts for your misdeeds against me may be made. The preparation for this will namely be made not only by that kind of earthquake and volcanic eruptions, that there will be a general lamentation ! There would also be made the further preparation for this by that kind of disease, famine and misery that catholic christendom would already be wholly extirpated from the earth, as soon as it would even not yet be separated by the earthquakes and volcanic eruptions from you paltry catholic parsons."

Others set about writing a book discussing the most important truths ; perhaps the third Testament, said a patient. The "heavenly giver of the marriage feast" fulfilled the parable by twice sending out the invitation in the form of comprehensive missives about the approaching millenium. The archbishop received a book weighing two and a half hundredweight. As, thereupon, nothing resulted except a complaint of disturbance of religion, the patient declared that he had now fulfilled his task, that he would acquiesce and would let perdition take its course. Another patient appeared on the streets of Munich decorated with silver gauze and with a board hanging from his neck on which was the following announcement :—

> "Hither and no further goes the Word of God. Do penance, for the end of Europe is near. For ten years you have still time to do penance and then in the whole of Europe there will not be a single human being left."

He also was arrested and returned quietly to his own home, as he had now done his duty. Another patient travelled over the world, crossed the ocean twelve times, felt himself impelled to go to the Jews, who keep the law. A female patient travelled with the assistance of her followers to Vienna, in order to exorcise the plague by her penance which she carried out in numerous churches. Many patients feel that they are called to reform the world, to make people happy. A Hebrew patient urged with the greatest obduracy and in ever repeated petitions to representative bodies the keeping holy of the Sabbath day, and the payment of tithes by the Jews, as also the free distribution of bread twice daily. He also desired that the fish in the sea should be fed and ascribed accidents at sea to this sin of omission. In a petition to the association of landlords he urged the hanging up everywhere of boards with rules for health printed on them : " One must never breathe through the mouth—One must never spit on the floor, and not on the street, only into a handerchief." On the road he reminded people that they should not sit down on stones, lest they should catch cold, advised policemen not to expose themselves with their helmets too much to the hot sun, but rather to walk in the shade.

The outward behaviour of the patients is usually in general quite orderly. For the most part they follow a calling, and frequently they appear to the people in their surroundings as specially gifted intellectually. They have usually great facility in speaking, can deliver long, flowery discourses of apparent profundity although very confused, in unctuous pulpit tone. A patient, already mentioned several times, regularly published for his followers a hectographed magazine, " From the School of Light," in which he spread himself at large over the most varied religious questions, but especially over the events at the creation, the discovery of fire, the life of antediluvian people. For his birthday a special number always appeared ; I reproduce the title-page of one of them (Fig. 49). In cases of death in the " congregation " announcements of the death were published, in which the pleasures of eternal life were promised to the departed who had taken an intimate part in all that happened in the sacred cause and had made great sacrifices to God of earthly possessions. His " spiritual God-man-nature " would enjoy these pleasures till the last day and then as a noble servant of God, risen anew in the body, would be sure of the greeting " My Allhighest Royal Majesty, the King's Son." The patients always exhibit great *self-consciousness*, sometimes concealed only by affected modesty. Many even try to express their sacred mission in their external appearance ; they let their hair and beard grow long and they put on a kind of garment such as Christ is represented as wearing.

Delusions of Grandeur, Eroticism.—This has still to be mentioned as a last form of paranoiac megalomania. The patient perceives that a person of the other sex, distinguished really or presumedly by high position, is kindly disposed to him and shows him attention which

FIG. 49.—Paranoiac Title-page.

cannot be misunderstood. Sometimes it is an intercepted glance, a supposed promenade before the window, a chance meeting, which lets this hidden love become certainty to the patient. A female patient noticed that the reigning sovereign bowed with special respect to her in the theatre, and made his children greet her. Kisses were blown to a patient. Others receive information about the affair only in circuitous ways by figurative allusions in their surroundings, advertisements in the newspapers, without perhaps their ever having seen the object of their interest.

Very soon the signs of the secret understanding increase in number. Every chance occurence, clothing, meetings, reading, conversations, acquire for the patient a relation to his imagined adventure. His love is an open secret and an object of universal interest ; it is talked about everywhere, certainly never outspokenly but always only in slight indications, the profound meaning of which he understands very well. *Pseudo-memories* are frequently mixed with these. Of course, this extraordinary love must meantime be kept secret ; therefore, the patient receives all messages in indirect ways, always through the mediation of others, by the newspapers, and in the form of concealed remarks. In the same way he can put himself into communication with the object of his love by the occasional dropping of hints. The flight of pigeons, which represent symbolically himself and his beloved, shows him that he has been understood, that after long struggles he will at last reach his goal. Anyone with whom he comes in contact, appears to him to be the chosen one, who has disguised herself in order to conceal her affection from the world, indeed, a secret prescience enables him at such a moment of recognition to ignore the most palpable dissimilarities, even the difference of sex.

A patient who importuned a rich lady with offers of marriage after having met her twice in a casual way, saw her again later under another name ; she cast glances at him. Then he met her quite changed under still another name as patient in one mental hospital, as nurse in another ; fellow-patients and the clergyman spoke about his affair in hidden words. After he had received a letter to her returned with the notice of her death—written by herself, as he perceived—he enquired after her and found her now married.

This peculiar delusion may for a long time be further

elaborated in the manner described, nourished especially by means of figurative advertisements in the newspapers, without anything wrong appearing in the remaining activities of the patient, who, indeed, tries to keep his affair secret. In the further course *dreamy hallucinations* not infrequently are associated with the delusion, the feeling of a kiss in sleep and similar things. The whole colouring of the love is at the same time visionary and romantic ; the real sexual instinct in the patient is often slightly developed or developed in an unwholesome way (onanism).

Finally, the patient resolves on further steps. He promenades before the window of his adored one, sends a letter to her or manages to have conveyed to her a proposal of marriage in due form. The refusals, which now follow, perhaps offend him profoundly at first, but then appear to him only as a means to put him on trial. In this view he is strengthened by the experience that the former mysterious relations continue. By means of advertisements in newspapers he is invited to a rendezvous ; remarks of passers-by indicate that he should go to his loved one ; he has a feeling as if he had neglected something if he does not do it. A female patient for several decades received news in the feuilleton of the newspapers from her highly-placed beloved, whom she then used to answer by letter. In this way she learned that he had dispatched a marriage contract to her, bought a house for her, and had set aside a yearly income of 30,000 francs for her.

Meantime, things take an unfavourable turn. In the case mentioned the loved one became unfaithful, as a captain's widow had bound him in the fetters of love for fifteen years. The marriage contract was suppressed ; people wished to prevent the marriage. Evil reports were spread abroad. A court lady set about boxing the ears of the patient publicly and so making her impossible ; the cook was incited by a jealous princess to poison her. Morphia was scattered in the beds ; there was poison in the night-light ; gas came up from below. Thus the loved one can become the enemy and the persecutor of the patient, or she will at least break his pride and then marry him. She sends spies everywhere after him, has his affairs secretly examined, prevents him from getting a good post. His name is wrongly written on letters, at the end the " yours most respectfully " is left out ; people jostle him on the street, put out their tongue at him, spit in front of him.

The food causes him stomach trouble and indigestion, evidently in consequence of admixtures injurious to health, so that he must do his own cooking ; on this account he writes threatening letters, and appeals for protection to the police.

As can already be seen from the descriptions given, the varieties of paranoia here kept apart from each other are by no means sharply delimited forms of disease. Rather do the individual forms of the delusion quite commonly combine with each other, but in an irregular way. As a rule, however, no great difficulty will be found in placing individual cases in the various groups, if the main direction of the development of the disease is taken into account. Now and then there are certainly cases whose assignment to one or other form is in some degree arbitrary. Of the individual forms of the delusion those of persecution, jealousy, and religion appear to me to be the most frequent ; but it may be that these morbid states have only more especial need of psychiatric care.

CHAPTER IV.

COURSE AND ISSUE.

THE general course of the malady has been repeatedly indicated in our description. The development always takes place *very gradually*, so that, as a rule, the beginning of the morbid manifestations can scarcely approximately be fixed. One speaks therefore of a period of preparation, in which, as precursors of the actual delusion, premonitions and conjectures emerge which again disappear, are forgotten, or perhaps rectified. Many patients express themselves with great reserve about their ideas even when from their whole conduct one is forced to the conviction that their system is firmly rooted. Such a patient came to ask if his ideas were insanity or reality.

The two opposed directions of the delusional formation may be from the beginning recognizable side by side. The patient perhaps already believes that he is not treated with due affection by his parents and brothers and sisters, but he is often misunderstood; for his peculiarity there is no comprehension. Thus a quiet opposition, gradually increasing, is developed between him and his surroundings. To his family he is as a stranger, as a being from another world; his relation to them is cold, external, unnatural, even hostile. "God is my father and the Church my mother," said a patient, who through frequent fasting wished to mortify his earthly self and so come into an intimate relation with God. The patient therefore withdraws himself from his family, behaves in a brusque, repellent way towards them, seeks solitude in order to be able to commune undisturbed with his thoughts, occupies himself with unsuitable reading which he does not understand. But at the same time a profound longing stirs in him after something great and high, a secret impulse to enterprise, the silent hope for an inconceivable happiness. More and more the conviction is strengthened in him that he was born for something "special." He believes in his "destiny," in his mission which he has to fulfil.

What in the end brings the delusion to definite recognition

appears not infrequently to be something in itself quite insignificant, as in the case described above of the patient who doubted as to the reality of his delusion. There also where the delusional formation is connected with *visions* or *ecstatic states*, one may assume a sudden emergence of the delusion. In other cases the delusional enlightenment begins in the patient, as is alleged, with experiences which are without doubt characteristic *pseudo-memories*.

The further development of the delusion takes place as a rule extremely slowly. In isolated cases, as Jaspers has shown, the delusional experiences may be crowded together in a very short period of time, so that afterwards there essentially follows only the working-up of them by logical conclusions and confabulating decoration. It has been already mentioned that occasionally also *hysterical*, or at least *psychogenic*, changes of consciousness may be interpolated; they have apparently a certain relationship with cases which we find in the delusion of persecution in prisoners and in induced insanity. Mostly, however, the formation of delusions proceeds only very gradually, perhaps indeed with greater or smaller exacerbations; the old circles of thought become wider and richer; new ones are added and they influence perception, interpretation, memory, and power of imagination in their own way.

Issue.—But generally a period of the disease can be distinguished, after which the delusion is in the main closed, and is no longer extended in its fundamental features, although it may be in details. The natural issue of paranoia accordingly is probably, as a rule, a *residual delusion*. The production of fresh delusions gradually abates, sometimes sooner, sometimes later, but the delusional system once built up generally continues unchanged in the main. Small extensions are perhaps still possible, and secondary features may fall into oblivion or even experience certain transformations, especially by pseudo-memories, but the essential delusional content remains the same. In the course of time, however, the strength of the emotional emphasis of the delusion and with that the driving-power for its development usually diminishes slowly. The patient brings, it is true, his delusional ideas to the front in the old way and at the same time also perhaps shows still a certain ardour, but they do not occupy him any longer continuously to the former extent, With that they also lose more and more their influence on his actions. The patient no longer resists the persecutions with the old energy, strives no longer passionately towards his high goal, but he yields to his fate, and tries, as well as he can, to come to terms with circumstances.

A patient sent the following document to me :—

" If I now am silent to all insults, the day will still come, when all that will come to the light of day, what a base game has been played with me. In Munich alone there are thousands who know that I am not insane, that I only must be insane in order to be deprived of my inheritance. But these stubborn gentlemen may wait for long till I take measures against my oppressors. Oh, no, I am not going to do such a thing in my old age and I am quietly waiting for the issue, whatever may come."

A patient, already mentioned above, who considered fasting, prayer, and silence necessary on religious grounds, wrote as follows :—

" As I have been deprived of my legal rights by the authorities and have been declared of unsound mind, it is absolutely justified that I should express myself in writing ; right is on this account absolutely on my side. But as this cannot be well carried out in practical life, I only make use of it in the case when conscientiousness compels me to do it, which namely is justified towards those who know my sad circumstances."

Genuine *weakmindedness* does not seem to be developed even after very long duration of the disease, although often the delusional ideas and what they are founded on, are fairly indistinct and senseless. I had the opportunity of observing a female patient till beyond her ninetieth year, who had fallen ill at the age of forty-three. Except a certain senile forgetfulness no sign of psychic weakness had appeared ; in carriage and behaviour also the patient displayed no disorder of any kind, while she firmly adhered to her old delusions throughout.

Only a cursory reference is required to the fact that the *development* described here of the paranoiac personality merely represents a morbidly distorted picture of the changes in general which human thought and endeavour undergo in the course of a lifetime. The exuberance of youth urging to great deeds and experiences ebbs gradually against the resistance of life, or it is guided into regulated paths by the ripening of volition which is conscious of a definite aim. Disappointments and hindrances lead to embitterment, to passionate struggles, or to resignation which takes refuge in trifling pursuits and consoling plans for the future. But gradually the elasticity disappears ; thought and volition are benumbed in the narrow circle of everyday life, only now and then are they revived by the remembrance of former hopes and defeats.

CHAPTER V.

FREQUENCY AND CAUSES.

THE frequency of paranoia in my experience does not nearly amount to one per cent. of the admissions, the reason of this probably being that the majority of the patients do not require institutional treatment or only require it temporarily. In Treptow Mercklin saw one paranoiac in about two hundred admissions. In order to throw light on these facts I give a survey of the duration of the disease up to the entrance into the institution for the small number of cases in which a fairly certain judgment could be made :—

Duration in Years	3	4	5	6	7	9	10	12	14	17	21	26	41	44
Cases	6	1	1	1	1	2	3	1	1	1	1	1	1	1

It is seen from this that the half of the patients lived undisturbed for more than nine years in freedom, before they came into the hands of the alienist ; not altogether infrequently over twenty years elapse up to that point, now and then over forty years. Even then the residence in the institution, as a rule, only lasted a comparatively short time, as the patients were ready and able to comply with the demands of the life of a community. Only the claimants to thrones and similar patients, who habitually trouble highly-placed individuals and the authorities in a querulant way or exploit other people, suffer a fairly long deprivation of freedom. For these reasons it is very difficult for the individual alienist to collect facts about paranoiac patients to any great extent himself, a circumstance which certainly must be made partially responsible for our defective knowledge of this domain and for the great differences of opinion.

As far as the small series of observations, which are at my disposal allows of a judgment, the male sex appears to have a considerably larger share in paranoia than the female ; almost 70 per cent. of my patients were men. They are specially in the majority, as can easily be understood, among inventors and founders of religions, while in erotic delusions and delusions of persecution women are fairly well represented. The age at the beginning of the disease was in two-thirds of the cases above thirty, relatively most frequent between the thirtieth and fortieth year. In isolated cases the traces of the disease could be followed back to the sixteenth or eighteenth year. On the other hand I have never been able to convince myself of a really "idiopathic" origin of the delusional ideas reaching back into early childhood, as Sander had in view in classifying as a separate form his "idiopathic paranoia." Much rather in such narratives of patients it invariably concerns *pseudo-memories*. The remarkable utterances and experiences narrated with extraordinarily exact detail occur to the patient subsequently, when he examines his whole life minutely like an open book ; before that they had made no impression at all upon him and were quite forgotten. Not infrequently, moreover, the cases idiopathic in this sense, belong to dementia præcox and quickly become demented ; others exhibit the picture of confabulating paraphrenia.

Hereditary Relations and Psychopathic Predisposition.—I scarcely venture to say anything about the hereditary relations of the patients, not only on account of the small number of observed cases, but especially also because the information about the family history in these patients, of whom two-thirds entered the hospital first after the fortieth year, is much too uncertain. A whole series of them had led such a wandering life that one was thrown solely on their own statements, naturally very unreliable. In such circumstances I place no value at all on the fact that in rather more than one quarter of the cases psychic disease was stated to be present in one of the parents. It is perhaps more important that in more than half of the cases personal peculiarities were reported to us, which allowed us to conclude that a *psychopathic predisposition* was present. An irritable, excited, occasionally rough and violent behaviour appeared to be the most frequent. Other patients were distrustful, self-willed, superstitious, or ambitious, aspiring, unsteady, untruthful ; still others were weak of will and poorly endowed. Several patients showed homosexual tendencies ; some had for long suffered from nocturnal enuresis. If accordingly in the meantime there can be no talk of a uniform paranoiac predisposition, so much may yet be said that the patients frequently exhibited from the beginning distinct personal peculiarities, which must have made the fitting into the life of a community essentially more difficult.

External occasions do not play any part at all in the history of origin, or at least only a very subordinate part. Even the unpleasant experiences now and then reported appear to me to be of significance at most for the content, but not for the origin of the delusion ; often they were obviously only the consequence of morbid behaviour. The insidious development of the malady might itself give evidence for the fact that the morbid process is engendered by *internal causes*, and general opinion tends to the assumption that we have before us in paranoia an expression of *degeneration*. If we agree to this view with regard to the peculiarity of the malady and to the frequency of preparatory psychopathic features, then we find the further question in front of us, which was sharply circumscribed especially by Jaspers, whether paranoia is to be conceived as the logical development of an abnormally predisposed personality, or as a process which from a given point of time onwards brings about a morbid transformation in a hitherto healthy individual.

The former view corresponding, perhaps, more to the opinions of the French investigators, has recently been represented among ourselves especially by Mercklin and Gaupp. Mercklin speaks directly of "paranoiac germs," which are said to come later to development in the disease. In support of this opinion the multiplicity of the delusional systems could in the first place be advanced, which in spite of the return of certain fundamental features, yet lends to each individual case its wholly personal stamp. Against it may be objected that even a morbid process, which perhaps only involves certain of the highest psychic capacities, would leave wide room for the play of the influence on the clinical state of the personal peculiarities of the patient. But, further, it is perhaps worthy of notice that the various directions, which the delusions take in paranoia, correspond in general to the *common fears and hopes of the normal human being*. They, therefore, appear in a certain manner as the morbidly transformed expression of the natural emotions of the human heart. Meanwhile we find similar relations also in severe, destructive diseases of the brain, as in paralysis and dementia præcox, a sign that just the content of the delusional ideas is everywhere determined partly by the common requirements of the *emotions*. It would, indeed, be difficult to understand whence otherwise the delusion should take its form.

But one may yet, perhaps, take up the standpoint that the connection of the delusion with personal peculiarity in paranoia is essentially more intimate than in the diseases mentioned. Without at all taking into account the fact that the million-blissfulness of the paralytic, the delusion of telepathic influence of the early dement is repeated much more uniformly, the roots of the delusion in paranoia, which appears later, can not at all infrequently be discovered in definite, preparatory features of character. The strong emotional emphasis of the experiences of life, and what is connected with that, the personal colouring of the relations to the external world in both hostile and friendly sense, appear to me very commonly to come into consideration here. Then also the feeling of personal uncertainty along with distrust plays a part and also the ambitious, passionate striving for recognition, riches, power, with measureless overrating of self. Here we have before us in a certain degree the component parts from which the development of a paranoiac view of life and the world could to some extent be explained. They carry in themselves the preliminary conditions not only for a lasting disproportion between wish and reality, but also for the influence on the whole view of life by this inward dissension. Specht has expressed the opinion that circumstances in life which bring about a conjunction of *high tension of self-consciousness with insufficient outward recognition* favour the development of paranoia; as example he mentions elementary school teachers.

If we now try to approach the question, under what premises in the one case the delusion of persecution, in the other the delusion of grandeur develops from the paranoid disposition, this might perhaps be thought of, that the original temperament, the tendency to a rosier or gloomier colouring of the experiences of life, guides the delusion formation sometimes in the one, sometimes in the other direction. If the previous history of our patients is examined minutely, a certain justification for this assumption cannot be withheld; an embittered, rancorous view of life appears indeed often to prepare for the development of the delusion of persecution, assured self-confidence for that of the delusion of grandeur.

Against such a simple assumption meanwhile the experience to some extent tells, that we find with extreme frequency both trends of delusion present *at the same time.* The attempt has usually been made to explain this con- junction by a kind of more or less clearly conscious deliberation. The patient fulfilled with ideas of grandeur is said to be forced to the assumption of hostile machinations by the resistance which he comes up against in the realization of his plans. On the other hand it may be objected that from those points of view a development of that kind might be expected invariably also in other diseases with delusions, which only happens to a rather limited extent. In any case the assumption may be defended that the struggles and difficulties in which the patient becomes involved partly by his delusions, partly on other grounds, are of considerable significance for the development of the delusion of persecution. Without taking the fact into account that in the prison psychoses we can follow with experimental directness the development of the ideas of persecution under the pressure of adverse fortune, we can also observe not infrequently that ideas of injury are added to the delusion of grandeur when the patients fall into difficult positions in life and come into collision with serious resistance.

But one may perhaps go still further and assume that in certain circumstances their insufficiency for the struggle with life arising from defective predisposition must be regarded as the root of their ideas of persecution. A man who is dominated by a secret feeling of uncertainty and sees himself hindered by his weakness in the fulfilment of his life wishes, is only too much inclined to suspect dangers and to lay the blame of his failures on external influences. Not infrequently we find that, when they have the opportunity, paranoiacs try from the outset to withdraw themselves from the serious struggles of life in the conscious- ness of their vulnerability ; they do not take a fixed situation, but wander restlessly about, occupy themselves only with amateur occupations, and avoid contact with life.

If the incomplete equipment for the surmounting of life's difficulties and the opposition to the surroundings which results, were an essential foundation for the delusion of persecution, its incurableness could also be understood. For this disproportion continues to exist and is permanent. While in the prison psychoses the mainsprings of the delusional formation are relaxed by the discharge of the patient to freedom, the feeling òf defencelessness towards the hostile forces of life is renewed here every day. That in spite of this the delusion generally begins only in the third or fourth decade, could be explained by the gradual loss of youthful elasticity which at first compensates for every failure by the awakening of fresh hopes for the future.

It must, however, be understood that in the paranoiac formation of the delusion still a further circumstance must play a part. We come across numerous psychopaths who are not equal to the battle of life and avoid it without developing ideas of persecution. What characterizes the paranoiac is his *resistance*, his passionate struggle against the injuries of life, in which he recognizes hostile influences. Just here it is seen that the delusion forms a component part of the personality. Failures are to the patient not chance events nor are they due to his own fault, but a wrong inflicted on him, against which he opposes himself. This manner of reaction appears to me to point to the fact, that in him even when he is permanently conscious of his inward uncertainty, an *increased self-consciousness* is present at the same time ; it is this which causes his special sensitiveness. If we might assume that, the frequency of exalted ideas along with the delusion of persecution could be in some measure understood.

The paranoiac delusion of grandeur has often been derived from the comprehensible estimation of the enormous sources of power which are at the command of the persecutors ; in this way, it is said, the patient acquires the idea of the very special significance of his own person. That appears to me to be an artificial assumption. We should then observe similar ideas in melancholic patients, but that does not occur unless manic admixtures are present. An egocentric direction of thought cannot be straightway connected with the delusion of grandeur in any case. Against that, besides the spinning of high-flying plans of youth across into riper years, still another source of paranoiac ideas of grandeur can be imagined, which possibly arises not far from the first one.

The struggle with life may favour this direction of thought in two ways. Humiliations may rouse to defiant and exaggerated self-appreciation, which in the strongly emphasized sense of personal value creates a counterbalance to the neglect shown him by the outer world, or else defeats and disappointments lead to submersion in a kindlier world of visions, as we have seen them do in the presenile delusion of pardon. If the delusion of grandeur in youth, full of the joy of hope, is intoxicated by its feeling of power because it does not know the seriousness of life and its resistances, the depressing experiences of life's struggle are here pushed aside because they cannot be conquered. Especially when the weapons fail, which are necessary for the conquest and subjection of the opposing hindrances, tenacity and endurance of volition, self-assertion is forced into one of these paths both of which lead to the delusion of grandeur, it may be by arrogant opposition towards the judgment of others, it may be by escape into hopes for the future which no misfortune is able to destroy.

Perhaps it will be possible some day to follow clinically the various developmental possibilities of the paranoiac delusion of grandeur. When it dominates the morbid state from youth up, we shall be able to think of its origin more from *self-complacent dreaming*. But when it develops in connection with ideas of persecution and first in riper years, it is probably more a *defensive measure against the depressing influences of life*. While the delusion in the former case betrays its history of origin in its romantic colouring, in its fund of pseudo-memories and delusional inventions, it is limited in the latter substantially to a measureless over-estimation of personal capacity. Lastly, likewise in later life, with or without connection with ideas of persecution, especially in weak-willed or otherwise insufficiently equipped natures, a delusion of grandeur may attain to development, which bears features similar to those in the first case, and which is a kind of *psychological compensation for the disappointments of life*. It must be left to the future to investigate whether these forms, in the first place derived from certain premises, can actually be found in experience; probably they will often blend with one another.

The emotional premises described above may well explain the development of delusional ideas, but not their peculiar paranoiac form. In any case by no means everyone who exhibits the peculiarities mentioned becomes paranoiac. There must be other circumstances which make the establishment and the psychic working up of the delusion possible. The surprising failure of criticism towards the emerging delusional ideas has often been pointed out here ; it lets the patient fall a victim to their influence without making any resistance. This lack of judgment has mostly been regarded as an indication of a certain psychic weakness. In reply it must first be remarked that the delusions of the paranoiac according to the explanations just given probably have their root in *emotional tensions*, such as in normal people also usually encroach to a great extent on the capacity of forming objective judgments. As is well known, the firm persistence of political and religious convictions illustrates this ; they are not acquired, as a rule, by personal psychic work, but are inoculated by the emotional influences of education and of example, and in this way " grow round the heart " ; even in regard to such convictions purely intellectual considerations often fail in an otherwise incomprehensible way.

Meanwhile without taking into account the emotional mooring of the paranoiac delusion, certain imperfections in the intellectual functioning in our patients might also essentially contribute to lessen their capacity for resistance to the emergence and interference of delusional ideas. As it appears to me, the delusional formation of the paranoiac exhibits many noteworthy points of agreement with *undeveloped thinking*. In the first place visionary longing for impossible goals not subdued by sober deliberation, ideals as they are apparently often formed by the foundation of the paranoiac delusion of grandeur, are found in similar manner in youth. Later, with the maturing of judgment the experiences of life surely and irresistibly lead to a restriction of hope to the attainable, while in the paranoiac the conviction becomes just then firmly rooted that he is near the fulfilment of his dreams. Even the peculiarly romantic colouring of the paranoiac delusional structure, the picturing of princely and kingly magnificence, the quietly blissful, sweet secret of the erotic delusion, the tendency to day-dreaming and to the transformation of the world according to immature personal wishes remind us strongly of similar creations of the power of imagination in youth. The same holds good for the bungling of the inventors, which we find again in the clumsy but laboured attempts · of our children enthusiastic for the wonders of technique.

Further, it must be pointed out that the egocentric trend of thought, the peopling of the external world with

friendly and with hostile powers, the superstitious interpretation of events, in short the whole foundation of the
delusion of reference represents a common peculiarity of
psychically undeveloped peoples and human beings.
Dromard [1] speaks in this sense of infantile features in the
thinking of the paranoiac. The more remote that thinking
is from the stage of purely sensuous experience, the more
conceptual general ideas are developed, all the more does
the personal colouring of intellectual functioning grow
pale, and all the more does judgment become objective.
But, lastly, it would still need to be emphasized that also
the sprouting up of fully formed convictions inaccessible to
doubt is a process which we find again in the same way at
the lower stages of the development of thinking. Certainty
is the natural, the self-evident thing ; doubt is the bitter
fruit of ripe experience.

We come, therefore, to the conclusion that a number
of peculiarities adhere to paranoiac thinking which we are
justified in regarding as an indication of *developmental
inhibitions*. They may lead to this, that habits of thought,
which otherwise are more and more overcome with the
ripening of the psychic personality, here continue permanently, and with corresponding emotional predisposition
gradually cause that falsification of the views of life which
characterizes our disease. If one will, one might say that
the world of ideas of a savage, who sees himself surrounded
by demons who lie in wait for him everywhere, and perceives
innumerable signs portending disaster or good fortune,
or of a medicine man, who has at his command the magic
powers of the fetish and produces supernatural effects by
his incantations, does not fundamentally differ very much
from paranoiac delusional systems. Only in the former case
it concerns stages of general culture, in the latter purely
personal morbid development.

It has further to be remarked that we must, of course,
not regard the paranoiac simply as a grown-up child. Rather
it might be assumed that in him an unsymmetrical development of the psychic personality had taken place, and so
only certain domains of the psychic life had remained
immature. It would accordingly concern a kind of
distortion of the psychic picture, in which the individual
features developed in various ways mutually influence and
disturb each other. Thus the firm tenacity also of the

[1] Dromard, Journ. de psychologie norm. et pathol., viii. 406.

paranoiac delusional system might be explained, which at first appears to be in contradiction to the susceptibility to influence of the imaginations of youth. The playful day-dreams of the undeveloped personality are built up in a mobile psychic life, and when this matures and becomes established they lose their foundation. But in paranoia the deficiencies of intellectual functioning described continue to exist in a personality already becoming crystallized ; they will, therefore, produce an essentially divergent and a more permanent effect.

Lastly, it must not be forgotten that the struggle for existence in the complicated conditions of civilization, the constant excitement due to the increased difficulties of life, must contribute to the peculiar character of the state which comes into existence under the premises described. If we, therefore, acknowledge that certain peculiarities of the paranoiac delusional formation can be derived from circumscribed developmental inhibitions and on this account exhibit points of agreement with the conduct of immature individuals and peoples, there are yet in other directions wide-spreading differences.

Peculiar disturbances of thought have been indicated by Berze[1] as the starting-point of paranoiac delusion formation. He thinks that in the paranoiacs there is a disorder of apperception which makes the grasping of psychic content in a momentary point of consciousness difficult. From this failure of " active apperception " a feeling of " suffering " is said to be developed which then probably smooths the way for the development of the delusion of persecution. The proof of these statements could scarcely be produced. On the one hand we observe that active apperception becomes difficult or ceases altogether in numerous morbid states, which are never, or only temporarily accompanied by delusion formation (mania, delirium, paralysis, idiocy) ; on the other hand there can be no question at all in paranoia of a general extension of the disorder named ; the systematic development of the delusion here definitely presupposes the firm hold of leading trains of thought and the selective preference for definite impressions and ideas.

Summary.—If we now summarize the discussion, it must approximately be said that *heightened self-consciousness* appears to me to be an essential foundation of paranoia.

[1] Berze, Über das Primärsymptom der Paranoia. 1893.

From it proceed the high-flying plans as well as the increased sensitiveness to the difficulties of the struggle for existence, which are especially great for the psychopath. At the same time by the strong affective emphasis of the experiences of life their personal interpretation and evaluation is favoured. Thus the preliminary conditions are provided for the development of ideas of grandeur and of persecution. But that it comes to delusion formation in the paranoiac sense rests on the *insufficiency of intellectual functioning in consequence of partial developmental inhibitions*, which cause certain primitive habits of thought to continue permanently. Here belongs the tendency to day-dreaming, to an egocentric view of life, and to uncritical yielding to any ideas that occur. In accordance with this view paranoia, as is also from clinical points of view feasible, would be brought into the neighbourhood of *degeneration hysteria*, in which we are likewise concerned with the persistence in isolated psychic domains of stages of development which have been surmounted.

If we have up to now exerted ourselves to explain the points of view from which the development of paranoia from a peculiar predisposition might be made comprehensible, reasons are also not wanting which might argue for the existence of an actual morbid process transforming the personality from a definite point of time. Since tangible external causes, as a rule, are not demonstrable, maladies must be thought of which are developed from *internal* causes. With regard to the indubitable relations of paranoia to degeneration, morbid germs might come into consideration, which were already present in the disposition, but only later develop in an independent manner, as in certain familial diseases of nerves, for example, Huntington's chorea. Of significance for this question is, firstly, the circumstance, that the roots of the paranoiac delusion can by no means always be traced back to a distant past ; the ideas often appear rather abruptly, at least according to the representations of the patients. Here it must certainly be taken into account that invariably the patients only come under our observation many years after the commencement of the malady, and that their statements very commonly are more or less strongly influenced by pseudo-memories.

Further, for the assumption of a morbid process the course in exacerbations which is seen fairly often, might be mentioned, the crowding together of delusion formation in relatively short periods of time with intervals lasting for years. It is evident that this argument would only have significance if the paranoiac development of the personality assumed above were conceived as wholly independent of external influences. But if one acknowledges, as we did, that for the coming into being of the paranoiac delusion the struggle with life is of authoritative significance, a course in exacerbations might very well result from external influences. Unfortunately up to now no adequate investigations of this question are to hand ; they might also come into collision with almost insuperable difficulties. It must, however, be said that in the development of a personality, probably also from internal causes, at any time more rapid transformations and likewise intervals may be interpolated ; the experiences of normal life seem to give evidence for this.

The circumstance is very noteworthy, that the content of the delusional ideas is sometimes extraordinarily far removed from normal thinking. It, therefore, is at first difficult to assume here a simple development from the normal latitude. Some evidence for our judgment may perhaps be got from the prison psychoses, in which we see very similar delusions, which in certain circumstances never again disappear, developing under the pressure of psychic injuries. Accordingly the possibility cannot be denied that a paranoiac delusion in spite of its senselessness may come into being solely through unfavourable emotional influences. Certainly we must here in all circumstances premise a well-marked paranoiac predisposition, since we are not concerned, as among the prisoners, with unusual fortunes in life, but with the effect of the everyday difficulties of the struggle for existence, which only here are felt as specially oppressive.

We come, therefore, to the conclusion, that at present definite evidence for the assumption of a morbid process as the cause of paranoia cannot be found, but that we have to reckon with morbid preliminary conditions in the form of quite definite insufficiencies of the predisposition. In so far points of contact with the view last discussed would be present. Only it would not concern the continued development of morbid germs to independent morbid processes reaching into the psychic life, destroying and distorting, but the natural transformations to which a psychic malformation is subjected under the influence of the stimuli of life.

It would have been impossible for the Freudian doctrines not to have taken possession of the question of paranoia. According to the results of psycho-analysis auto-eroticism, narcism, homo-sexuality, form the starting-point of paranoia. The disease sets up the defensive symptom of distrust towards others in order to overcome the unconsciously reinforced homo-sexuality. The delusional formation is in reality an attempt at cure after the catastrophe. Since these assertions are not supported either by a clearly defined conception of paranoia or by evidence at all acceptable, it might be unnecessary to occupy oneself further with them.

CHAPTER VI.

DELIMITATION.

THE delimitation of paranoia is not less difficult than the search into its character. We have already in the introduction mentioned the changes which the extent of the conception of paranoia has gone through in the course of the last decades. If dementia paranoides, the paraphrenias, and a series of other paranoid diseases are kept apart, as has been done here, there remain still two directions in which there are important questions of delimitation to solve. In one it concerns the decision whether there are *curable forms of paranoia running an abortive course.* Certainly now we shall no longer be able to agree with the view of Westphal, who in his time regarded cases of compulsion insanity as abortive paranoia, but it remains still to investigate whether paranoiac delusion formation must continue permanently in all circumstances. The French have described " bouffées délirantes ", which they are inclined to place in relation to paranoiac diseases, and among ourselves also one speaks of delusion formations in degenerates, for which according to their history of origin a relationship with those of the paranoiacs would probably have to be acknowledged. With reference to the assumption made by Wernicke of an " idea of over-estimation," which may for a longer or shorter time dominate the patient, Friedmann has, as was mentioned above, published observations about " mild delusional forms." Here in immediate connection with external events agitating the emotions (disappointed hopes of marriage), a systematized but circumscribed delusion appeared, namely, the *delusion of respect,* which gradually faded again after two or three years without any exact rectification ; it concerned mostly women thirty or forty years of age. Lastly, Gaupp has mentioned cases of educated men with " depressive-paranoid " predisposition, in whom under the pressure of painful circumstances a distrustful delusion of reference with a certain amount of insight and fluctuating course insidiously developed without leading to rigid systematization.

It is not easy to take up a position in relation to all these experiences. One of the principal difficulties at present is, in my opinion, *diagnostics*. I have, namely, convinced myself that there are cases of *manic-depressive insanity*, which on account of the many delusional ideas which appear and the inconspicuous colouring of the background of mood, may with extreme ease be taken for abortive cases of paranoia. In spite of attention specially directed to this point it has happened to myself till quite recently, that I have regarded such attacks as paranoiac exacerbations. The possibility will, therefore, always have to be reckoned with that one or other case of paranoid disease having a favourable course, although without acquiring full morbid insight, must be interpreted in the sense mentioned. We shall have to come back to this question.

The delusion formations of the *degenerate* are, so far as is known at present, invariably of *psychogenic* origin and are connected with a *definite, tangible occasion*, as far as they at all exhibit a certain similarity with paranoia. In this point they thus differ throughout from the insidious development of paranoiac delusion formation. It appears to me, therefore, suitable to separate them from it. But it will have to be admitted, that there may be transitions here, according to whether a larger or smaller rôle falls to the personal peculiarity on the one hand, to the external obstacles on the other, in the history of origin of the morbid phenomena. Paranoia and psychogenic delusion formation may, perhaps, be regarded as the end-links in a chain in which all possible intervening links are represented.

From this standpoint no objection could on principle be raised against the occurrence of " *mild*," *psychogenic forms of paranoia* resulting in *cure*. It would only have to be assumed that here a " latent " paranoia exists permanently, which not in all circumstances, but only on special occasions leads to delusion formation. Thus it would also be comprehensible that the delusion formation would again come to a standstill, when the occasion was removed or its effects counter-blaanced. Any other event in life might then later in a similar way cause the disease. We should thus be concerned more with the permanent *tendency* to delusion formation, with isolated attacks of delusion, not, as in developed paranoia, with an inexorably progressive delusional transformation of all the views of life in a definite direction.

It cannot be said at present with certainty, whether and how far the views here developed can be brought into agreement with clinical experiences. In any case it appears to me that there are predispositions, which, indeed, carry in themselves the germ of continued development in a paranoiac direction, but only develop it further to a transitory and indistinct delusion formation. Mercklin speaks of personalities which throughout their whole life are on the way to paranoia. Even among the more pronounced cases of paranoia, many are found in which the system of delusions exhibits a less rigid and closed form than it is customary to assume from an academic point of view. Among the psychopaths who resort to our hospital I have come across a certain number of personalities, certainly not very large, whom I might call " paranoid," in as far as they appeared to me to exhibit essential preliminary conditions for the development of paranoia ; some of them even displayed the rudiments of it, yet without an actual delusional system attaining to development. I shall try, as far as the limited experiences at my disposal allow, to give a short description of this group of paranoid personalities.

Paranoid   Personalities. — In the majority of the patients *ideas of persecution* were in the foreground of the clinical picture, probably because they most frequently give occasion for a consultation with the alienist. The most conspicuously common feature was the feeling of uncertainty and of distrust towards the surroundings, which expresses itself in the most varied forms. The patient feels himself on every occasion unjustly treated, the object of hostility, interfered with, oppressed. His own people treat him badly ; his fellow-workmen do not like him ; they teaze him, make remarks about him, look at him derisively as at some one mentally unsound, laugh at him. Everything presses on him ; he has to endure a martyrdom, he complains about his " life crushed and trodden on ". A patient spoke of "pecuniary ill-usage continued for years ", when his guardian in consideration of his small means was not able to satisfy all his excessive financial claims. People want to drive him from his situation ; the foreman aims at him. In indefinite hints he speaks of secret connections, of the agitation of certain people. Things are not as they ought to be ; everywhere he scents interested motives, embezzlement, intrigues ; the wire-pullers of the injuries from which he suffers are known to him, but he will not speak out. One patient could read off the faces of people the evil in them. The physicians whose duty it is to examine him, give a prejudiced opinion ; the authorities show partiality. A patient, who thought that his wife had put the virus of gonorrhœa in the soup, asserted that the police did not wish to have the affair investigated, because he had no money to pay. Another complained that he had been wrongfully declared to be mentally unsound, while the verdict had been pronounced in favour of his mental health. Some patients expressed ideas of jealousy ; one patient noticed that his wife did not concern herself about him ; she showed him by her behaviour to others " that she was perhaps unfaithful to him." He wanted to get rid of her, but when she was gone, he had a great longing for her, and then when she returned, he immediately re-commenced the old reproaches.

Such delusional ideas, which emerge sometimes on one occasion, sometimes on another, are closely accompanied by great *emotional irritability* and a *discontented, dejected mood*. The patient is difficult to get on with, is fault-finding, makes difficulties everywhere, perpetually lives at variance with his fellow-workers, on trivial occasions falls into measure-less excitement, scolds, blusters, and swears. He composes long-winded documents full of complaints, threatens his wife, ill-uses the children, applies for a divorce, speaks of shooting the foreman. Others withdraw themselves, refuse to have anything to do with the people round them. One patient communicated with his wife in writing only ; another obstinately refused to obey judicial summons.

The patients have no understanding for the insufficiencies of their personality, which appear in their whole conduct. They are impatient and obstinate, think that they are perfectly within their rights, that their unusual actions are quite in order, hold firmly and stubbornly to their ideas. On the other hand they are often extremely credulous in regard to communications, which lie in the direction of their thoughts ; they accept without hesitation every piece of gossip as truth, let themselves be imposed upon, get into scrapes.

As a rule, heightened self-consciousness can be easily demonstrated. The patients boast of their performances, consider themselves superior to their surroundings, make special claims, lay the blame for their failures solely on external hindrances, without which they would undoubtedly have been in a position " to do useful and beneficial work ". I have also come across a few cases which might be regarded as in the initial stages of the *paranoiac delusion of grandeur* in its various forms.   I saw some inventors who occupied themselves with perpetual motion, and hoped by their future successes to gain money and honour on a considerable scale ; one of them expected great things from savings-bank stamps with business advertisements.   Other patients were conspicuous by their high-flying plans and ideas for benefitting the world, which were quite out of proportion to their knowledge and ability.   They thought of themselves as having a mission which they had to fulfil, although they were not able to meet the most commonplace claims of life. I have also met indications of erotic delusion, patients, who in spite of the most unequivocal refusal, yet ever again pursued the supposed beloved and tried by entreaties and threats to make her yield.

Intellectual endowment was on the average fairly good in the patients discussed here ; all the more striking was the failure of judgment in regard to their delusional ideas. Capricious behaviour with frequent change of mood was often observed, the influence of which could also be recognized in a restless, adventurous conduct of life. Occasionally there were hypochondriacal complaints, twinges of pain in the back, constriction in the breast.   Several times great sexual excitability was reported.   Some patients made suicidal attempts, occasionally repeated.   In isolated cases hysterical disorders appeared, convulsive weeping, fainting fits, diminution of the pharyngeal reflex, concentric restriction of the field of vision.   Many patients at times took excessive alcohol.   Almost all lived permanently in freedom, mostly without any special difficulty ; they were only on some special occasion once in a while brought temporarily to the hospital.

What distinguished the delusions of these patients from those of pronounced paranoia was their *vagueness* and the *absence of systematic working up*.   Their fears and hopes were of a more indefinite kind, were brought forward as indications and conjectures, or they consisted in a strong personal valuation of actual events, which was not too far removed from the one-sidedness of normal individuals. As far as could be known, no internal connection of the individual component parts of the delusion with a paranoiac view of life had taken place. They did not appear to have actually passed into the flesh and blood of the patients ; they appeared and receded again, yet without quite vanishing. It may naturally be objected that the patients, perhaps, kept their innermost trains of thought secret, or that the development of a delusional system will still take place later. Further experience must decide about these possibilities. At present the assumption appears to me to be well founded, that cases of undeveloped, " rudimentary " paranoia would not only fit in with our view of the character of the disease, but also come actually under observation.

It will certainly be often doubtful in the individual case whether and when we are right in calling a morbid personality, in the sense here delimited, " paranoid." It seems to me to be essentially a *combination of uncertainty with excessive valuation of self*, which leads to the patient being forced into hostile opposition to the influences of the struggle for life and his seeking to withdraw himself from them by inward exaltation. Further, a strong personal colouring of thought by vivid feeling-tones, activity of the power of imagination and self-confidence, might be of significance. If these peculiarities lead to isolated or general delusions without systematization, the paranoid psychopath would with that be approximately characterized.

The great restriction which the conception of paranoia has suffered in the course of the last few decades, frequently led to the prophecy, that it would soon wholly disappear. Indeed, Specht has made the attempt to solve the whole morbid state of paranoia. He thought that querulant delusion first, but then next paranoia contained in itself " the whole inventory of mania," the pressure of talk and writing, the restlessness, the digression, the readiness of repartee. For him accordingly the disease only signifies the reaction of a *manic-depressive predisposition* to an event which excites emotion. It must be admitted that some of the features mentioned are now and then found in paranoiacs, further, that there are manic patients with abundant delusions mentally worked up, who on account of the slightness of their excitement may for a considerable time be held to be paranoiacs. On the other hand the view of Specht appears to me to shoot far beyond the mark. There are numerous paranoiacs in whom the peculiarities resembling those of manic patients are altogether absent.

But when they are present, they invariably have a history of origin and a significance quite different from the similar manic phenomena. Pressure of speech and writing are explained by the active endeavour to defend themselves against persecution or to advance their own high claims, restlessness by the incapacity for persevering, useful work in consequence of the delusional disorders, digression by the heightened activity of the power of imagination, readiness of repartee by increased self-consciousness and by the mental working up of the content of the delusions, which has long ago solved all difficulties, although often in an extremely inadequate manner.

CHAPTER VII.

DIAGNOSIS AND TREATMENT.

THE diagnosis of paranoia presents scarcely any difficulties to attentive consideration of the slow development, of the peculiar, connected delusion formation, of the excellent preservation of intelligence as well as order in the train of thought, in conduct, and in activity. Certainly there are a number of diseases which may temporarily exhibit a similar picture. The delimitation of the malady from the " paranoid " mental disorders we have already considered. That there can be no question of transitions between paranoia in the sense here delimited and dementia præcox, as has been assumed by some observers, needs no special discussion.

Schizophrenia.—On the other hand at this point the possibility must shortly be discussed, that many cases of apparent paranoia might really be imperfectly developed schizophrenias. In the individual case it is not always easy to decide this question. The delusional system of the paranoiac is internally more closed, more rounded off, more thought out ; it takes account up to a certain degree of objections, tries to explain difficulties, in contrast to the abrupt delusional ideas of the paranoid schizophrenics, which are often contradictory to each other and also change frequently. In the latter, moreover, the signs of emotional devastation will not be missed, the slight internal interest not only in the surroundings, but also in the delusion, which at most leads to occasional outbursts, but provides no permanent motives for activity. In the paranoiac also we meet now and then a reserved, repellent manner, and peculiarities of many kinds in the conduct of life. But his conduct is invariably far more grounded on deliberation or emotional processes than the impulsive peculiarities of the schizophrenic. The whole personality in spite of its morbid features appears more comprehensible, more natural, more susceptible to influence. It is much easier by intelligent treatment to come into inner relations with it than with the capricious, inaccessible schizophrenic.

Schneider has described a case, which I consider a genuine paranoia, as a paranoid terminal state of dementia præcox, as I believe, without sufficient foundation.

Paraphrenia.[1]—We have further still to discuss the distinction of paranoia from the paraphrenic diseases, especially from the *systematic* form. In the first periods of the malady the similarity of the clinical states is so great that it will be very difficult to keep them separate. The circumstance seems to me to be of significance, that in paranoia exalted self-consciousness appears more distinctly from the outset; if the delusion of grandeur dominates the morbid state from the beginning or at least very soon, it is probably a case of paranoia. With this difference the fact is, perhaps, also connected, that the paranoiac is usually not nearly so much tormented by his ideas of persecution, and also not so much influenced in his actions as the paraphrenic patient. The latter proceeds far more regardlessly against his supposed persecutors, soon has resource to self-help and with all means in his power, so that invariably he comes to the institution comparatively early and often has even to be kept there permanently. At the same time he carries on the struggle with the greatest acrimony. In contrast to that the paranoiac possesses far more self-control, restricts himself to legal methods of fighting, yields to obvious supremacy, and understands how to avoid permanent deprivation of freedom by circumspect behaviour and concession. The compulsion of the morbid change by no means subjugates the personality to the same extent as in paraphrenia. Moreover, we have before us in the latter disease a constantly, although slowly progressive course, while the paranoiac may exhibit for decades a fairly uniform state, and often learns also to come to an agreement, practically endurable, with the difficulties resulting from his delusion. Besides that the delusion in paraphrenia gradually becomes always more extraordinary; hallucinations and exuberant ideas of grandeur are added, and the patients in their whole conduct are seen to be so strongly dominated by the morbid phenomena that they now can scarcely any longer be confused with the orderly and sociable paranoiacs who mostly are even able to earn their living.

Many cases of the " délire d'imagination " or " rétrospectif," which by the French are taken together with

[1] *Dementia Præcox and Paraphrenia*, p. 283.

" délire d'interprétation," our paranoia, probably belong to *confabulating* paraphrenia. In it the extraordinary abundance of pseudo-memories is noteworthy ; they serve by no means only for the development of a definite delusion as in paranoia, but they bring to light all possible trifles frequently of no importance at all. The delusional interpretation, conjectures, and presentiments which are always in the foreground in paranoia and are only supplemented and confirmed by pseudo-memories, go quite into the background here behind the regardless confabulation. The development of the malady is usually accomplished with considerably more rapidity than in paranoia ; at the same time the indications of psychic weakness, striking lack of judgment, emotional dulness, incoherence, for the most part appear fairly soon in an unmistakable manner.

Manic-Depressive Insanity.—Essential difficulties may, as Lähr[1] among others has shown, occasionally arise in distinguishing paranoia from delusional states of manic-depressive insanity, as just attacks of that kind occasionally exhibit a very " extended " course and comparatively few conspicuous emotional disorders. To this there may be added discharge by an external occasion, alternation or mixture of morbid phenomena of various kinds and tardy recovery without genuine insight. As to detail, it must be remarked that in the forms with depressive colouring more exact observation can still distinctly recognize the permanently depressed or anxious mood, which characterizes states of that kind. In contrast to that the paranoiac appears in general less constrained emotionally ; he only becomes irritated and embittered, when he is telling of the wrongs done to him. Abrupt fluctuations of mood, especially a sudden outburst of jocularity, pleasure in enterprise, indications of flight of ideas, likewise the appearance of ideas of sin, hopelessness, despair, give evidence for manic-depressive insanity.

Hypomania.—In hypomanic patients one will have specially to take into account their volitional restlessness, which is ever going after new plans in contrast to the steady, uniform pursuit of a definite aim by the paranoiac. Further, the demonstration of heightened distractibility and susceptibility to influence from the surroundings is of significance. The delusion formation mostly betrays a playful, bragging character, and also probably changes its content, while the

[1] Lähr, Schweizerhof, 3, Bericht, 59, 1903.

paranoiac, true to his convictions, holds fast to the same ideas once they are developed. Lastly, the manic mood inclining to outbursts of anger or to self-derision is characteristic, and essentially different from the dignified reserve or the naive confidence of the paranoiac.

For the assumption of manic-depressive insanity, independent of the colouring of the actual clinical picture, the fact that other attacks with a favourable course have preceded is of great weight. On the other hand the absence of other attacks before and after cannot be made use of for the diagnosis of paranoia, even when the history of the patient is followed, as Thomsen has done, for many years. We have, indeed, already seen that the free intervals in manic-depressive insanity may extend over three or four decades, but above all that well-characterized cases with only one attack in a lifetime are by no means rarities. That is also the reason, why I, with Kleist, must very decidedly call in question the cured " acute " forms of paranoia, in so far as they do not come under the heading of " abortive " paranoia described above.

Liars and Swindlers.—With the paranoid personalities, so far as they exhibit ideas of grandeur, morbid liars and swindlers may have a certain external similarity. Only in the latter it concerns not genuine delusions, but " delusional imaginations ", sudden fancies, which are brought forward more in a playful manner, and come and go without acquiring any authoritative influence on the internal aspect of the personality. The content of these inventions is usually far more variegated and extraordinary than the monotonous delusions of the paranoiac, which conform more to the actual circumstances of life. With regard to the wrongful claimants to thrones, claimants to money, and benefactors of the people, the question will occasionally emerge, how far it concerns paranoiacs or conscious swindlers. The circumstance is here decisive, whether the individuals in question themselves believe in the justice of their claims or in their mission. It can usually be ascertained by somewhat long observation whether they utilize their proceedings solely for the attainment of selfish ends, or whether the matter itself really lies next their heart, whether they also hold fast to it when they get nothing but suffering from it.

Treatment.—There can be no question of real treatment of the paranoiac in the nature of the case. Of course, one may hope that a life without any specially strong emotional stresses or strains, protected from excesses, and filled with well-regulated activity, may contribute to prevent the development of the slumbering paranoiac germs, and make exacerbations of the malady, which might appear, run an abortive course. The cure of a pronounced paranoia by direct psychic influence could probably be expected only by a psycho-analyst. Bjerre has published a case of that kind, in which he, certainly without actual psycho-analysis, but by a kind of cautious art of persuasion, cured a delusion of persecution which had existed more than a decade. Unfortunately the diagnosis of paranoia admits of grave doubts. Thus we shall in the meantime have to restrict ourselves to keeping our patients by distraction and occupation as much as possible from being absorbed in their delusional ideas. That frequently succeeds, in favourable circumstances for decades, so well, that the patients in spite of the most marked delusions are yet capable of living without too great difficulty in freedom. Every effort will, therefore, be made to save them, as far as it can at all be done, from seclusion in an institution.

INDEX

MANIC-DEPRESSIVE INSANITY

PARANOIA

Classics in Psychiatry

the Ayer Company collection

American Psychiatrists Abroad. 1975

Arnold, Thomas. **Observations On The Nature, Kinds, Causes, And Prevention Of Insanity.** 1806. Two volumes in one

Austin, Thomas J. **A Practical Account Of General Paralysis, Its Mental And Physical Symptoms, Statistics, Causes, Seat, And Treatment.** 1859

Bayle, A[ntoine] L[aurent] J[esse]. **Traité Des Maladies Du Cerveau Et De Ses Membranes.** 1826

Binz, Carl. **Doctor Johann Weyer.** 1896

Blandford, G. Fielding. **Insanity And Its Treatment.** 1871

Bleuler, Eugen. **Textbook Of Psychiatry.** 1924

Braid, James. **Neurypnology.** 1843

Brierre de Boismont, A[lexandre-Jacques-François]. **Hallucinations.** 1853

Brown, Mabel Webster, compiler. **Neuropsychiatry And The War: A Bibliography With Abstracts and Supplement I,** October 1918. Two volumes in one

Browne, W. A. F. **What Asylums Were, Are, And Ought To Be.** 1837

Burrows, George Man. **Commentaries On The Causes, Forms, Symptoms And Treatment, Moral And Medical, Of Insanity.** 1828

Calmeil, L[ouis]-F[lorentin]. **De La Folie:** Considérée Sous Le Point De Vue Pathologique, Philosophique, Historique Et Judiciaire, Depuis La Renaissance Des Sciences En Europe Jusqu'au Dix-Neuvième Siècle. 1845. Two volumes in one

Calmeil, L[ouis] F[lorentin]. **De La Paralysie Considérée Chez Les Aliénés.** 1826

Dejerine, J[oseph Jules] and E. Gauckler. **The Psychoneuroses And Their Treatment By Psychotherapy.** [1913]

Dunbar, [Helen] Flanders. **Emotions And Bodily Changes.** 1954

Ellis, W[illiam] C[harles]. **A Treatise On The Nature, Symptoms, Causes And Treatment Of Insanity.** 1838

Emminghaus, H[ermann]. **Die Psychischen Störungen Des Kindesalters.** 1887

Esdaile, James. **Mesmerism In India,** And Its Practical Application In Surgery And Medicine. 1846

Esquirol, E[tienne]. **Des Maladies Mentales.** 1838. Three volumes in two

Feuchtersleben, Ernst [Freiherr] von. **The Principles Of Medical Psychology.** 1847

Georget, [Etienne-Jean]. **De La Folie:** Considérations Sur Cette Maladie. 1820

Haslam, John. **Observations On Madness And Melancholy.** 1809

Hill, Robert Gardiner. **Total Abolition Of Personal Restraint In The Treatment Of The Insane.** 1839

Janet, Pierre [Marie-Felix] and F. Raymond. **Les Obsessions Et La Psychasthénie.** 1903. Two volumes

Janet, Pierre [Marie-Felix]. **Psychological Healing.** 1925. Two volumes

Kempf, Edward J. Psychopathology. 1920

Kraepelin, Emil. **Manic-Depressive Insanity And Paranoia.** 1921

Kraepelin, Emil. **Psychiatrie:** Ein Lehrbuch Für Studirende Und Aerzte. 1896

Laycock, Thomas. **Mind And Brain.** 1860. Two volumes in one

Liébeault, A[mbroise]-A[uguste]. **Le Sommeil Provoqué Et Les États Analogues.** 1889

Mandeville, B[ernard] De. **A Treatise Of The Hypochondriack And Hysterick Passions.** 1711

Morel, B[enedict] A[ugustin]. Traité Des Degénérescences Physiques, Intellectuelles Et Morales De L'Espèce Humaine. 1857. Two volumes in one

Morison, Alexander. **The Physiognomy Of Mental Diseases.** 1843

Myerson, Abraham. **The Inheritance Of Mental Diseases.** 1925

Perfect, William. **Annals Of Insanity.** [1808]

Pinel, Ph[ilippe]. Traité Médico-Philosophique Sur L'Aliénation Mentale. 1809

Prince, Morton, et al. **Psychotherapeutics.** 1910

Psychiatry In Russia And Spain. 1975

Ray, I[saac]. **A Treatise On The Medical Jurisprudence Of Insanity.** 1871

Semelaigne, René. **Philippe Pinel Et Son Oeuvre Au Point De Vue De La Médecine Mentale.** 1888

Thurnam, John. **Observations And Essays On The Statistics Of Insanity.** 1845

Trotter, Thomas. **A View Of The Nervous Temperament.** 1807

Tuke, D[aniel] Hack, editor. **A Dictionary Of Psychological Medicine.** 1892. Two volumes

Wier, Jean. **Histoires, Disputes Et Discours Des Illusions Et Impostures Des Diables, Des Magiciens Infames, Sorcieres Et Empoisonneurs.** 1885. Two volumes

Winslow, Forbes. **On Obscure Diseases Of The Brain And Disorders Of The Mind.** 1860

Burdett, Henry C. **Hospitals And Asylums Of The World.** 1891-93. Five volumes. 2,740 pages on NMA standard 24x-98 page microfiche only